ADAPTIVE ARCHITECTURE

'*Adaptive Architecture* is a rigorous and thoughtful guide, full of important precedent studies, for architects and building professionals navigating an increasingly complex, fluid, and interdependent world of sociocultural, economic and climatic design challenges.'

Philip Horton, *The Design School, Arizona State University, USA*

The constant in architecture's evolution is change. *Adaptive Architecture* explores structures or environments that accommodate multiple functions at the same time, sequentially, or at periodically recurring events. It demonstrates how changing technological, economic, ecological, and social conditions have altered the playing field for architecture from the design of single purpose structures to the design of interacting systems of synergistically interdependent, distributed buildings. Including contributors from the US, UK, Japan, Australia, Germany, and South Africa, the chapters are woven into a six-part framework which provides a broad and unique treatment of this important and timely issue.

Wolfgang F. E. Preiser held a Ph.D. in Man–Environment Relations from Penn State, and several architecture degrees from Virginia Tech, Karlsruhe Tech (Germany), and Vienna Tech (Austria). Unfortunately, Wolfgang passed away in August 2016, before the publication of this book.

Andrea E. Hardy, Creo Architects, holds a Master's degree in Architecture from Arizona State University (2012) and a Bachelor of Science in Architectural Engineering Technology from Wentworth Institute of Technology (2007).

Jacob J. Wilhelm holds a Bachelor of Science in Design in Architectural Studies from Arizona State University (2016).

ADAPTIVE ARCHITECTURE

Changing Parameters and Practice

Edited by Wolfgang F. E. Preiser, Andrea E. Hardy, and Jacob J. Wilhelm

LONDON AND NEW YORK

First published 2018
by Routledge
2 Park Square, Milton Park, Abingdon, Oxon OX14 4RN

and by Routledge
711 Third Avenue, New York, NY 10017

Routledge is an imprint of the Taylor & Francis Group, an informa business

© 2018 selection and editorial matter, Wolfgang F. E. Preiser, Andrea E. Hardy, and
Jacob J. Wilhelm; individual chapters, the contributors

The right of Wolfgang F.E. Preiser, Andrea E. Hardy, and Jacob J. Wilhelm to be
identified as the authors of the editorial material, and of the authors for their individual
chapters, has been asserted in accordance with sections 77 and 78 of the Copyright,
Designs and Patents Act 1988.

All rights reserved. No part of this book may be reprinted or reproduced or utilised in
any form or by any electronic, mechanical, or other means, now known or hereafter
invented, including photocopying and recording, or in any information storage or
retrieval system, without permission in writing from the publishers.

Trademark notice: Product or corporate names may be trademarks or registered
trademarks, and are used only for identification and explanation without intent to
infringe.

British Library Cataloguing-in-Publication Data
A catalogue record for this book is available from the British Library

Library of Congress Cataloging-in-Publication Data
Names: Preiser, Wolfgang F. E., editor. | Hardy, Andrea, editor. | Wilhelm,
    Jacob J., editor.
Title: Adaptive architecture : changing parameters and practice / edited by
    Wolfgang F.E. Preiser, Andrea E. Hardy, and Jacob J. Wilhelm.
Description: New York : Routledge, 2017. | Includes bibliographical
    references and index.
Identifiers: LCCN 2017004346| ISBN 9781138647268 (hb : alk. paper) |
    ISBN 9781138647275 (pb : alk. paper) | ISBN 9781315627113 (ebook)
Subjects: LCSH: Architectural design. | Buildings--Performance. |
    Architecture and society.
Classification: LCC NA2750 .A197 2017 | DDC 729--dc23
LC record available at https://lccn.loc.gov/2017004346

ISBN: 978-1-138-64726-8 (hbk)
ISBN: 978-1-138-64727-5 (pbk)
ISBN: 978-1-315-62711-3 (ebk)

Typeset in Bembo and ITC Stone Sans by
Servis Filmsetting Ltd, Stockport, Cheshire

In memory of Wolfgang F. E. Preiser: colleague, teacher, mentor

CONTENTS

List of illustrations	*xi*
About the editors	*xvi*
About the contributors	*xviii*
Foreword by Robert G. Shibley	*xxix*
Preface by Wolfgang F. E. Preiser, Andrea E. Hardy, and Jacob J. Wilhelm	*xxxiii*
Acknowledgments	*xxxv*

PART I
Introduction   1

Introduction   3
*Wolfgang F. E. Preiser★, University of Cincinnati; Thomas Fisher,
University of Minnesota; and Andrea E. Hardy, Creo Architects, Phoenix, AZ*

PART II
Concepts and processes for future flexibility   13

Preamble   15
Allison Lenell Magley, DWL Architects + Planners, Phoenix, AZ

1. Challenges of large-scale housing in the developing world: the Habitat
for Humanity Global Village project in Ethiopia   17
Allison Lenell Magley, DWL Architects + Planners, Phoenix, AZ

★ Wolfgang F. E. Preiser, also Emeritus College, Arizona State University, USA

viii Contents

2. Predesign planning for flexibility   25
Robert G. Hershberger, University of Arizona, Tucson, AZ and Molly E. Smith, thinkSMART Planning, Phoenix, AZ

3. Multi-performance spaces: assessing the impacts of an innovative LEED™ platinum educational complex on the triple bottom line   34
Ihab M. K. Elzeyadi, University of Oregon, Eugene, OR

4. Mixed-use development using air rights above the JR train station at Nagoya, Japan   44
Gen Taniguchi, Nagoya University, Akikazu Kato and Shiho Mori, Mie University, Japan

5. Prospects for adaptive, inclusive design: lessons learned from children's museums   52
Korydon Smith and Beth Tauke, University at Buffalo

Reflections on Part II   59
Michael J. Crosbie, University of Hartford, USA

PART III
Rooms/settings scale   **63**

Preamble   65
William Fawcett, Cambridge Architectural Research Ltd, Cambridge, UK

6. The measurement and efficiency of adaptive design strategies   67
William Fawcett, Cambridge Architectural Research Ltd, Cambridge, UK

7. Finding the balance: a model of assessment for commercial floor-plate performance   77
Jeffrey L. Morgan, Grimshaw Architects, Sydney, Australia

8. Beyond the cellular office: adaptable offices for medium-sized companies   86
Martin Hodulak, Nextspaces, Munich, Germany

9. Adaptive architecture of the London Science Museum: a needs assessment   95
Kristin E. Hibbs, Science Museum, London, UK

10. Post-occupancy evaluation of a multi-tasking environment: the University of Kentucky Medical Center's emergency department   105
Lindsey L. Fay, University of Kentucky, Lexington, KY

11. A construct of generosity in Navajo culture: the Hogan   114
Jaclyn M. Roessel, Heard Museum, Phoenix, AZ

Contents **ix**

Reflections on Part III *Michael J. Crosbie, University of Hartford, USA*	119

PART IV
Building scale
123

Preamble
Wolfgang F. E. Preiser, University of Cincinnati*, and Jacob J. Wilhelm, Arizona State University
125

12. Keren Or Center for Blind Children with Multiple Disabilities in Israel
Wolfgang F. E. Preiser, University of Cincinnati*, and Jacob J. Wilhelm, Arizona State University
127

13. Omgivning: transforming historic icons through adaptive reuse
Karin Liljegren and Kelly Kish, Omgivning, Los Angeles, CA
136

14. Strategies for planning, designing, and operating adaptable facilities
John P. Petronis, Faye Whittemore, and Andy L. Aguilar, Architectural Research Consultants, Incorporated, Albuquerque, NM
149

15. Native meets high-tech: the Sobeloff Center, Sealaska Heritage Corporation
Zane M. Jones, MRV Architects, Juneau, Alaska
158

16. Building with boxes: the New Jerusalem Children's Home
Mia L. C. Anfield, 4d and a architects, Johannesburg, South Africa
168

Reflections on Part IV
Michael J. Crosbie, University of Hartford, USA
177

PART V
Urban scale
181

Preamble
Andrea E. Hardy, Creo Architects, Phoenix, AZ
183

17. Reappropriation of city infrastructure: alleyways
Andrea E. Hardy, Creo Architects, Phoenix, AZ
185

18. Concourse to campus: transforming Berlin TXL Airport into a higher education space
Una Rath, Senate Administration for City Planning and the Environment, City of Berlin, Germany, and Martin Hodulak, Nextspaces, Munich, Germany
195

* Wolfgang F. E. Preiser, also Emeritus College, Arizona State University, USA

x Contents

19. An adaptive evolution from Prussian artillery barracks to intelligent
campus buildings   204
Ulrich Schramm, Bielefeld University of Applied Sciences, Germany

20. A case study on the design of the Scottish Crime Campus   214
Gordon Murray, Ryder Architecture, Glasgow, UK

21. Multi-tasking architectural computer programs: BIM   227
Akikazu Kato and Shiho Mori, Mie University, and Gen Taniguchi,
Nagoya University, Japan

Reflections on Part V   233
Michael J. Crosbie, University of Hartford, USA

PART VI
Epilogue   **237**

22. The International Space Station: adaptive human accommodations in
an extreme, isolated environment   239
David Fitts, Jennifer L. Rochlis, Mihriban Whitmore, and Alexandra
Whitmire, NASA, Houston, TX

Appendix: The habitability paradigm – key elements and concepts for
a humane architecture   *249*
Wolfgang F. E. Preiser★, University of Cincinnati; Andrea E. Hardy, Creo
Architects, Phoenix, AZ; and Jacob J. Wilhelm, Arizona State University

Index   *258*

★ Wolfgang F. E. Preiser, also Emeritus College, Arizona State University, USA

ILLUSTRATIONS

Figures

I.1	Influences of globalization and adaptability in commercial building design.	4
I.2	Scales of adaptivity.	6
1.1	Habitat for Humanity worldwide.	18
1.2	Habitat for Humanity International Ethiopia; Debre Birhan housing project.	19
1.3	Habitat for Humanity International Ethiopia; Debre Birhan; construction and labor.	21
1.4	Habitat for Humanity International Ethiopia; Debre Birhan; construction and labor.	22
1.5	Habitat for Humanity International Ethiopia; Debre Birhan; existing versus new construction.	22
2.1	Covenant Baptist master plan.	27
2.2	Typical office tower plan.	29
2.3	Tent structure.	29
2.4	Relocatable church concept.	31
2.5	Horton Plaza: mall.	31
3.1	Design strategies of multi-performance spaces.	36
3.2	Adaptive architecture place experience system model.	37
3.3	The Lewis Integrated Sciences Building (LISB).	38
3.4	Energy and resource consumption in EUI of LISB.	39
3.5	Multi-performance space example – meeting office space.	40
3.6	Singular-performance space example – laboratory space.	41
3.7	Low-performance space example – computational office space.	42
4.1	JR Towers building site and railway platform.	46
4.2	Façade of JR twin-tower building.	47
4.3	Office plan of Taisei Corporation Nagoya branch office.	49
4.4	Office layout of smaller tenants of JR Office Tower.	50
4.5	Office layout of Kokuyo Nagoya branch office.	50

xii List of illustrations

6.1 The McMaster University Health Sciences Centre (MHSC) at Hamilton, Canada, was designed by Eberhard Zeidler of Craig Zeidler & Strong and opened in 1972. 69

6.2 The feasibility matrix for the healthcare clinic worked example. 72

6.3 Scattergram showing the cost and adaptive performance (% of the 10,000 simulated demand profiles that can be accommodated) for 50 design strategies. 73

7.1 Floor-plate assessment criteria: (1) net-to-gross ratio, (2) wall-to-floor ratio, (3) average distance to façade, (4) daylight penetration, (5) floor-plate visibility, (6) floor-plate connectivity. 79

7.2 Assessment grid of points generated for square floor-plate with central core. 80

7.3 Generic floor-plate analysis typologies. 80

7.4 Grasshopper parametric algorithm. 84

8.1 Cycles of demand for office concepts. 87

8.2 Town hall, Plauen. 88

8.3 Typical cellular office plan. 89

8.4 Traditional versus open-space principle. 90

8.5 Typical open-space floor layout. 92

8.6 Aims and goals referring to new office concepts. 93

9.1 Site plan for the new building of the Science Museum. 98

9.2 The Jubilee exhibition in the East Hall of the Science Museum. 100

9.3 Gallery view of "Cosmonauts: Birth of the Space Age" exhibition. 101

9.4 Gallery view from the mezzanine toward the Rugby Tuning Coil at the center of the Information Age gallery. 101

9.5 Gallery view during construction for the new mathematics gallery designed by Zaha Hadid Architects. 102

9.6 The bicycle tour was installed in 2012 to inspire delight and nostalgia in visitors upon entry. 102

9.7 The Making the Modern World gallery is one of the Science Museum's most popular spaces for dinners and parties. 103

10.1 University of Kentucky Medical Center and emergency department entrance. 106

10.2 University of Kentucky emergency department's linear configuration with a central core. 107

10.3 Behavioral mapping and communication documentation. 111

12.1 Street view of the Keren Or Center for Blind Children with Multiple Disabilities. 128

12.2 Upper level 4 floor plan: dormitories and residential activities. 129

12.3 Main entry level 3 floor plan: administration and classrooms. 130

12.4 Lower level 2 floor plan: therapy rooms, kitchen, and dining. 130

12.5 Lower level 1 floor plan: synagogue and staff apartments. 131

12.6 Special, double handrails in staircase, color coded in yellow for better visibility. 134

13.1 1951 – historic exterior view of the May Company Department Store. 137

13.2 Historic exterior view of Sears Roebuck Distribution Center. 138

13.3	The Broadway Building main floor.	138
13.4	The Broadway Building typical floor today.	139
13.5	Broadway Building existing penthouse.	140
13.6	Proposed rendering of exterior façade on Broadway and 8th Streets.	141
13.7	Proposed rendering of exterior façade on Hill and 8th Streets.	141
13.8	Existing exterior photo of Sears Building.	142
13.9	Proposed rendering of central hub.	142
13.10	Existing interior photo of typical floor of the Sears Building.	143
13.11	Existing interior photo of tower at the Sears Building.	143
13.12	Proposed rendering of new lightcourt at the Sears Building.	145
13.13	Proposed rendering of new lightcourt at Broadway Building.	146
13.14	Proposed rendering of partial roof amenities at the Broadway Building.	147
14.1	Strategies for planning, designing, and operating adaptable facilities.	150
14.2	State of New Mexico's space request process.	151
14.3	Open versus closed work environments.	151
14.4	Huddle room.	152
14.5	Conceptual diagram of a flexible floor-plate.	153
14.6a and 14.6b	Photo/diagrams of a local architectural firm office.	155
14.7a and 14.7b	Screen captures from a web-based tool for utilization and capacity analysis.	156
15.1	Example of the Tlingit Naanyaa.aayí clan house known as the Chief Shakes House in Wrangell, Alaska.	159
15.2	Soboleff Center context view.	162
15.3	Soboleff Center entrance view.	163
15.4	Soboleff Center floor plan 1.	164
15.5	Soboleff Center floor plan 2.	165
15.6	Soboleff Center section 1.	165
15.7	Soboleff Center section 2.	166
16.1	Typical informal housing.	169
16.2	Container House by Adam Kalkin.	170
16.3	3D image generated for a client presentation.	171
16.4	Architectural ground floor plan.	172
16.5	Architectural first floor plan.	172
16.6	Mosaics were used to decorate the concrete plinths supporting the containers.	173
16.7	Two of the children of the New Jerusalem Children's Home.	174
16.8	The completed house.	175
17.1	Le Corbusier's versus Frank Lloyd Wright's illustrated spatial utopian theories.	186
17.2	Graphic illustration of possible arrangements of Gehl's comfort levels/sizes within the size limitations of an alley.	188
17.3	Photograph of a typical Phoenix alley adjacent to residential properties.	189
17.4	Collage by author outlining possible uses of alleyways by displaying historic and potential future uses in or off of alleyways.	189
17.5	Mural by Lalo Cota and El Mac, south-facing wall at Barrio Café on Calle 16.	191

xiv List of illustrations

17.6	Mural by Douglas Miles, Native American Women with historical and present images in their hair.	192
17.7	Plans of Sliver House designed by Boyarsky Murphy Architects.	193
18.1	TXL concept – from idea to market production.	197
18.2	Extent of university site with field laboratories.	198
18.3	Schematic section of terminal building converted to university use.	198
18.4	Building life cycle.	200
18.5	Organization structure of an integral planning.	202
19.1	Map of the artillery barracks.	205
19.2	The former men's quarters turned into the main building on the Minden Campus.	207
19.3	The former blacksmith's workshop now used as a computer lab.	208
19.4	The new campus building (middle) with the auditorium (left) and the former tower of the fire department (right).	210
19.5	Map of Minden Campus, Bielefeld University of Applied Sciences, 2016.	211
19.6	Atrium of the new library, located on the second floor of the new campus building.	212
20.1	View of campus.	215
20.2	Chromosome and DNA patterns.	216
20.3	Site plan of Campus.	217
20.4	View south in atrium showing level changes.	218
20.5	View of atrium.	219
20.6	Glazed wall on north end of atrium.	221
20.7	Evening view of campus.	222
20.8	Detail of façade.	224
21.1	PICU of Aichi Children's Hospital, photographed immediately after building completion.	229
21.2	BIM view of PICU with expected medical equipment and furnishings.	230
22.1	Exterior view of ISS.	240
22.2	Rack system within ISS habitable volumes.	241
22.3	Crewmember Naoko Yamazaki prepares to transfer sub-rack experiments during transfer vehicle docking; ISS rack showing integration of smaller sub-rack experiment packages.	242
22.4	ISS interior volume configuration analysis for resolving conflicts.	243
22.5	Graph showing NASA-recommended NHV as a function of mission duration.	244
22.6	Graph showing NASA historical spacecraft NHV as a function of mission duration.	245
22.7	The Expedition Two and Space Shuttle crews convene for a group portrait aboard the ISS.	248
A.1	Habitability paradigm elements.	250
A.2	The triad of facility programming/building performance evaluation/database development.	252
A.3	Elements and phases of habitability research.	255

Tables

1.1	Habitat for Humanity International Ethiopia; cost of deliverables and fund allocation.	23
6.1	A sample of 20 simulated demand profiles for consecutive time periods.	71
6.2	Summary statistics for the 10,000 simulated demand profiles.	71
6.3	Data for the design strategies highlighted in the scattergram (Figure 6.3).	74
12.1	Evidence-based design guidelines for blind persons with multiple disabilities.	132

ABOUT THE EDITORS

Wolfgang F. E. Preiser held a Ph.D. in man–environment relations from Penn State, and several architecture degrees from Virginia Tech, Karlsruhe Tech (Germany), and Vienna Tech (Austria). He had over 40 years of experience in teaching, research and consulting in the evaluation and programming of environments, including healthcare facilities, public housing, public libraries, cross-cultural and universal design, as well as design research in general.

He published 20 books and over 130 chapters, monographs, and articles. His most recent books include: *Architecture Beyond Criticism: Expert Judgment and Performance Evaluation* (Routledge, 2015), *Enhancing Building Performance* (Wiley, 2012), *Universal Design Handbook* (McGraw-Hill, 2010) and *Designing for Designers: Lessons Learned From Schools of Architecture* (Fairchild, 2007). Preiser lectured worldwide at 69 venues and conferences in the United States and Canada, as well as 86 overseas. He served on national committees with the American Institute of Architects, the Building Research Board of the National Academy of Sciences, and the National Institute for Disability Rehabilitation Research.

Preiser received many awards, including two Progressive Architecture Awards, two Professional Fellowships from the National Endowment for the Arts, the Career Award from the Environmental Design Research Association (EDRA), and two EDRA Achievement Awards, as well as other awards while at the University of Cincinnati.

Andrea E. Hardy, Creo Architects, holds a Master's degree in architecture from Arizona State University (2012) and a Bachelor of Science in Architectural Engineering Technology from Wentworth Institute of Technology (2007).

She worked in architecture offices for several years while studying for her degrees. After working professionally in Boston and Phoenix, and studying public architecture through Arizona State University in Buenos Aires, Argentina, Hardy is currently an associate and registered architect working at Creo Architects in Phoenix, Arizona.

While at Arizona State University, Hardy was a member of the American Institute of Architecture Students, served one term as secretary for the American Institute of Architecture Students, was a teaching assistant for a design studio and history class, received multiple scholarships, and participated in non-academic activities such as working on multiple design competitions, workshops, and volunteer work.

Recently, Hardy was published as co-editor and co-author in *Architecture Beyond Criticism: Expert Judgment and Performance Evaluation* (2015), contributed to updating *Improving Building Performance,* NCARB Monograph series (2016), and is currently working as an editor on the forthcoming second edition to *Building Performance Evaluation* (in press).

Jacob J. Wilhelm holds a Bachelor of Science in design in architectural studies from Arizona State University (2016). Currently an architectural designer in Denver, Colorado, he is the recipient of many awards and grants based on his work in design and publication. While at Arizona State University, Wilhelm held various leadership roles, serving with Alpha Rho Chi as president and with the American Institute of Architecture Students, Students for the New Urbanism, and the Student Planning Association. Both as an individual and collaborating with students in the fields of architecture, industrial design, urban planning, and more, Wilhelm has been awarded in multiple local design competitions as sponsored by Arizona Residential Architects, the Scottsdale Museum of Art, and Arizona State University. He is committed to expanding architectural discourse through interdisciplinary study, research, and theory, and his current focus is in architectural practice and publication.

ABOUT THE CONTRIBUTORS

Andy L. Aguilar holds a Master of Architecture degree from the University of New Mexico (1995) and a Bachelor of Arts degree in architecture from the University of New Mexico (1984). He is a project manager at ARC, with an emphasis on facility programming, feasibility studies, and long-range master planning. He has 31 years of experience in facility programming, needs assessments, and physical facility condition assessments for a variety of governmental and educational clients.

Mia Anfield was born in the United Kingdom and lived there until 1980, when, at the age of 15, she and her family relocated to South Africa. This adjustment to the then apartheid way of life and the subsequent turbulent period in South Africa (until the first multi-racial democratic elections in 1994) had a huge effect on the young girl from London. She flourished with the imposition of order, structure, lines, boundaries, and began to create these by hand in her technical drawing classes at high school. She excelled in this subject and as the only girl in her class loved the male-dominated environment. Her decision to take this subject which had not been available to her in the United Kingdom was a huge contributor to her decision to become an architect.

Anfield holds a Bachelor's Degree in architecture from the University of Natal, Durban (1989). She has practiced in various architectural firms for the last 25 years. Since 2002, she and her husband, Sean, are partners at their architecture firm 4d and a architects.

Mia creates architecture of timeless simplicity and proportions. She is committed to practical, simple, functional designs. She understands that architecture is more than just the design of spaces and buildings; it's about people. She has a client-responsive approach to architecture which results in a service-orientated standard. Her design philosophy centers around the creation of architectural projects, from the smallest alteration to a new office building, generated from a sensitive response to the context and the individual client's requirements.

Mia is registered with the South African Council of Architects and is also a member of the Green Building Council of South Africa. She resides in Johannesburg with her husband and two teenage children.

Michael J. Crosbie, Ph.D., FAIA, has made significant contributions in the fields of architectural journalism, research, teaching, and practice. He studied architecture and received his Doctor of Philosophy degree from The Catholic University of America. He has served as an editor at *Architecture: The AIA Journal, Progressive Architecture, ArchitectureWeek.com*, and since 2001 he has served as editor-in-chief of *Faith & Form*, a quarterly interfaith journal on religious art and architecture. He is also a frequent contributor to *Oculus* magazine, *Architectural Record*, and writes about architecture and design for the *Hartford Courant*. He is the author of more than 20 books on architecture (including five books for children) and has contributed to two dozen others. Dr. Crosbie is Professor of Architecture and former Chair of the Department of Architecture at the University of Hartford, and has served as an adjunct professor at Roger Williams University and Catholic University (where he was the visiting Walton Critic in 2015). He has lectured and served as a visiting critic at architecture schools in North America and abroad, among them the University of California (Berkeley), the University of Pennsylvania, Yale University, and the Moscow Architectural Institute. Dr. Crosbie has practiced with Centerbrook Architects and Steven Winter Associates, is a registered architect in the State of Connecticut, and elected to the College of Fellows of the American Institute of Architects.

Ihab M.K. Elzeyadi, Ph.D., FEIA, LEED^{AP} is a professor of architecture and the director of High Performance Environments laboratory (HiPE) and Façade Innovative Technologies (FIT) testing facility at the School of Architecture & Allied Arts, University of Oregon. Dr. Elzeyadi has been engaged in the design, construction, and research of high-performance buildings for more than 25 years. He has conducted post-occupancy evaluations, building performance assessments, and field studies of more than 75 buildings, 30 of which are LEED™ and LBC rated. Professor Elzeyadi teaches design studios and lectures in building performance and metrics; integrated design and delivery; indoor environmental quality, as well as environmental impacts of buildings on human performance and health.

Dr. Elzeyadi conducted grant-supported research on the relationship between people and buildings including the impact of the physical environment on health, productivity, and other aspects of wellbeing as they relate to sustainable design strategies in commercial and educational environments. His studies produced evidence-based design guidelines and design-assistance services on various commercial projects with an emphasis on energy and resource effective design. He recently completed a number of research projects investigating cost and financial benefits of green and LEED™ educational environments, livable communities' physical infrastructure, and the Green Classroom Toolbox Project for energy retrofits of existing schools. He has been published in journals and international conference proceedings and is a featured speaker at various schools of architecture and international conferences around the world.

William Fawcett is an architect who favors mathematical analysis of architectural challenges. His Ph.D. from the Martin Centre in Cambridge University's Department of Architecture was *A Mathematical Approach to Adaptability in Buildings* (1979, supervisor Lionel March). He worked in conventional architectural practice and taught in the Department of Architecture at Hong Kong University (co-authoring *Architecture: Formal Approach* with Jerzy Wojtowicz, 1986), and was one of the co-founders of the multi-disciplinary consultancy Cambridge Architectural Research Ltd (CAR) in 1987.

xx About the contributors

At CAR a major interest is in functional issues – this led to design guidance publications (*Design for Inherent Security*, with Barry Poyner, 1995; *Refurbishing Occupied Buildings*, with Jason Palmer, 2004), and briefing ('pre-design') studies for specific projects. Design for flexibility is a continuing interest. This theme connects with a new approach to life-cycle evaluation based on real options that takes account of future uncertainty (*New Generation Whole-life Costing* and *Whole Life Sustainability*, co-authored with Ian Ellingham, 2006 and 2013). The argument is that flexibility for changing needs is a primary component of long-term value. Cambridge Architectural Research Ltd was a participant in the European Commission-funded CILECCTA consortium (2009–13), which developed software for real-options-based life-cycle costing (LCC) and life-cycle assessment (LCA).

William Fawcett was appointed to the Chadwick Fellowship in Architecture at Pembroke College, University of Cambridge (2005–10) to develop the Activity-Space Research initiative, using mathematical models to investigate the changing ways that buildings are used in a digitally connected world. This work is recorded in *Activity-Space Research* (2016).

Lindsey Fay, Assistant Professor in the School of Interiors at the University of Kentucky, is creating an extension of the academic learning environment for design professionals and students through advancements in the participatory design process and evaluations of extant environments. As an advocate of evidence-based design, her research has examined healthcare, learning, and community-based environments to assess the intercultural conditions and exchanges that exist within these spaces. Currently, her research utilizes post-occupancy evaluation to assess the design of healthcare spaces and their impact on care delivery. It further implements this methodology as a learning tool and immersive learning experience for interior design students. Fay has been published in a number of peer-reviewed journals and is a frequent presenter at national conferences.

Thomas Fisher is a professor in the School of Architecture, Director of the Metropolitan Design Center, and former Dean of the College of Design at the University of Minnesota. A graduate of Cornell University in architecture and Case Western Reserve University in intellectual history, he was the editorial director of *Progressive Architecture* magazine and was recognized in 2005 as the fifth most published architecture writer in the United States. He has written over 50 book chapters or introductions and over 400 articles in professional journals and major publications. His books include *In the Scheme of Things, Alternative Thinking on the Practice of Architecture* (2000), *Salmela, Architect* (2005), *Lake/Flato, Buildings and Landscapes* (2005), *Architectural Design and Ethics, Tools for Survival* (2008), *Ethics for Architects* (2010), *The Invisible Element of Place, The Architecture of David Salmela* (2011), *Designing to Avoid Disaster* (2013), and *Designing our Way to a Better World* (2016).

David J. Fitts worked for the National Aeronautics and Space Administration (NASA) for 27 years before retiring in 2015. In his career with NASA he was deeply engaged in the three major human spaceflight programs of his era: the Space Shuttle Program, the International Space Station (ISS) Program, and the next-generation Constellation Program for deep-space exploration. During ISS and Constellation development phases, Mr. Fitts served the Agency as the Chief of the Habitability and Human Factors Branch, which focuses on ensuring human capabilities and limitations are strongly integrated into human spaceflight programs' systems engineering and management processes. In one noteworthy accomplishment during the early construction phases of ISS, Mr. Fitts developed an ISS Interior Volume Configuration Process which the Program uses to prioritize and ensure human accessibility to the limited resource of usable, habitable space within the vehicle. During the Constellation Program, Mr. Fitts' team participated in basic design trade studies, such as determining the size of the habitable volume of the Orion spacecraft and writing the Program's contractually binding Human Systems Integration Standards. As Constellation transitioned to current, ongoing, and future deep space human exploration programs, Mr. Fitts worked within the Agency to ensure human concerns would continue to receive equal consideration to hardware and software development concerns through pressing for agency-wide requirements for human/systems integration practices and processes. Mr. Fitts holds a Bachelor of Architecture degree from the University of Arkansas.

Robert G. Hershberger, professor and dean emeritus of the University of Arizona, resides in Payson, Arizona. He is working with Molly Smith and Andrea Hardy on two books: updating his 1999 book titled *Architectural Programming and Predesign Manager* for a second edition to be titled *Predesign Planning for the Environmental Design Professions,* and preparing eight or nine mini-monographs on predesign planning for the National Council of Architectural Registration Boards (NCARB). He is completing work on a biography titled *My Life with Deanna: Charging Woman* and a related book titled *Journey into Unknowing and Death: Diary of an Alzheimer's Caregiver.*

Hershberger is dean emeritus and was a professor in the College of Architecture at the University of Arizona from 1988 to 2002, dean from 1988 to 1996. He was a professor of architecture at Arizona State University from 1969 to 1988 and assistant professor of architecture at Idaho State University from 1961 to 1965 During these years he taught courses on and published research relating to architectural programming (predesign planning) and maintained an active architectural and predesign planning practice, receiving recognition and numerous awards for the quality of his work.

Hershberger received a Bachelor of Fine Arts from Stanford University in 1958, a Bachelor of Architecture from the University of Utah in 1959, a Master of Architecture degree in 1961 and a Ph.D. degree in 1969 from the University of Pennsylvania.

He was born in Pocatello, Idaho in 1936 and was married from 1961 until his wife's death in 2015. He has two children and six grandchildren. He has travelled extensively on six of the seven continents and enjoys skiing, fly-fishing, golf, tennis, travel, sketching, painting, and writing.

Kristin E. Hibbs has a B.S. in architecture and a Master of Architecture from the University of Cincinnati.

Hibbs is Head of Design at the Science Museum in London. She joined in 2012, having authored their masterplan the year before. She is the creative director for their design studio and is the champion and client for design across the museum, playing a central role in the implementation of the masterplan.

She has studied, worked and lived in Copenhagen, London and Berlin. It was an internship in London, where she worked on the masterplan for the Victoria & Albert Museum in 2000, that had the most profound impact on her career path. She observed first-hand how powerful a tool master planning can be.

Kristin is a specialist in museums. She knows how they operate technically as buildings;

how they support the care of collections; how they need to be run as commercial businesses; and most importantly how they provide transformative experiences for their visitors. Kristin has worked with museums big and small during her seven years with Metaphor, in London. As director for master planning, she worked with cultural institutions in the UK, Europe and the Middle East, often at the top level – Ministries of Culture and Tourism. Most notably, she worked for five years on the masterplan and exhibition design for the Grand Egyptian Museum in Cairo, Egypt.

Martin Hodulak is a facility programming and workplace strategy consultant, providing services to government and commercial clients. Over the past 18 years, he has been leading or conducting more than 70 projects on facility programming and workplace design for automotive, pharmaceutical and IT industries, as well as for governmental institutions and higher education facilities. His projects range from small-scale workplace designs up to large programs on the urban design scale, such as the conversion of Berlin Tegel Airport.

Apart from project work, he has been refining methodologies for programming and workplace design. He co-authored the first guidebook on programming for the German market (Hodulak, M. and Schramm, U., *Nutzerorientierte Bedarfsplanung*, Springer, 2011). Martin has lectured on programming and workplace design, and is published in national and international conference proceedings. He was trained as an architect at the University of Karlsruhe and the University of Bath and holds a Ph.D. from the University of Stuttgart. In recent years, he has worked as a project leader, senior consultant and managing director for various architectural and consulting practices.

Zane M. Jones holds a Master's degree in architecture from Arizona State University (2012). He holds an undergraduate degree in English literary studies from Utah State University (2007). Zane also has a certificate in fundamentals of Arctic engineering from University of Alaska Anchorage (2013). Zane has worked for MRV Architects in Juneau, Alaska for several years. Previously he worked for the design-build firm Construction Zone, in Phoenix, Arizona. Prior to his career and education in architecture, he worked in various construction trades, specializing in finish carpentry. He spent two years studying and living in Norway, and speaks fluent Norwegian. Northern climates and design have been a prominent area of his study.

Currently, Zane lives and works in Juneau, Alaska. He is currently the chair of the Juneau Historic Resource Advisory Committee, a board member on the Juneau Commission on Sustainability, and a board member of the Juneau Jazz and Classics Festival. He actively participates in Southeast Alaska culture and design.

Akikazu Kato is Professor of Architecture at the Mie University Graduate School of Engineering in Japan. His appointment includes teaching and research responsibilities in the fields of architectural planning and facility management. Previous positions involved serving as faculty member at other national universities and working as a licensed architect at Kume Architects. He received his doctorate in engineering from Nagoya University, has published a number of books and refereed papers, and has presented at various international symposia. He also planned and designed a number of architectural projects, mostly in the healthcare field. These include those winning architectural prizes such as the 1991 Minister of Health Award for Hekinan City Hospital and the 2001 Minister of Construction Award for the Asahi–honmachi Housing for Elderly.

Kelly J. Kish received his Bachelor of Arts from UC Berkeley in the history of art in 1988. With construction as his background, he entered the Graduate School of Architecture and Urban Planning at UCLA. There he studied under Frank Israel and Ben Refuerzo, receiving his Master's degree in architecture. After his studies he has worked with several notable architecture offices in both Los Angeles and Santa Barbara including Pleskow + Rael, Kanner Architects, and Shubin + Donaldson. He has established his own firm, Konstruct, and now focuses his attention on construction management.

Karin Liljegren founded Omgivning in 2009, located in downtown Los Angeles. Karin began her architectural career studying at the University of North Carolina, Charlotte, where she received her Bachelor of Arts in architecture. She studied under such notable instructors as Ken Lambla and Lebbeus Woods. She continued her studies at UCLA receiving her Master of Architecture in 1994. There she studied under Thom Mayne and Craig Hodgetts. At UCLA Karin began developing her notion of spatial experience; a notion that would later serve her well working on re-shaping and re-formulating of the historic structures of downtown Los Angeles.

With the completion of her education, Karin began employment with Killefer Flammang Architects. It is here that her love for and passion to breathe new life into the historic structures of downtown Los Angeles was spawned. During her 15 years with KFA, Karin assumed the position of senior associate where she was in charge of the firm's adaptive re-use projects. Karin designed and managed to completion the conversion of 12 historic high-rise office buildings. While preserving and restoring as much historic fabric as possible, these buildings were stripped and were given new life as residential units. Karin was personally responsible for the construction of approximately 3000 new live/work units.

After her tenure with KFA, Karin created Omgivning. She has employed 25 architects and designers, and Omgivning is now recognized as one of the authorities of adaptive re-use in LA. As an office, Omgivning has worked on over 200 of the city's historic downtown buildings and high rises. Karin was instrumental in the development and adaptation of the LA's Adaptive Re-Use Ordinance, which came into effect in 2013.

Allison Lenell Magley holds a Master's degree in architecture from Arizona State University (2012). She has been practicing in the field of architecture and design for several years, prior to and while obtaining her degree. While working towards her architectural degree and working professionally in Phoenix, Magley began to focus her study on healthcare and architecture in the developing world through a semester abroad in Rwanda.

Magley is a registered architect at DWL Architects + Planners, with a focus on the design and development of higher education in the advanced medical sciences. She is continuing to expand on her Master's thesis of healthcare design in Rwanda through humanitarian architectural endeavors led by Habitat for Humanity Global Village. Magley traveled to El Salvador in 2013, Ethiopia in 2014, Cambodia in 2015 and is preparing for her next Global Village trip to Chile in 2017.

Jeffrey L. Morgan is Associate Principal with Grimshaw Architects in Sydney, Australia with over 17 years of international experience working for renowned architectural practices, including previously Foster and Partners and Future Systems, across a diverse range of project sectors including commercial, institutional, retail, hospitality, and residential typologies.

xxiv About the contributors

During his time at Foster and Partners, Jeffrey worked on a number of high-rise commercial projects and was also based in Abu Dhabi for three years delivering the first phases of the Masdar Institute, the first buildings as part of Foster and Partners' master plan for Masdar City – the world's first designed carbon neutral city. At Grimshaw, he has continued to diversify his project portfolio to include master planning and transport infrastructure projects, whilst broadening his commercial sector experience as project architect for 333 George Street, a new boutique commercial offer tower in Sydney's CBD.

Shiho Mori is an associate professor of architecture at Nihon Fukushi University in Japan. She is engaged in consulting on master plans of medical and welfare facilities, focusing on the relation between the management and the space planning. She has presented at international congresses, and worked as a lecturer in a training course for the position of facility director of nursing homes. Her previous positions include a post at Mie University, and as a planner at a housing manufacturer in charge of universally designed household appliances, such as prefabricated modular bathrooms and kitchens. Using the experience from previous posts, she is currently participating in projects from detached houses to a large-scale housing complex focused on universal design.

Gordon Murray has practiced in Glasgow and across Scotland for 35 years. His work has been exhibited at the Royal Institute of British Architects in London, at the Royal Scottish Academy and RIAS in Edinburgh, Rotterdam, and Marseilles – as well as in the 2004 Venice Biennale. He was appointed Professor of Architecture and Urban Design at the University of Strathclyde in 2007. He has occasionally taught in schools of architecture across the UK, as well as the Bauhaus in Dessau, Berlin and in Bilbao at the University of the Basque Country. In 2008 he participated in a conference and workshop in New Zealand on behalf of the Scottish Government and OECD on inclusion and integration through innovation in design. He also acted as design advisor to the City of Melbourne on its new special needs school in 2009/10.

Murray was president of the Royal Incorporation of Architects in Scotland 2003–5 and a trustee of the Lighthouse, Scotland's Centre for Architecture and Design, from 2003–9. A member of the Board of Architects Professional Examination Authority Scotland from 2005–7, he was also chair of SCHOSA – 2010/12 – the Standing Council of Heads of Schools of Architecture across the UK. He is a lead enabling participant with Architecture and Design Scotland.

He merged GMA into Ryder Architecture in 2011/12 and became a partner. Within the practice he is responsible for the Scottish office, which he carries out in parallel with his university activities. The office is involved in commercial, education, healthcare and sustainable energy projects across the country. In 2014 he published a paper: 'Holl and Mackintosh. A Comparative Study of the two buildings by Charles Rennie Mackintosh and Steven Holl at GSA' (*Architectural Research Quarterly,* Vol. 18, No. 2).

John P. Petronis, AICP, AIA founded Architectural Research Consultants, Incorporated (ARC) in 1976. This is the largest and longest-established planning firm in the state. It specializes in facility programming and master planning, and has successfully completed and implemented hundreds of projects. Mr. Petronis holds a Bachelor of Arts degree from Gettysburg College, and Master's degrees in architecture and business administration from the University of New Mexico. He is both a licensed architect and a certified planner. Mr. Petronis' work has been featured in a number of facility planning and programming text books.

Una Rath is a senior project manager in the department for large and significant construction projects at the Berlin senate authority for urban development. She studied building services engineering at the University for Applied Sciences in Erfurt, Germany. She has a professional background in building services engineering, planning, and construction management. Recent projects include the refurbishment of the Berlin Olympic stadium for the Word Soccer Championship in 2006, refurbishment of the Berlin International Congress Center, and the re-use of Tegel Airport in Berlin.

In her projects, Una Rath promotes holistic concepts and an integrative planning approach. Characteristic for this approach is the intense involvement and collaboration of all relevant stakeholders and professional disciplines throughout the various planning and realization phases. Una's focus is on sustainable building operation, overall economy, energy efficiency, and resource conservation in the context of the building life cycle. She regards interdisciplinary collaboration and merging of architectural and engineering skills as key challenges, but also as a factor of success of sustainable building projects. She is currently completing her Master's thesis on energy and resource efficiency at the Beuth University of Applied Sciences in Berlin.

Dr. Jennifer L. Rochlis received her Ph.D. in aeronautics and astronautics from the Massachusetts Institute of Technology in Cambridge, MA, and her certification in Human Systems Integration (HSI) from the Naval Post Graduate School. She has been working at the NASA Johnson Space Center in Houston, TX in areas including human systems integration, human factors engineering, commercial partner integration, requirements management, human rating, teleoperation and telerobotics.

Dr. Rochlis is currently the space human factors and habitability element manager for the NASA human research program. In this role she manages a multi-center, multi-discipline research, and technical team responsible for burning down the top risks to human health and performance for future NASA missions in areas including habitability, microbiology, dust, advanced food, human computer interaction, training, human automation and robotic interaction, task design, and occupant protection.

She is also the lead for the NASA Office of Chief Engineer HSI Steering Committee, and the Johnson Space Center Lead for the Agency Human Factors Capabilities Leadership Team. She has received a Center Director's Innovation Award for her work on telerobotics projects including Robonaut, the next generation lunar/Martian rovers, and ground control of Space Station and Space Shuttle arms. She has authored book chapters for the Human Factors and Ergonomics Society and for Springer's *Bioastronautics Encyclopedia* (in progress). She is a member of the Human Factors and Ergonomics Society, and a committee co-chair for the National Defense Industrial Association.

Jaclyn M. Roessel's work as an arts and museum professional cultivated Roessel's belief in the value of utilizing cultural learning as a tool for developing communities and engaging community members. Driven by her own experience being born and raised on the Navajo Nation, her work asserts the value of the first-person narrative and traditional American

Indian philosophy in communicating and creating culturally responsive educational programming. She applies these efforts in her role as education and public programs director at the Heard Museum in Phoenix, Arizona.

Roessel is a digital media content producer. Through public speaking engagements, her podcast, and writing on her blogs, she examines the influence of traditional American Indian history and teachings on modern American Indian culture and society.

Ulrich Schramm is a professor in the field of architecture and civil engineering at the Bielefeld University of Applied Sciences, Minden Campus, in Germany. His appointment includes teaching and research responsibilities in the field of facility programming, building performance evaluation, and building technologies. He is a trained architect and an experienced facility programmer. He received his doctorate in architecture from the University of Stuttgart and a post-doctoral fellowship from the German Research Foundation (Deutsche Forschungsgemeinschaft, DFG) for his stay at the University of Cincinnati as visiting professor of architecture. Results of his studies within the International Building Performance Evaluation (IBPE) consortium and the campus-based research project Intelligent Building Technologies (InteG-F) have been presented at conferences of the Environmental Design Research Association (EDRA) since 1995 and published in several articles and book chapters. He has recently written some chapters that were published in *Enhancing Building Performance* (Wiley-Blackwell, 2012) and *Architecture Beyond Criticism: Expert Judgment and Performance Evaluation* (Routledge, 2015). He also co-authored the first book on facility programming in Germany *Nutzerorientierte Bedarfsplanung: Prozessqualität für nachhaltige Gebäude* (Springer, 2011). Currently, he is serving at the German Institute for Standardization (Deutsches Institut für Normung, DIN) in Berlin as expert and co-chair of the revised edition of the German building standard DIN 18205 *Brief for Building Design*.

Robert G. Shibley, FAIA, FAICP, is a professor and dean at the School of Architecture and Planning, University at Buffalo (UB) where he also serves as the campus architect. His tenure with UB dates back to 1982, when he was recruited as a professor and chair of the Department of Architecture. He has authored, co-authored or edited 13 books, 14 book chapters, 14 US government publications and over 100 articles dedicated to place making, urban design and evidence-based design. Among many lifetime achievement awards he was recognized with the James Haecker Distinguished Leadership Award from the Architectural Research Centers Consortium and the 2014 Thomas Jefferson Award from the American Institute of Architects. The Jefferson Award for public architecture recognized Bob's role in preparing a national and international award-winning suite of economic development, comprehensive and urban design plans still guiding development for the City of Buffalo, the University at Buffalo, and the Buffalo and Niagara region in western New York.

Korydon Smith is a professor in the Department of Architecture at the University at Buffalo-SUNY, where he teaches undergraduate and graduate courses in architectural design, theory, and methods. His primary research focuses on design for social justice. Recent books include *Just Below the Line: Disability, Housing, and Equity in the South* (University of Arkansas Press, 2010), *Universal Design Handbook,* 2nd edition (McGraw-Hill, 2010), *Introducing Architectural Theory: Debating a Discipline* (Routledge, 2012), and *Diversity and Design: Understanding Hidden Consequences* (Routledge, 2015).

Molly Smith is an educational planner, facilitator, writer, researcher, speaker, and community member. She is a certified planner – a designation awarded by the American Planning Association. Her consulting firm, thinkSMART Planning Inc., is committed to the creation of learning environments that support the latest thinking in teaching and learning. Her broad-ranging experience includes facility programming, master planning, space utilization analysis, budget and financial analysis, and site selections for over 20 million square feet of educational space. Ms. Smith is a nationally recognized authority on all aspects of K–12 planning as well as career technical facilities and adaptive reuse for education. She has written and spoken extensively on school planning techniques and school facilities' connection to student improvement. Currently, she is collaborating with Robert Hershberger on a second edition to his book *Architectural Programming and Pre-design Manager*, co-writing new standards for the planning portion of the NCARB exam, and assisting Mr. Hershberger with a mini-monograph series on planning for architects. She holds both a Master's and Bachelor's degree in architecture from Florida A&M University.

Gen Taniguchi is a former presidential advisor on facility management at Nagoya University in Japan. He served as head of the facility management office, as well as a professor of architecture. He was involved in the development of a campus master plan and townscape management, and also asset management of public facilities. His previous positions include professorships at various universities. He worked as a licensed architect at INA Architects, has published a number of books and refereed papers, and has planned and designed a number of hospitals and welfare facilities.

Beth Tauke is Associate Professor in the Department of Architecture at the University at Buffalo-SUNY, and a project director in the Center for Inclusive Design and Environmental Access (IDEA), the leading research center on universal design in the built environment in the US. Her research focuses on design education and inclusive design, especially the empowerment of minority groups through design. Her primary professional goal is to encourage university administrators to include courses in their general education or core programs that address the relationship between design and diversity issues, an essential element of 21st-century education.

Dr. Alexandra Whitmire has been with Wyle, prime contractor for NASA Johnson Space Center in Houston, Texas, since 2006. She began as a research coordinator for the Behavioral Health and Performance Element (BHP) in the Human Research Program, then became a BHP Portfolio Scientist focusing on research related to circadian, sleep, and workload-related risks on orbit. In 2014, she became the Deputy Element Scientist for NASA BHP, where she currently serves. In addition to strategic planning for the BHP risk mitigation strategy – which also targets research related to optimizing team cohesion and performance, as well as mitigating adverse behavioral and cognitive outcomes – she has helped to develop clinical practice guidelines for mitigating circadian misalignment caused by jet-lag and overnight shifts, for NASA and international space agencies. She has also helped to lead the development of evidence-based requirements for a lighting system on the ISS, and to develop recommendations for acceptable net habitable volume for future spaceflight vehicles.

During her time with BHP, Dr. Whitmire pursued and received her Ph.D. in industrial organizational psychology (with a focus on occupational healthy psychology) from

Capella University. She previously received her Masters of Science degree from University of Texas at San Antonio and her Bachelors of Arts degree in English and psychology from the University of Texas at Austin. She has received several awards including the JSC Director's Innovation Group Achievement Award NASA Exceptional Service Medal for her work as a lead on the ISS Flexible Lighting Team. She has published several manuscripts as NASA Technical Memorandums including a comprehensive report on sleep-related issues with 76 Shuttle Astronauts.

Dr. Mihriban Whitmore received her Ph.D. in industrial engineering from the Wichita State University in Wichita, KS, and her certification in HSI from the Naval Post Graduate School. She has received numerous awards including NASA Exceptional Service Medal for her work as the Orion HSI Lead and Health and Medical Technical Authority Delegate, and Human Factors and Ergonomics Society Alexander Williams Design, and NASA Astronauts Personal Achievement (Silver Snoopy) Awards for her work on the ISS glovebox and crew restraints design. She has authored a book chapter on the fundamentals of aerospace medicine and published manuscripts in numerous journals including the *International Journal of Industrial Ergonomics,* and the *Journal of Aviation, Space and Environmental Medicine.*

Dr. Mihriban Whitmore is currently the space human factors and habitability element scientist for the NASA Human Research Program. In this role, she oversees the strategic planning and execution of multi-center, multi-discipline research for future NASA exploration missions on human factors (human computer interaction, training, human automation and robotic interaction, task design), habitability, microbiology, dust, advanced food, and occupant protection. She is also the operating board member of the DoD HFE Technical Advisory Group (TAG), and the chair of the DoD HFE Extreme Environments Sub-TAG.

Faye Whittemore, AIA, LEED AP BD+C, NCARB, is a licensed architect and LEED AP BD+C for ARC. She has 13 years of experience in a variety of project types, including schools, healthcare and government facilities, and multifamily housing. She is a project manager focusing on master planning and programming for educational institutions. Ms. Whittemore received a Master of Architecture from the University of Michigan in 2005, and a Bachelor of Science in architecture, with a minor in environmental science, from the University of Virginia in 2001.

FOREWORD

Adaptive Architecture was in the final stages of going to press when the consortium of authors and collaborative editors were notified of co-editor Wolfgang Preiser's death. As we celebrate his life, we can take comfort in the fact that Wolf, with many other collaborators, produced well over 25 books, scores of conference and workshop events, as well as hundreds of research projects and published articles. Through this process he has mentored thousands of students, colleagues, and friends. All of this means that he will live on for decades, if not centuries. Even with that said, he will be missed.

It is hard for me to imagine a world without Wolfgang Preiser in it. Wolf asked me to write the foreword to this new book, *Adaptive Architecture: Changing Parameters and Practice,* and I gladly accepted as I have known him and respected his work since 1973. We first met at the third conference of the rapidly maturing Environmental Design Research Association. It is an honor to offer my comments and thoughts on this, one of his last books, and I will deviate a little from the normal foreword format to include a bit of a eulogy to this special researcher and human being.

Adaptive Architecture was developed with a large contingent of very solid contributors and extraordinary efforts by co-editors Wolf Preiser, Andrea Hardy, and Jacob Wilhelm to explore the idea of adaptability in design. The introduction to the book suggests the importance of a deeper and more nuanced look at "new and interacting systems, showcased through case studies that identify and investigate the variety of ways that adaptability has influenced and been addressed in architecture today, and how that may continue to revolutionize this field in the future."

The book is a call for us to understand the inevitability of change and the promise of the built world we make, manage, and sustain to adapt to such change – or maybe even lead the changes through the agency of the places we influence and the collaborative design methods we employ. This book demonstrates the ongoing making of architecture through the practice of placemaking, focusing on the relationships between people and the places they live and work, as well as the relations among people in such places over time.

One might assume that the book is a series of disciplined case studies of how buildings and people react to changes occurring largely out of their control. My interpretation of the

xxx Foreword

work of the authors, the subjects of their case studies, and the passions represented, however, reveal that people and places are far from passive reactors. The case histories and critical reflections they offer give agency to both place and the processes by which changes to place are proposed. Examples demonstrate even very special purpose facilities are reused often and function beautifully for all users. Churches become apartments, school buildings are transformed into co-housing facilities, gas stations become restaurants, and federal office buildings become mixed-use hotel, conference center, and condominium projects.

My own School of Architecture and Planning at the University at Buffalo, Hayes Hall, was once an asylum for the insane designed according to the Kirkbride model popular in the late 19th century. It was later a home for unwed mothers before becoming the administrative office of the University at Buffalo, and in its latest incarnation, home of the architecture and planning school. The latest restoration brought with it a listing on the national register for historic places and it is designed to exceed Leadership in Energy and Environmental Design (LEED) gold standards. Well-made spaces have served a variety of functions over almost a century and a half: supporting psychiatric care, education, historic preservation, universal design, environmental systems design, and the study of architecture and planning in the modern university. We all live in such adapted buildings and landscapes, and without doubt Hayes Hall will likely have yet more reincarnations.

The authors assembled here champion the intention for the built world to not just accommodate but actually facilitate achieving the human aspiration to live life well with the environment they inhabit. They have neatly rolled up over half a century of critical inquiry and precedent framing a response to, "where to from here," for habitability study and the broad range of topics and scales connected to creating an adaptable yet clearly beautiful and life-supporting world.

The life work of Wolfgang Preiser and many of his co-editors and authors are embedded in the intellectual traditions and the evolution of our understanding of placemaking. Their reflections on case studies reinforce the interface of environmental, organizational, and cultural forces. Not understanding their interaction can result in facilities that exclude some populations. In *Adaptive Architecture: Changing Parameters and Practice* the editors and their authors give new meaning to the very idea that we can only know what we are organized to know as they frame clearer and ever more proactive ways to ensure that the built environment is made adaptable to changing circumstances.

So how do we think of the spaces among many forces in the context of a specific project or place? Jacob Bronowski's brief text titled *Science and Human Values* (1965) offers us a way to understand the richness the editors have brought to the subject of adaptable environments. Bronowski identifies three core elements essential to understanding meaningful science and, I would argue, a meaningful address to making places. He calls for "a habit of truth," a "sense of human dignity" and "a creative mind." Preiser, Hardy, and Wilhelm assembled authors that exhibit each of these elements of Bronowski's way of thinking about science.

Adaptive Architecture is filled with cases that demonstrate respect for evidence-based design. The cases embody the use of the social and physical sciences and clearly engage the habit of truth as a grounding ethic. They do this as a matter of course, not as some form of heroic departure from what was often described as the norm in the practice of design. The integrity of the work is woven throughout the book.

But honesty is not enough. It needs to come with a more nuanced understanding of built-in bias related to the structure of inquiry. We really can only know what we organize to know, and honesty through science, absent an understanding of the biases presented by the limited set of questions it can answer, often leaves out the nuances that make us human.

Bronowski suggests that, when practiced with a sense of human dignity, science can, and often does, find a way to sustain its habit of truth even as it embraces what it cannot know, respects competing value systems, and allows for multiple and often conflicting ways of knowing. There is richness to the cases offered in this book as it presents sites of inquiry that were not easy to research. Many of the chapters involved very complex collaborations among people from very different intellectual traditions. The authors and the people involved in the case histories reported were as interested in the behavior settings they explored as they were in the challenges in relationships among people and places. Diversity and inclusion give emphasis to the human side of our time in place. In the aggregate, the work engages a mix of ages, incomes, cultural conditions, and abilities.

The body of work also tends to avoid simple assertions of cause and effect and, from my reading, avoids the presumption that knowing what to do actually translates into getting it done. Good science is not evidence that tells us what to do, but rather offers help in understanding what is really going on. This evidence needs to blend with an understanding of how this reality is valued by those affected by the behavior setting being considered, and what the range of alternative ways of making might be that would relate both the evidence and its value. All this may then also need to be tempered by limits to tolerance. Human values cannot wish away the real consequences of our actions. Gravity is real; so also are the dramatic changes we are experiencing in our climate due to our addiction to fossil fuels.

Perhaps the most important element of Bronowski's lens on science is the mandate to exercise a creative mind in the conduct of our science. The creative act of framing the questions to be asked involves thinking about how the research will add value to the conversation on what to do and how we should think about alternative responses. This is when the habit of truth, the sense of human dignity, and the creative mind are fully engaged.

This, one of Wolfgang Preiser's last collaborative books, affirms his understanding of the complexity of placemaking as an ongoing practice whether in programming for new construction, evaluating operations, or developing adaptive reuses for existing building. He was a pioneer in his insistence that people come with their worlds and environments, and that those who make buildings are doing so for real flesh-and-blood human beings who have requirements and desires of their own.

Personally, I remember him as a mentor and colleague who invited me to EDRA 4 to present my first academic paper in April of 1973. I was, at this time, a new university graduate serving as a second lieutenant in the special projects office in the US Army Office of the Chief of Engineers. The mission of our small unit was nothing less than to support the Army's transition from a conscription to a volunteer force. I worked with Preiser and many other scholars and practitioners in the development of guidelines for these facilities. These men and women were the leaders in the emerging discipline of environmental design and founded the Environmental Design Research Association in the early 1970s.

In his introduction to the proceedings of that 1973 conference, Preiser described the symposium in language that envisioned his trajectory as a scholar:

> (The symposium) … focuses on the consideration of need fulfillment on the individual, social, and ecological levels of functioning. Realization of research potential requires institutional innovation to … enable coordination of effort among mission-restricted

institutions and agencies whose combined effort is essential to resolve environmental problems. Public awareness of issues needs to be increased and the communications gap between design researchers and policy makers needs to be bridged. Furthermore, only holistic theory can form the basis for actions that will contribute to system stability with options for adaptive evolution. (Preiser, 1973, p. v)

Adaptive Architecture: Changing Parameters and Practice is in a great tradition of research and practice in environmental design. As the case studies demonstrate, we work with imperfect but ever improving models that describe our understanding of the constantly changing pressures to adapt, the methods of adaptation, and the consequences of both. We collectively do this work to improve the quality of life for all people, deploying as we can Bronowski's habit of truth through disciplined science, sense of human dignity through our respect for the people we study and build for, and by using as best we can a creative mind.

The case studies in this volume are asking about what an ethic and practice of fully adaptable, universal, and ecological design might mean as we continue to make and unmake our world. It explores the use of new tools and ways of thinking brought to us by the way computing allows the designer's model or drawing to get closer to the full capacity to fabricate and construct. Some of these tools and thought processes also bring us closer to systematically analyzing the consequences of one kind of action over another, giving us the capacity to model alternative "shared economies," materials, tectonics, typologies, social structures, behaviors, and their associated ecological and cultural impacts. As Preiser's work over his lifetime demonstrates, we can work to proactively adapt as scholars and placemakers with our shifting worlds. Thanks Wolf.

Robert G. Shibley, FAIA, FAICP,
Professor and Dean,
School of Architecture and Planning,
University at Buffalo

Bibliography

Bronowski, J. (1965). *Science and Human Values*, New York: Harper & Row.
Preiser, Wolfgang F. E. (1973). *Environmental Design Research: Volume Two Symposia and Workshops*, Stroudsburg, PA: Dowden, Hutchinson & Ross.
Schneekloth, L. and Shibley, R. (1995). *Placemaking: The Art and Science of Building Communities*, New York: John Wiley & Sons.

PREFACE

In 1943, Winston Churchill famously and astutely observed in the Commons: "We shape our buildings, thereafter they shape us." This insight certainly applies to *Adaptive Architecture: Changing Parameters and Practice*, as it reflects upon the relationships between the physical environment, especially the designed and built environment, and its occupants. The mutual dependency between all species and their adopted habitats can change from year to year and from country to country, depending on climate and many other factors.

In an age when technological revolutions take place on a regular basis, adapting architecture and its occupants is a foregone conclusion and necessity. Both need to be flexible and need to be willing to adopt different attitudes and spatial configurations that can take on multiple functions over time. This movement was underscored in the article "WeWork's Top Rival: Anyone and Everyone" (Brown, 2016). In a "sharing economy" they must make economic sense, because of the enormous expenditure for designing and building for clients with changing populations like workers, schoolchildren, and hospital staff. As the Introduction to *Adaptive Architecture* shows, emerging trends of our time are multi-faceted and frequent. This reality provides the backdrop for the chapters that follow, organized in the six parts of this book.

These parts contain different aspects of *Adaptive Architecture,* including concepts and processes for future flexibility; rooms/setting scale; building scale; and urban scale. This is followed by the Epilogue in which the International Space Station's design, construction, and use are described by NASA staff. As such it points into the future of habitable environments under extreme conditions. Each one of these parts of the book has a unique preamble and reflections element. Preambles are authored by the first chapter author of each part, giving an overview of each chapter and highlighting possible connections among the chapters. Reflections are by Michael J. Crosbie on significant discoveries and lessons learned in each of the parts of the book.

The book's Appendix highlights theoretical considerations and presents the habitability paradigm, which is the conceptual foundation for much of the discussion in this book.

Most of the authors in this book have collaborated over the years in one way or another, whether in book chapters, research articles, or book projects. Tom Fisher, for example, was

xxxiv Preface

a co-editor of *Designing for Designers: Lessons Learned From Schools of Architecture* (2007) and was formerly editor of the journal *Progressive Architecture,* which sponsored the annual P/A Awards for many years in categories such as Design, Urban Design, and Applied Research.

The process of programming for flexibility is highlighted by Robert G. Hershberger, who authored the book *Architectural Programming* (1999), and Molly E. Smith. They emphasize the different values and methodologies that steer the architectural programming process.

"Challenges of Large-Scale Housing in the Developing World: The Habitat for Humanity Global Village Project in Ethiopia" by Alison L. Magley shows the global dimension of adaptive architecture. In this case the project, sponsored by Habitat for Humanity International, is promoting self-help in housing for a poor and uneducated population, using local materials and customs in assembling them.

Another example of changing situations in the world of design and construction is the concept of sustainability. Ihab Elzeyadi presents a multi-performance space assessment using the green LEED approach to fostering sustainability in the case of a university building.

A chapter on indigenous peoples in the United States is also included, with a focus on the one-room dwelling of traditional Navajo culture called the Hogan. This chapter allows the book to not only look at the future aspects of adaptive architecture, but also very similar, relevant, and practical historical examples.

Finally, this book covers the example of ingenious utilization of air rights in a country where space is very scarce, e.g., Japan. A multi-functional mixed-use development above the Japan Rail (JR) Nagoya station illustrates how creative and imaginative combinations of uses can result in new perspectives on urban life. The J. R. Central Towers complex, among other things, contains a sky mall 12 floors up from the ground level, a concept that would never appeal to shoppers in Western countries where shopping at street level or several levels near the ground is common.

As far as building types are concerned the range includes: museums; emergency rooms in hospitals; offices; educational facilities; cultural centers; and the re-utilization of airports for transformation into higher education space.

From a cultural perspective, countries like the United States, Australia, Japan, Canada, the United Kingdom, South Africa, Israel, and Germany are represented.

Wolfgang F. E. Preiser
Andrea E. Hardy
Jacob J. Wilhelm

References

Brown, E., (2016). "WeWork's Top Rival: Anyone and Everyone." *Wall Street Journal*, Wednesday, July 13, P. C6.
Hershberger, R. G. (1999). *Architectural Programming and Predesign Manager*. New York: McGraw Hill; re-issued, (2015) London: Routledge.

ACKNOWLEDGMENTS

The idea for this book was born in conversations between the editors, with their different perspectives, ideas, and experiences. The first editor, Wolfgang F. E. Preiser, was an active member of International Building Performance Evaluation (IBPE) and the Environmental Design Research Association (EDRA) since their conception. With Preiser's long history with these two organizations, and the experience in designing flexible, multipurpose spaces of the second editor, Andrea E. Hardy, the concept of the book blossomed to combine a career spanning many decades and continents with professional practice and research as they are understood today. Through the support of the Arizona State University Emeritus College the third editor, Jacob J. Wilhelm, brought a fresh perspective, refinement, and research to support the future-oriented nature of the book, completing a team that unites authors from around the globe.

As the table of contents indicates, contributors to this volume come from Europe, Africa, North America, Australia, and Asia, bringing with them local experience in evaluating facilities at different scales. The six major parts of this book are structured accordingly.

Part I serves as an introduction to emerging trends and innovative forces that are currently shaping our changing world. Part II deals with new technologies and conceptual approaches to designed, built, and occupied environments. Part III progresses to environments at the setting or room scale, followed by Part IV covering the building scale, and Part V discussing the campus and urban scale. A complete timeline of historical and future environments is investigated, ranging from indigenous design practices to the complex outer reaches of space stations as identified in Part VI of the book, the Epilogue.

First, we thank all of our authors, many of whom crossed language and geographic barriers to further the discourse on architectural design, construction, and building evaluation. Chapter contributions share the authors' projects, research, and findings from architecture firms around the world and reveal inspiring dedication to asking more of the built environment.

We thank all of the organizations that were clients to the editors and authors, who provided releases of information, quoted text, illustrations, and photography, as well as Deirdre Price, who helped process dictations for various parts of this book.

xxxvi Acknowledgments

Thanks are owed to our significant others, family, and friends who have supported us during the multiple-year journey of developing, producing, and editing this book project.

Finally, Jacob and Andrea want to extend a special thanks to Wolf, who passed away before this book could be published. We are forever grateful for the knowledge, guidance, and optimism he shared with us, and his mentorship will be missed.

PART I
Introduction

INTRODUCTION

Wolfgang F. E. Preiser, Thomas Fisher, and Andrea E. Hardy

I.1 Synopsis

Adaptive architecture can accommodate multiple purposes at the same time, sequentially, or at periodically recurring events. While most buildings—and the structures, materials, and environments that comprise them—have adaptable qualities, adaptive architecture has emerged as an important issue because of changing technology and economic dislocations that have drastically altered the field. For example, look at the impact of Uber (Barbaro and Parker, 2015). A globally successful car-sharing company, Uber allows individuals to use their personal vehicles as taxi cabs and to communicate with potential clients needing transportation through innovative applications downloaded to one's smartphone. This same evolution of a "sharing economy" has changed architecture from the conceptualizing, designing, and constructing of buildings to the creating of interacting, synergistically interdependent, distributed systems, fueled by the invention and global use of the Internet. WeWork, provider of shared office space for small companies and technology start-ups, earned a market valuation of ten billion dollars after only six months since its first offering. This phenomenon affects retail merchandising and urban infrastructure as much as the design and construction of architecture. The chapters that follow explore such new and interacting systems, showcased through case studies that identify and investigate the variety of ways that adaptability influences architecture today, and how they may continue to revolutionize this field in the future.

This book also explores the transformation happening in architectural practice as a result of the digital revolution, which has changed the world dramatically in the last several decades. Because of digital technology, practitioners must be aware and knowledgeable about a variety of innovative topics, and be able to accomplish many more tasks within ever shorter timeframes. As described in "Déjà vu" by Michael Totty (2002), the developments of the printing press, telegraph, radio, railway, airplanes, and the Internet historically made it easier for professionals, academics, designers, and people in general to share ideas and conceive new ones rapidly. While all of these inventions greatly influenced communication among people, with each step in technology there is an implicit expectation that we obtain

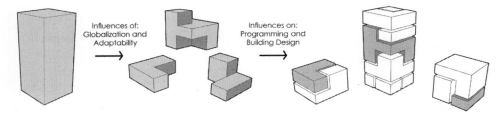

Most companies start with a main headquarters. With the influences of globalization and the internet, they are given opportunities to expand. This then means that there are smaller "pods" of the company in many other locations. These smaller pods share larger buildings with other companies, ultimately changing the trend in architecture from one-tenant design to a multi-tasking, adaptive multi-tenant building design.

FIGURE I.1 Influences of globalization and adaptability in commercial building design.
Source: Jacob J. Wilhelm.

more information, interpret it, and then put it to use for the benefit of society at large: an adaptability of knowledge and communication (Totty, 2002). Through the development of digital technology and the global economy, companies can now quickly share documents and information over long distances, allowing organizations to divide major headquarters into smaller segmented entities of the business in locations around the world (Figure I.1). Not only does this allow businesses to extend their global reach, but it also creates a new architecture of shared spaces, which can lead to collaboration among industries. This book has, as its main premise, flexibility at numerous levels, highlighted by the concepts and execution of the case studies that follow.

I.2 Historical development of adaptive architecture

Change remains the only constant in the evolution of architecture. Hence, this book examines architecture as it has changed from utilitarian edifices serving basic community needs like fortifications for defense, aqueducts for water supply, harbors, roadways, and other hubs of transportation, all the way to today's highly fragmented and specialized creation of spaces for living, working, producing, and conducting commercial activities, which are reflected in the popular phrase "Live. Work. Play" now used by many developers and designers. The book will also address facilities for schooling and education, healthcare, public services, recreation and entertainment, as well as other building types.

Such fragmented spaces continue to shape our culture and, in turn, our culture affects the design of our built spaces. The iterative influences between culture and architecture would not be possible without studies and analysis on functionality and habitability. Through the exploration of post-occupancy evaluations (POEs), building performance evaluations (BPEs), as well as research on "habitability," designers are able to push the envelope of architecture forward by learning what buildings need and envisioning how they can adapt.

I.2.1 Functionality of adaptive architecture and flexible spaces

As a sub-discipline of architecture, a systematic approach to architectural programming originated in the 1950s, with POEs pioneered in the mid-1960s and universal design as a movement taking off in the mid-1980s. All of these subfields are concerned with the quality of the built environment as the end users experience it, and thus, they help us understand the functionality and habitability of adaptive spaces.

With constantly changing technology and with spaces increasingly programmed for multiple functions, it is becoming important to evaluate the levels of performance of buildings: their health and safety, their functional and task performance, as well as their level of social and psychological comfort and cultural satisfaction (Preiser and Hardy, 2015). By conducting research, observations, and interviews of these performance levels, we can assess the usefulness, habitability, and need for multi-functional, multi-tasking, and adaptive spaces. Through the evaluation of a building's actual uses, we can begin to understand the habitability of its spaces.

I.2.2 Habitability and adaptive architecture

The emergence of the design and behavior field dates back to the mid-1960s. Variously referred to as environmental psychology, architectural psychology, ecological psychology, socio-physical technology, person–environment relations, man–environment relations, and human factors, its name depends upon which discipline or agency originates and sponsors it. We use the name "design and behavior field" to signify its relevance and utility to architecture and planning, and to a lesser degree to the social sciences.

Elements of the design and behavior field, or what some call the "Habitability Paradigm" (see the Appendix), include buildings/settings, occupants, and occupant needs. It deals with the physical environment on a setting-by-setting basis, and builds up in scale from the immediate or proximate environment of people. Each higher order scale of the environment is comprised of units at lower scales, leading to the following hierarchy:

- region—an assembly of communities at the geographic scale;
- community—an assembly of city blocks or neighborhoods;
- facility—a complex of buildings such as a military base or campus;.
- building—an assembly of rooms or spaces;
- room—an assembly of workstations or activity/behavior settings;
- activity setting—the proximate environment in which behavior occurs, e.g., a workstation.

Adaptive Architecture covers not only the process of creating built environments but also the majority of the scales listed above. The past, present, and future habitability of a project directly relates to its adaptive capability, and the Appendix provides further insight into the theory and evolution of the "Habitability Paradigm."

Habitability also relates to the many guidelines and code requirements that influence how the architecture profession responds to the continuously developing design and behavior field. Code requirements that reflect and enforce the American Disabilities Act (ADA), for example, have led to Universal Design, which transcends the ADA in spirit. The current trend toward adaptive public and private spaces shows the need to relate people to their surrounding spaces on one hand, and through universal design, to make products, buildings, transportation systems, and information technology accessible to all people on the other. Universal design follows the democratic principle of equality for all, regardless of disabilities, ethnicity, or culture (Preiser and Ostroff, 2001; Preiser and Smith, 2011). While information generated by the design and behavior field needs to become more easily accessible to and usable by architects, it is hoped that the applications of behavioral science in architecture and

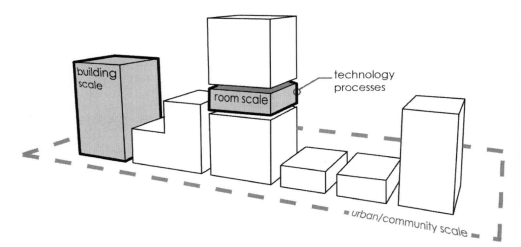

FIGURE I.2 Scales of adaptivity.
Source: Jacob J. Wilhelm

environmental design will continue to improve the quality of our everyday environment in the long run.

The design and behavior field emphasizes the interrelationships, rather than cause–effect relationships, among environmental influences and people, which rules out architectural determinism. Like any other living species, humans seek equilibrium with a dynamic, ever changing environment, and through the use of analogies—such as living systems, organisms, and living species—we can more easily relate to and better understand the world around us. "[Analogies] make complicated things easier for people to grasp by stripping them to their essence. The very best analogies make things as simple as possible—but no simpler" (Pollack, 2014). Through analogous, combinatorial thinking, designers can generate new and stimulating solutions to current-day issues, and create a more adaptive architecture in the process.

I.3 Future trends

Since before the Industrial Revolution, companies have sought ways to streamline their operations through quicker production, fewer people, and faster assembly lines; although we now know that repetitive motion does not necessarily create healthy environments, quality products, and profitable companies. Thomas Petzinger argues that companies should stop mimicking machines and start relating more to living systems and human ecologies. By doing this, "[companies] are leading business back to its roots as a nature and fundamentally human institution" (Petzinger, 1999). That idea underpins the new human-centered economy emerging in our midst—one that the economist Jeremy Rifkin has called the "Third Industrial Revolution" (Rifkin, 2011). This is good news for the architectural profession. Industrial revolutions require the redesign of almost everything, and if the profession can cast aside some of its old practices and assumptions about what architecture entails and recognize the vast array of design opportunities that the new economy has created, the profession will see no end to the work it has to do.

Although Rifkin pays relatively little attention to architecture in his book, his argument has profound implications for the profession's future: how we will plan cities, design buildings, practice architecture, and educate architects. The Third Industrial Revolution "will fundamentally change every aspect of the way we work and live," Rifkin writes. Small-scale, crowd-funded fabrication will gradually replace large-scale, capital-intensive manufacturing; nimble, networked organizations will steadily prevail over big, hierarchical companies; and the global movement of digital files will increasingly supplant the global trade of goods. If the steam engine became the iconic technology of the First Industrial Revolution, and the assembly line that of the second, 3D printing may well become the icon of the third.

The field of architecture has experienced such massive economic disruptions before. The modern profession emerged during the First Industrial Revolution in the 19th century, as the mechanization of manual labor led to the need for new types of buildings, and as technology allowed us to build larger and taller. The profession as we still largely practice it today arose in the 20th century, as the mass production and consumption of the Second Industrial Revolution inspired the rise of specialized architectural firms able to mass-produce big buildings. It also gave birth to star architects (so called "starchitects") able to create signature structures suitable for mass-media consumption.

Although the Second Industrial Revolution isn't over yet, it has entered what Rifkin calls its "end game," with an unsustainable dependence on fossil fuels and unsupportable levels of debt. Meanwhile, the Third Industrial Revolution has emerged at a staggering pace: consider how quickly social media has transformed the news business, online streaming has upended the music industry, and Google has become one of the most valuable companies in the world in just 15 years.

I.3.1 Wiki architecture

Adrian Smith + Gordon Gill Architecture's design for the World Expo 2017 in Kazakhstan represents one of the first architectural explorations of Rifkin's ideas. Comprising a globe-like national pavilion surrounded by streamlined structures for exhibits, meetings, and performances, the expo will have features that Rifkin sees as "pillars" of the new economy: renewable energy, hydrogen fuels, smart grids, and electric vehicles.

Expo 2017 will broadcast the idea of a Third Industrial Revolution to a global audience. But the real impact of this revolution on architecture will happen as we shift from an economy of mass production and consumption to an economy based on mass customization. That may not seem like a threat to architecture, as our field knows how to customize design to meet client needs. The challenge will come from learning how to mass customize architecture in an economy in which everyone may become a producer as well as a consumer of design.

Alastair Parvin, a U.K.-based designer, shows how this might happen: he and his team developed an open-source design of a small, extremely low-cost "WikiHouse" and demonstrated how ordinary people can download the file, cut out the parts on a computer-controlled machine, and erect the rectangular, gable-roofed structure themselves, without the need of tools or construction skills. If the 20th century "democratized consumption," Parvin says, the 21st century will "democratize production," with mass customization efforts like his.

I.3.2 Digi-cities

Think of what this might mean for cities. Most of us still inhabit the unsustainable model of the Second Industrial Revolution: living in residential areas, commuting to work in commercial districts, and buying goods often produced at a large scale in distant places. The Third Industrial Revolution may flip that equation. Consider the many software and digital fabrication companies that have sprung up in cities all over the U.S.: their staffs increasingly live, work, and make things—even grow things—all in close proximity.

Fostering such economic activity may require a rethinking of public policies that still largely support the old economy of mass production and consumption. The separation of residential, commercial, and industrial zones, for example, has become a barrier to innovation, which increasingly depends upon maximizing the interactions among diverse people and enterprises. This may, in turn, cast New Urbanism in a new light. More walkable communities and denser mixed-use and mixed-income neighborhoods will now have economic benefits as well as social and environmental ones.

I.3.3 Customizable buildings

The Third Industrial Revolution, much like the previous two, may also lead to new kinds of buildings. Just as we separated cities in the 20th century into single-use zones, we constructed a lot of buildings for singular purposes, full of special-use spaces. That made sense in the old economy based on disaggregation and specialization, but in the new economy—characterized by a fluidity between living, working, and making—purpose-built structures will quickly become obsolete.

To see the future, we might look at where many businesses at the vanguard of the Third Industrial Revolution have gone: to the warehouse districts of cities. They have done so not because entrepreneurs like exposed brick but because older warehouses often have the spatial flexibility and structural capacity to accommodate a wide variety of uses. This suggests that the buildings that will thrive in the new economy will have an adaptive character, with high ceilings, hefty construction, and open plans that allow people to mass customize their own space.

Developers like Artspace have shown how to do this in new and old buildings, working with architects in several cities. Their projects accommodate a wide range of creative business and artistic practices, with residential, commercial, and production activities occurring in the same building and often on the same floors.

I.3.4 The rise of public interest

Architectural practice may also change in dramatic ways. For example, public-interest design, now a marginal practice in the profession, seems likely to grow and thrive in the Third Industrial Revolution. This stems partly from the mass customization that becomes necessary when we view the planet's seven billion-plus people as potential "clients." Many of them will require extremely inexpensive, easily fabricated systems (much like Parvin's project) that they can download and adapt to their particular needs.

But public-interest design also prompts a type of practice ideally suited to what Rifkin sees as the collaborative and distributed nature of the new economy. The need to develop low-cost, culturally appropriate solutions has led public-interest designers to form nonprofit firms like Mass Design Group, teaming with NGOs like Partners in Health. In contrast to the medical profession's model of practice long followed by the design community—providing customized responses to individual needs—public-interest firms have begun to evolve a public-health model of practice, mass customizing architecture like the FlatPak House by Lazor Office, or the Wee House by Alchemy Architects.

1.3.5 Non-invasive architecture

Rifkin also sees companies morphing in the Third Industrial Revolution "from primary producers and distributors to aggregators," able to "manage the multiple networks that move commerce and trade." Architects in the Second Industrial Revolution became the primary producers and distributors of building designs. But in the Third Industrial Revolution, this specialization has started to marginalize architects, at least in the minds of many clients, who face all sorts of design problems that do not involve the construction or renovation of buildings.

While a growing human population will still need a lot of buildings, architecture firms may morph along with the rest of the business world to become more the managers of networks and aggregators of expertise, with building design becoming just one of many services. Indeed, given the expense and impact that buildings have on the planet, they may also become a solution of last resort, after architects have explored every other alternative to meet clients' needs. And construction, when it occurs, may have to become, like modern surgery, more non-invasive and minimally disruptive, many examples of which are featured on websites like www.inhabitat.com and https://impactdesignhub.org/ (both accessed March 25, 2017).

1.3.6 Polyculture practices

This may, in turn, change the composition of firms. As Rifkin suggests, the Second Industrial Revolution encouraged monocultures in everything from how we grow food to how we organize businesses. While monocultures create efficiency and predictability, they also make it hard, in the case of architecture, for clients to tell the difference between one firm and another, with each offering similar services, standard practices, and—at least to some clients—indistinguishable results.

Rifkin sees the Third Industrial Revolution rewarding those who create polycultures instead of monocultures. That may lead architecture firms, long dominated by the design disciplines, to cultivate a richer and more diverse ecology of staff and consultants from a wider range of backgrounds and fields, able to embrace what Rifkin describes as the dominant value of the new economy: a "biosphere consciousness" of the impact of every decision on the planet.

Polyculture design firms have begun to emerge, like McDonough Braungart Design Chemistry, which is devising new recyclable and biodegradable products, and Ideo.org, led by a designer and by an anthropologist (Patrice Martin and Jocelyn Wyatt) who strive to understand the beliefs and behavior of people in different cultures. Such firms may serve niche markets but they also have very little competition, and, in a globally connected world, a large number of potential clients.

I.3.7 Beyond assembly-line education

The Third Industrial Revolution may have equally dramatic effects on higher education. Like the modern professions, universities have changed with the economy. The public land-grant universities of the mid-19th century responded to the needs of the First Industrial Revolution, educating students in the "mechanical arts," and the large, research-oriented universities of the 20th century reflected the demands of the Second Industrial Revolution, molding graduates able to participate in the mass production and consumption of goods and services.

Universities, though, struggle to adapt to the Third Industrial Revolution. Most recognize the value of interdisciplinary, collaborative education, and embrace ideas like empathy and inclusivity that Rifkin views as essential in the new economy. But, academic structures and accreditation standards still seem mired in the past. Academic departments, for example, represent a kind of disciplinary monoculture, and standardized curriculums remain a mass-production approach to educating students.

Likewise, accrediting bodies tend to reinforce the assumptions of the Second Industrial Revolution: the focus on building design in our accreditation standards for architecture, for instance. While architects will continue to need to know how to design and detail buildings, the accreditation process gives scant attention to the increasing demand in the Third Industrial Revolution for design thinking applied to a client's and community's organizational and spatial problems, which may or may not require a building.

I.3.8 Lateral learning

Nevertheless, design studios offer one possible model of what education in the Third Industrial Revolution might look like. Rifkin argues that schools must create a more "distributed and collaborative educational experience," in which students acquire not only disciplinary depth, but also interdisciplinary breadth in how to apply knowledge to the grand challenges we face. Studio education has reflected some of the bad habits of the old economy, with overworked students pulling all-nighters and overly packed curriculums preventing them from taking many courses in other disciplines. The exploratory, synthesizing nature of the design studio seems like an ideal setting to learn the creative and collaborative skills needed in the new economy.

I.3.9 Deep play

Of all the skills that architects have to offer in the Third Industrial Revolution, maybe the most important constitutes what Rifkin calls "deep play." In the previous two revolutions, he says, "we lived to work." In the third one, success—and happiness—will come to those who value creativity and connectivity, those who "live to play."

I.4 Book structure and content

This book is structured to highlight the multiple scales of adaptive architecture: urban planning, building design, spatial design, and the process of design, and therefore, is divided into six parts. Part I, the Introduction, is followed by the four scales of case studies: II: Concepts and Processes for Future Adaptivity; III: Urban Scale; IV: Building Scale; and V: Rooms/Settings Scale; and the book concludes with Part VI: Epilogue. The chapters will cover various regions around the world and will identify one or more case studies that relate to the scale of that particular part. Regions covered throughout the book include: North America, Europe, the Middle East, Australia, Asia, Africa, and the International Space Station.

An important quality of this book is that professionals currently working in their respective fields have written the majority of the chapters. This provides the reader with a "behind-the-scenes" look at the design process of adaptive projects. Through multi-disciplinary design teams led by some of the foremost professionals in discovering and resolving the many challenges of adaptivity within urban planning, architecture, and other design related fields, these projects are followed from conceptualization to execution.

The case-study parts provide a variety of examples ranging from urban to building to room size scales, as well as examples of architectural processes. Each case study provides an in-depth exploration of the adaptivity of the project functions, spatial planning, or re-use. A preamble introduces each part of the book, further identifying the theories pertinent to that scale. Each part will then conclude with reflections on the case studies provided, and their relation to the theories outlined in the preamble.

Adaptability is a phenomenon appropriate for our time. From a social perspective, adaptive spaces provide benefits at the workplace, and in many other building types, as well as environments at the urban, building, and room/setting scales. This book will identify current conceptualizations and future implications of architectural adaptivity, and how they will influence the functionality, efficiency, and transformation of social environments in a new and dynamic architecture practice.

I.5 References

Barbaro, M. and Parker. A. (2015). "Uber's Much More Than Just a Ride Service in This Presidential Race." *The New York Times*, July 17.

Petzinger, T. (1999). "A New Model for the Nature of Business: It's Alive!" *The Wall Street Journal*, February 26.

Pollack, J. (2014). "Four Ways to Innovate through Analogies." *The Wall Street Journal*, November 7.

Preiser, W. F. E., and Hardy, A. (2015). "Historical Review of Building Performance Evaluation." In: Preiser, W. F. E., Davis, A. Salama, A. and Hardy, A. (eds.) (2015) *Architecture Beyond Criticism: Expert Judgment and Performance Evaluation*. New York: Routledge.

Preiser, W. F. E and Ostroff, E. (eds.) (2001). *Universal Design Handbook*. New York: McGraw-Hill.

Preiser, W. F. E. and Smith, K. (eds.) (2011). *Universal Design Handbook* (2nd edn). New York: McGraw-Hill.

Rifkin, Jeremy (2011). *The Third Industrial Revolution, How Lateral Power is Transforming Energy, the Economy, and the World*. New York. Palgrave Macmillan.

Totty, M. (2002). "Déjà vu." *The Wall Street Journal*, July 15.

PART II

Concepts and processes for future flexibility

Preamble

Allison Lenell Magley

The increasing emphasis on the flexibility of the built environment speaks to the current era of a human condition dependent on digital technology and rapid information sharing. On a local scale, the appropriation and development of property is evident through the seemingly overnight construction of urban infill projects. These isolated interventions serve only to provide a visual contrast that emphasizes the disparity between past and present conditions. The economic and social transition of the built environment, combined with the dominance of the information technology age, begins to suggest the concept of developing for future flexibility. The chapters in this part address instances of flexibility through cross-cultural immersion, habitability of immediate space, education, complexities of intersecting transportation infrastructures, and the influence of age on sensory perception of space.

Chapter 1 considers the influence of cross-cultural immersion in order to initiate exposure to individuals and cultures that remain isolated by immediate surroundings. The rapidly expanding opportunities of globalization aid to ensure the evolution of mankind. In order to facilitate such measures, controlled spatial environments require a system of perpetual redesign. This chapter discusses how Habitat for Humanity International addresses basic infrastructural needs at a local and global scale, thus establishing a neutral platform for adaptability through architecture to evolve worldwide.

Hershberger and Smith, in Chapter 2, look to critical development of the pre-design planning process in order to establish the functionality of adaptable multi-use space. This chapter evaluates a diverse spectrum of building conditions that challenge the success of future adaptability when inhibited by a traditional formulaic approach. The current ranges of elements demanding flexibility are growth, change, adaptability, resilience, and redundancy. Specifically, with the arrival of the computer and the Internet, the necessity to accommodate instantaneous spatial modification established flexibility as a critical component of the built environment. The pre-design planning process becomes increasingly predominant through intimate interaction of divergent disciplines so that the evolution of flexibility and spatial dynamics remains fluid.

Elzeyadi, in Chapter 3, assesses the extension of the design process beyond construction completion to include critical evaluation and user input following owner occupancy.

Through critical analysis of the LEED Platinum design process of an educational complex in Eugene, Oregon, USA, the socio-spatial attributes of the built environment are drawn through all phases of the design process. The adaptability of architecture is considered through the integration of building systems with response to fluctuating occupant needs. User response to building performance is based on the ability to influence interactive, responsive spaces, considered on levels of performance classification: low/singular performing, and high/multi-performing. The adaptability of architecture through systems integration relies on the multi-performance capabilities of the space in lieu of static function based designs. In order to assess its relevance to the adaptable architecture practice paradigm, Elzeyadi looks at user response to interacting with live spaces.

Taniguchi and co-authors, in Chapter 4, propose design cohesion of complex parts to replace current forms that serve as an accumulation of isolated functions. The adoption of this universal approach will create additional services and innovative adaptations to urban living. This chapter issues a comparative study to evaluate the influence of vertical and horizontal design on building performance. The Japan Rail Twin Towers and the Kyoto Station Building introduce the complexities of intersecting transportation infrastructures integrated with mixed-use urban living conditions. The goal of this advanced technology, to challenge historical barriers of space and time, ultimately challenges the overall reconfiguration of the metropolitan structure and current way of life. This dynamic interface serves as a critical point of interest as mobility increases worldwide.

Smith and Tauke, in Chapter 5, distinguish the sensory experience of a child as an interpretation critical to the built environment. This chapter identifies the children's museum as an archetype for the increasing drive toward ethics based, inclusive humanitarian design. The critical component of programming, based on the psychology of the user, is further challenged when the disparities of age, maturity, and communication capabilities inhibit translation. Designing the built environments to serve the sensorial capacities of a child, as interpreted through the eyes of an adult, epitomizes the adaptive role of the architect. While designing for inclusive environments, the architect must assume the role of spatial mediator for youth. The children's museum represents a level of such adaptive architecture that exemplifies emotional continuity and cognitive transformation at all ages through interactive spatial design. This chapter challenges the adult perspective inherent in spatial, material, formal, and technological translation in built form, identifying the sensorial experience of a child as an opportunity to expand inclusive design.

1

CHALLENGES OF LARGE-SCALE HOUSING IN THE DEVELOPING WORLD: THE HABITAT FOR HUMANITY GLOBAL VILLAGE PROJECT IN ETHIOPIA

Allison Lenell Magley

1.1 Introduction

While change represents the predominant constant in the evolution of architecture, the basic human need for shelter remains. In a profession increasingly dependent on adaptability for existence, the necessity to repurpose the foundations of antiquity in order to facilitate a sustainable practice increases. In its simplest form, shelter is defined as a structure that covers or protects. This universal understanding of spatial form provides a primitive foundation that accentuates the technological advances that challenge cultural interpretations of an inherently personal space. Building forms historically represent isolation and separation, and thus conflict with the freedom of movement offered by modern technology. The need to challenge traditionally static forms based on structural boundaries, and re-define architecture to epitomize mobile adaptability increases with the instantaneous sharing of information.

Current modern urban areas re-purpose land for sustainable mixed-use development, allowing individuals to live, work, and play without commuting. This movement allows individuals the opportunity to travel further and experience more diverse contexts. As a product of the Industrial Era, in the United States, the separation of residential and commercial zones creates a barrier to innovative technologies that depend on maximizing interaction among diverse people and economies. Immersion in global communities distinguished by rich traditions enhances the potential for the architecture field to facilitate larger scale adaptation based on cultural iterations of shelter and community. This opportunity is made possible through active organizations similar to that of Habitat for Humanity International (HFHI). This chapter will discuss how HFHI addresses the human condition at a local and global scale, establishing a neutral platform for culturally adaptive architecture worldwide.

1.2 Humanitarian/development aid

Between 1970 and 2008, funds allocated to developing countries in the sectors of economic infrastructure, production, and commodity support infrastructures decreased, while the sectors of humanitarian aid, administrative donors, and non-governmental organizations

(NGOs) increased (United Nations, 2010). This long-term study supports the sustainability of the HFHI model, as distinct from larger, more complicated economic agendas. While both approaches prove critical, they benefit from separation of duty, allowing support to the developing world regardless of fluctuations in political and social climates. The increased adaptability of architecture will allow for cooperation between such fragmented entities. Habitat for Humanity International is distinguished in its approach by its unique model and success in the face of geopolitical complexity.

The World Health Organization (WHO) establishes two distinct levels of aid based on duration of assistance. This differentiation is critical in the establishment of a sustainable model structured to provide basic sanitation and hygiene conditions to all populations. Humanitarian assistance is aid undertaken on an impartial basis in response to human needs resulting from complex political emergencies and natural hazards. By contrast, development assistance is aid given to support the economic, social, and political growth of developing countries, and is distinguished by its long-term approach to alleviating poverty (WHO, Glossary of Terms, www.who.int/hia/about/glos/en/, accessed April 2, 2017). While development aid focuses on a co-operative partnership between donor and recipient, humanitarian aid offers an immediate response to populations faced with unanticipated conflict. In addition, aid is either provided bilaterally, from one country directly to another country, or multilaterally, from the donor country to an international organization or NGO, which is then distributed to developing countries. In the face of perpetual political pressure and complex divisions of financial aid policy, individuals are able to participate through multi-lateral agencies without requiring intrinsic political affiliation or representation. Habitat for Humanity is an international non-governmental, non-profit organization established in 1976 in Americus, Georgia, which offers a platform for advancing the adaptability of architecture through worldwide interdisciplinary collaboration.

The establishment of "national offices" and community level "affiliates" exemplifies a sustainable measure of the Global Partnership Model that positions Habitat for Humanity International in all 50 U.S. states and more than 70 countries around the world (Habitat

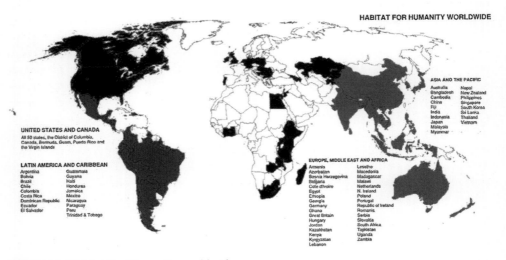

FIGURE 1.1 Habitat for Humanity worldwide.
Source: Author, 2014.

for Humanity International, 2014). Instead of handing out funds, HFHI works to empower already existing communities to manage self-sustaining efforts of internal development. This strategic system of building homes and improving the infrastructure of local communities allows vulnerable populations to improve standards of living. The collaboration between HFHI and local governments empowers communities in poverty to take ownership of recovery and continued development. The long-term success of the HFHI goals rely on the effectiveness of the organization's internal special initiatives and programs designed to provide a hand-up versus a hand-out. Examples include the Funds for Humanity, a revolving fund for future construction; the principle of sweat equity, the homeowner's down payment in the form of 500 work hours; and the Global Village Project, established in 1993.

1.3 Habitat for Humanity International Ethiopia

Habitat for Humanity International Ethiopia (HFHE) National Office was established in 1993 in the capital city Addis Ababa. HFHE focuses on what they term "WASH": water, sanitation, and hygiene, assisting vulnerable populations in home construction, and developing partnerships to create long-term educational and societal impacts. Ethiopia is the largest landlocked country in the world, with 91 percent of the population living in rural areas sustaining the 85 percent agriculture based economy. Countrywide, 90 percent of urban houses and almost all rural houses are in poor condition (Central Statistical Agency Ethiopia and ICF International, 2012), access to safe drinking water is 49 percent, and 20.7 percent of the population has access to adequate sanitation. The capital city of Addis Ababa has an area of 203 square miles (525 square kilometers), and a population of 3.4 million people.

The following information focuses on the HFHI Global Village Project in Debre Birhan, located 75 miles (120 kilometers) northeast of Addis Ababa. The Global Village project in Debre Birhan has become the largest community of homes built within the HFHI organization worldwide. Over 600 homes have been transferred to individual families, with more than 40 under construction at the time of this publication, and still 900 families on the waiting list. Debre Birhan has an area of 5.68 square miles (14.7 square kilometers), and a population of 110,408 people. For purposes of comparison, New York City is less

FIGURE 1.2 Habitat for Humanity International Ethiopia; Debre Birhan housing project. *Source*: Author, 2014.

dense, at an area of 470 square miles (1,217 square kilometers) and a population of 8.5 million people.

The Global Village Project in Debre Birhan utilizes the donations, labor, and participation of individual volunteers to aid in the HFHI Ethiopia Affiliates work nationally. Project teams consist of 10–14 individuals from locations worldwide and 1–2 team leaders. Due to the condensed trip length, typically 10–14 days, individuals establish a relationship instantly, and together adapt to the local community. Habitat for Humanity International Ethiopia provides a local representative to join the team for the duration of the project, and act as mediator and facilitator between participants and community members. The team leaders and the affiliate representative establish a work-week itinerary that begins construction where the Global Village volunteer group from the previous week left off. The community has appointed multiple project construction supervisors and attendants that oversee building activities on a daily basis. The supervisors work in unison with the volunteers, and are difficult to distinguish from other workers. Community members work in traditional garb, women in long skirts and men in casual clothing or full suits.

While practicing local construction methods, HFHE identifies design quality standards to establish a baseline for home and site planning responsive to environmental conditions. Each person in a household requires a minimum usable covered floor area of 280 square feet (26 square meters) or a minimum of two rooms (Habitat for Humanity International Ethiopia, 2016). There is equitable access to adequate storage of water for drinking, cooking, and personal and domestic hygiene. Public water points are located within a sufficiently close distance to the households to minimize water waste. The siting and locating of structures, including homes, kitchens, and toilets, identifies the locations of drainage in order to avert the health risks posed by water erosion and standing water, both domestic and environmental.

1.4 Cross-cultural context and the digital revolution

The immersion of the GV volunteer in the cultural context represents a significant mission of the HFHI model. The objective distribution of goods and funds serves a necessary yet singular goal of direct aid. The HFHI model aims to challenge the volunteer to transcend individuality and transition to increasing levels of involvement. Prior to travel, the GV team communicates through email regarding social customs volunteers must learn prior to arrival. The cultural practices identified by the GV Ethiopia project include a slower pace of life, the significance of greeting and recognition, holding hands regardless of gender in friendship, giving with the right hand while touching the forearm with the left hand, and walking around two people rather than between as a sign of respect. Such cultural practices emphasize the high regard volunteers carry for Ethiopian customs and values.

After driving 75 miles (120 kilometers) in 3 hours on one of the country's few paved roads, volunteers are welcomed by a line of community members clapping and singing in celebration. Individuals are assigned to several homes each at varying phases of construction. In order to understand the entire process, team members rotate working with different trades and community members. The use of local materials and building methods stimulates local economy and labor, which further emphasizes principles of the HFHI model. Community members work alongside volunteers and educate them in traditional customs and practices, intensifying an environment of growth.

FIGURE 1.3 Habitat for Humanity International Ethiopia, Debre Birhan; construction and labor. *Source*: Author, 2014.

The traditional home is built using large boulders for foundation work, posts cut from eucalyptus trees as poles for framing, purlins for reinforcing, full-length splinted wood as fill for the space between structural posts, and corrugated metal for roofing. Volunteer tasks begin with manual excavation using local shovels, and transporting individual large boulders using a two-person hand trolley made of left over eucalyptus poles and corrugated roofing metal. Labor practices are manual and independent of mechanical equipment throughout the project, so the pace of construction varies from day to day.

Stripped splints of wood are soaked in water and used as wraps to bind intersecting structural members. As is customary in the Ethiopian tradition of home construction, a mixture of soil, water, and straw, called *chika,* is applied to the exterior walls, serving a purpose similar to that of plaster and lath. *Chika* is mixed and prepared on site using one's feet until it reaches the required consistency. The rudimentary application technique of throwing handfuls of this mixture onto the wall requires precision, as adhesion is dependent on the appropriate level of applied pressure. Laborers use sticks to puncture closely spaced shallow depressions across the *chika* exterior. Chicken wire is then embedded in the *chika,* serving to initiate a mechanical bond and form an integral unit of the exterior finish plaster layer and the supporting structure.

Volunteers complete interior finish work applying a boiled mixture of gypsum, animal fat, and water for the interior walls. This exposure to the traditional construction process introduces all participants to levels of development typically unavailable through indirect distribution of monetary aid.

The final afternoon in Debre Birhan is spent celebrating the work completed and the relationships established over the short, intimate time constructing homes. The close bond that forms is demonstrated when the initial formal receiving line of community members fragments into an emotional scattering of individuals sharing reluctant farewells. The intensity of the experience emphasizes the profound benefits of a multilateral aid model that HFHI practices, and the power that immersion in a culture half a world away can ignite.

FIGURE 1.4 Habitat for Humanity International Ethiopia; Debre Birhan; construction and labor.
Source: Author, 2014.

FIGURE 1.5 Habitat for Humanity International Ethiopia; Debre Birhan; existing versus new construction.
Source: Author, 2014.

1.5 Influence of scale and mobility on the capacity for short- and long-term change

The cost effectiveness of the HFHI model as compared to alternative low-cost housing initiatives represents a common controversy. It is argued that the multilateral approach to distributing aid results in a depleted amount of funds reaching the country (Kharas, 2007). Bilateral distribution of aid sees funds delivered directly from the donor government to the recipient government. While statistically monetary totals appear higher through direct distribution, the multilateral approach recognizes more diverse and varied levels and locations of need. Moreover, the pouring of large amounts of funds by rich countries for economic

TABLE 1.1 Habitat for Humanity International Ethiopia; cost of deliverables and fund allocation.

COST OF DELIVERABLES (Currency in US Dollars)	
New House with Toilet	$ 2,500.00
New House with Toilet (For Vulnerable Families)	$ 2,900.00
Existing House with Toilet (Renovation based on Size)	$ 1,800.00
Existing Kitchen Improvement	$ 1,500.00
Community Toilet (Six Latrines)	$ 4,900.00
Community Water Stand Pipe	$ 2,900.00

Source: Data from Habitat for Humanity International Ethiopia (2016); table generated by author.

and political purpose disregards the existing traditions and identities of the recipient culture. "Business persons have raised concerns about the entry of substandard merchandise, dumping by Chinese suppliers, unfair competition and displacement of small Ethiopian businesses" (Shinn, 2014). Continued active involvement, both bilateral and multilateral, while serving potentially conflicting means, allows for the neutral issue of poverty to be addressed despite the rise and fall of political conflict and economic agendas.

The primary role of mediator that HFHI uses to model is a significant factor in the success of large-scale housing efforts in developing nations. Ethiopia maintains a strict system of fund allocation and documentation of cost of deliverables. This separation of goods, services, and administrative overhead, allows for a critical evaluation of the HFHI model, which operates toward more sustainable measures. The HFHI model can be compared to the proverb "give a man a fish and you feed him for a day; teach a man to fish and you feed him for a lifetime" (source unknown). The model reflects an inter-relationship with the recipient community, as compared to a cause–and–effect relationship, which responds to immediate need based on extreme conditions that have been allowed to progress. While natural disasters occur and require intervention, the long-term growth of poverty remains constant.

1.6 Conclusion

The HFHI model and the Global Village Project activate aid distribution through interdisciplinary networking of volunteer diversity worldwide. This platform of multilateral aid challenges the limitations of traditional humanitarian bilateral aid beyond isolated monetary exchange. The program's flexibility allows individuals from all economic levels to participate, and facilitates networks that continue translating aid beyond the individual project. Individual volunteerism expands to include collaboration between industries and enterprises, aiming to increase the sharing of space and responsibility in the midst of political pressure.

Habitat for Humanity International further challenges the architect's understanding of shared spaces to include collaborating with industries and nations beyond the local economy. With the increasing speed of sharing information and technology, medium and large-scale entities are increasingly challenged to diversify the range of services offered beyond stick and mud structures. The architecture establishment represents an industry responsible for addressing areas where planning and design guidance is non-existent. Like the French aid organization Doctors Without Borders, the architecture professional is challenged to establish a more critical presence in the design and planning for vulnerable populations. This step represents a larger scale translation of the current trend toward adaptable architecture.

The remnants of an era that existed to mimic industrial machinery and materials in order to maximize the size, speed, and erection of structures stands to symbolize the current challenge of adaptability. Existing systems reliant on extensive networks of utility and support infrastructure, force professionals to exercise in transitioning toward a built environment based on future flexibility. The repurposing of existing urban areas to facilitate the sustainability of environmental design, and the engineering of systems based on the speed of technology, requires the redefining of architecture from concrete institutions to dynamic systems of mobility. Habitat for Humanity International serves as a platform for utilizing the advanced systems of the digital world to activate global immersion into traditional cultural communities. In this instance, the Internet exposes individuals to worldwide participation through direct human contact, instead of the contained isolation of media sharing through bilateral distribution of aid. This simple model promotes awareness of worldwide issues inherent within volatile political societies, while constructing the basic infrastructure needed to enable proper education and access to hygiene and sanitation. "This same evolution of a 'sharing economy' has changed architecture from the conceptualizing, designing, and constructing of buildings to the creating of interacting, synergistically interdependent, distributed systems, fueled by the invention and global use of the Internet" (Preiser, Fisher, and Hardy 2017). In a century of rapid change and instantaneous replacement of technology, the existing brick and mortar environment requires an architecture practice defined by adaptability.

1.7 References

Central Statistical Agency Ethiopia and ICF International (2012). *Ethiopia Demographic and Health Survey, 2011.* Addis Ababa, Ethiopia, and Calverton, MD, USA: Central Statistical Agency and ICF International, Unicef.

Habitat for Humanity International (2014). *Program Milestones FY2014.* June, 2014. Americus, GA, USA: Habitat for Humanity International.

Habitat for Humanity International Ethiopia (2016). *Habitat for Humanity Ethiopia,* www.habitatethiopia.org. Accessed March 20, 2017.

Kharas, H. (2007). *Trends and Issues in Development Aid.* Working Paper No. 1. Washington D.C., Wolfensohn Center for Development.

Preiser, W. F. E., Fisher, T. and Hardy, A. E. (2017). "Introduction" In: Preiser, W. F. E., Hardy, A. E. and Wilhelm, J. J. (eds.) *Adaptive Architecture: Changing Parameters and Practice.* London: Routledge.

Shinn, D. H. (2014). Ethiopia and China: When Two Former Empires Connected. *International Policy Digest,* https://intpolicydigest.org/2014/06/11/ethiopia-and-china-when-two-former-empires-connected/. Accessed April 2, 2017.

United Nations (2010). *Retooling Global Development; Towards A New Aid Architecture; World Economic and Social Survey 2010.* New York: United Nations.

2

PREDESIGN PLANNING FOR FLEXIBILITY

Robert G. Hershberger and Molly E. Smith

2.1 Introduction

Flexibility, by definition, requires "the ability to change readily to meet new circumstances" (Soanes and Stevenson, 2004). A formulaic approach to predesign planning does not promote such flexibility. A case in point is the *problem-seeking* approach to predesign planning (Pena *et al.*, 1969–2015). Starting with four pre-assumed issues like function, form, economy, and time may work when repeatedly dealing with the same problem, but if the design problem is different, or has changed, an important issue may be overlooked. The authors of the aforementioned book assert that any discovered issue can fit into one of the above categories. But if a new, equally crucial issue is discovered and treated in this way, will it assume appropriate importance? Probably not.

Some original advocates for Operations Research stressed the importance of composing research teams of persons with widely divergent disciplinary backgrounds to discover critical issues (Ackoff *et al.*, 1962). These advocates believe that having diversity on a team increases the likelihood of discovering important issues that might be missed by a single-discipline team. The authors advocate a value- or issue-based approach to predesign planning, in which a diverse team involving the client, users, community members, appropriate consultants, and designer first identify the most important values or issues, then direct subsequent research to these issues (Hershberger, 1999).

2.2 Flexibility

Design aspects missed in predesign planning relate to various facets of flexibility: growth, change, adaptability, resilience, and redundancy, whether planning for a building, interior, urban area, landscape, spaceship, or other kinds of accommodation.

Specifically, predesign planning for primary and secondary education is changing profoundly toward flexibility as teaching and learning relate more to individual and group problem solving. Various educational facilities can be made more flexible and effective learning environments by providing programmatic additions not traditionally associated with

2.3 Growth

Many architectural design commissions occur because an organization has outgrown existing facilities. In fact, most successful enterprises expand or reconfigure physical facilities numerous times during their existence. Sometimes they do this on the original site. Often they move because the site on which the existing facilities are located is not large enough to accommodate expansion.

The predesign planner must discover if a facility has a potential for development, determining what particular areas and manners of growth are most likely to occur and include strategies acceptable to the client for accommodating it. The absence of such a consideration is a glaring problem in many traditional predesign plans and may result in added future costs to clients when they discover that new growth is difficult to accommodate given the location or configuration of existing facilities.

Churches can be striking examples of this. They often begin with a small group of people meeting in a home, grow into a rented facility such as an elementary school's multi-purpose room, and then build or move into a small church of their own. If they have the financial resources or denominational support, they often purchase a parcel of land of sufficient size to accommodate projected growth, beginning with only one or two buildings large enough to contain their present congregation. Once the first phase is complete and the congregation size is near capacity, the church typically begins a second phase of predesign planning, design, construction, and so on, until the capacity of the site is reached. At such time, the church faces the prospect of limiting growth, finding a larger site to begin the process of growth again, or possibly spinning off smaller churches to absorb new members. In some cases, initial worship facilities are enlarged to achieve greater capacity. In other cases, old worship facilities are converted to new uses, such as education or fellowship, and a new larger worship facility is built. It is important that growth potential be recognized as an issue in predesign planning so adequate provision can be made for future additions and new facilities.

The master plan for Covenant Baptist Church by Hershberger-Kim Architects responded to a predesign plan calling for a much larger future sanctuary, several more classrooms, and expanded parking to account for expected future growth, but the site plan also allowed for unknown future buildings and parking to utilize the site fully.

University campuses and buildings are prime examples of the need to provide for growth by securing enough land for new facilities and leaving enough space around buildings to allow them to expand individually. The State of Arizona initially provided the University of Arizona and Arizona State University large land parcels on which to build their campuses. This approach worked well for many years, but as the institutions grew, the allotted land proved inadequate. So, both universities had to acquire adjacent residential and commercial property, demolish existing structures, and build new campus-related facilities in their place, often with resistance from the neighboring community. Similarly, most of the smaller initial campus buildings have been demolished and replaced by much larger new facilities, so only a symbolic handful of original buildings remain. This scenario has been repeated at nearly every major public university in the country.

Predesign planning for flexibility **27**

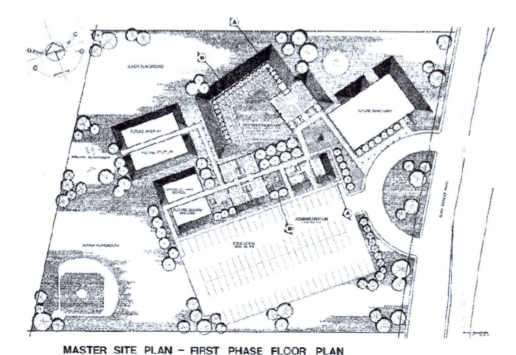

FIGURE 2.1 Covenant Baptist master plan.
Source: Hershberger – Kim Architects.

Wide spacing of campus buildings to allow for future growth makes sense but creates conflict when beloved green space between buildings is threatened or two adjacent departments need to expand into the same area. At GBQC Architects in Philadelphia, Robert Geddes, one of the design principals, responded to a university's predesign requirements for future growth by proposing central circulation splines with various-size building units attached to them. This approach allowed for growth both away from the spline and to either side of the individual building units. Similarly, several buildings at the University of Arizona, including the main library, were designed to allow for future additions several stories above the initial structure. Other buildings on campus were built with two or three additional floors of unfinished space to accommodate predicted growth.

2.4 Change

Another characteristic of university buildings is the likelihood of internal change. A university's building stock is in constant flux, and it is rare for an academic building to be used for the same purpose over time. A building may begin as a liberal arts college, be taken over by a larger department, then be given over to still another department as the first outgrows the facility and is moved elsewhere. Between actual moves, there may be almost constant internal change as a department's focus changes from teaching to research, as equipment and furnishings become outdated and are modernized, as new faculty are fitted into already crowded office space, and so on. The predesign planner must discover if such change is likely and make this clear in the predesign plan.

Louis I. Kahn, after reviewing the initial predesign plan for the Richards Building on the University of Pennsylvania campus, analyzed existing medical research laboratories and determined that a square laboratory space, 45 foot on each side, could accommodate the requirements for the never-ending changes in research. The adjacent office and service spaces worked as intended, but the laboratory space was found to be too large, too small, or too low in some cases. When Kahn worked with a new client on the Salk Center in La Jolla, CA, it became clear during predesign planning that a wide, high, and indefinitely long laboratory space enveloped top and bottom with "interstitial" service spaces would provide the flexibility needed to house the ever-changing requirements of bio-medical research. In both cases, the need to accommodate change was identified but requirements for appropriate change were not articulated sufficiently until the inadequacy of the first design became apparent. The invention of the computer and the Internet required planning for wire management at laboratory workbenches, with one design solution incorporating split benches to accommodate changing wiring configurations. Miniaturization of laboratory equipment has further altered experimental setup, to the point where what once took up an entire room is now a desktop-sized piece of equipment.

Similar problems occur in high-rise office buildings. Many early high-rise structures were planned and designed for specific-use spaces, with executive offices at the corners and individual offices between to provide exterior light and ventilation to each office. Just inside the offices were open spaces for secretarial pools, while the central core was dedicated to service space including elevators, restrooms, copy and storage rooms, and the like, with stair towers at the ends of the building to allow safe egress to the exterior. This fixed approach proved awkward as the housed organizations changed over time. Eventually the clients, predesign planners, and architects of high-rise office buildings determined that a more flexible floor plan would better serve the changing needs of tenants. As a result, many recent high-rise office buildings have unobstructed spans from the central core to the exterior walls, with moveable partitions to accommodate changing tenants and uses over time. In many of these buildings, the stair towers are incorporated in the core with fireproof access to the exterior at the ground level.

The issue of change is rarely articulated in planning for residential design. Frank Lloyd Wright epitomized a "tailored" approach to meeting client requirements even to the point of designing fixed furnishings within each space. This approach does not work well for growing families. Architects do predesign planning with clients at a certain stage of their life, say, when their children are young. In doing so, the client may articulate the needs of children of that age, resulting in small or shared bedrooms flanked by a playroom. It is unlikely that this arrangement will be appropriate when the children are in their teens. The architect, as a predesign planner, must introduce past experience to the predesign planning process to help the client understand that family needs change over time.

Most building types are affected by the need to change internally as technologies become obsolete and new equipment and systems are introduced. It is often hard to predict the nature of this change. Making spaces more general, with free spans from exterior walls to the core may help accommodate change and avoid costly renovations. Over-sizing ducts, chases, and other service systems may also help to mitigate the problem.

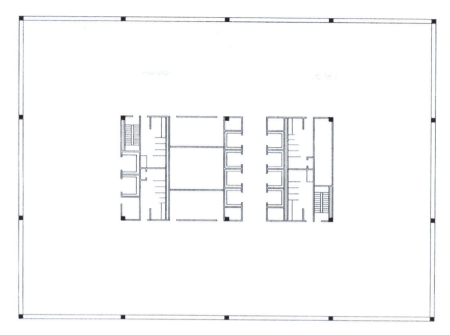

FIGURE 2.2 Typical office tower plan.
Source: Author, Robert Hershberger.

FIGURE 2.3 Tent structure.
Source: Richard Larry Medlin Architect, Inc.

Some buildings change even more dramatically. International events and exhibitions, from the Olympics to the Venice Biennale, require buildings and pavilions to be designed so that they can be dismantled at the end of the proceedings and other use can be made of the fairground site. More temporary structures, like those at circuses or festivals, are designed to be erected and dismantled repeatedly in different locations.

2.5 Adaptability

There are many instances in which adaptability is an important issue in the design of buildings. For instance, a client may wish to take advantage of the sun's ability to heat an interior or exterior space in the winter using passive solar design principles but want to shut out sun penetration in the summer, when, if anything, cooling will be needed. The client may also want to take advantage of the benign exterior temperature of the swing seasons by opening the building to cross ventilation. Information about desired adaptability should be included in the predesign planning document.

A common instance of adaptability is for multi-use facilities, whether interior or exterior. An example from one of the authors' predesign planning and design practice was a small start-up church in Tucson, Arizona. The area minister wanted the denomination to own a re-locatable church building that could be placed on a permanent site at the same time as the newly assigned minister arrives. However, he wanted this temporary church to remain on the site no longer than five years, when it would be moved to yet another site to begin a new church. He believed that a high-quality initial facility for exclusive use of a new congregation would enhance church commitment and growth. This approach gave the congregation three years to gain members, hire an architect to design permanent facilities, and have them built before the end of the fifth year, allowing the initial building to be moved to start a new church elsewhere. The program required that the building accommodate all typical activities of a congregation of 100 persons, including a minister's office, kitchen, restrooms, foyer, storage, and multi-use space for church school, worship, coffee hour or even a brunch, all taking place in the same morning.

The design used four completely furnished and movable units built off-site that could be transported on lowboy trailers for on-site assembly to form a 50 foot long by 50 foot wide facility. As designed, the building met the functional, aesthetic, code, and cost requirements required in the predesign document, using easily moved partitions and folding chairs and tables in the assembly space.

Jon Jerde's design for Horton Plaza, a major shopping center in downtown San Diego, and many of his other similarly designed facilities, responded to requirements for change at a more urban scale, but in a slightly different way. Jerde advocated "scripting" places in the city for a variety of uses at different times of the day, week, and year, so that changing activities could be accommodated seamlessly. He was successful at designing for these changes, because he recognized change as a critical urban design issue.

2.6 Resilience

With all of the expected and unexpected changes resulting from climate change, architects are talking about designing buildings that can remain fully functional during and after extreme weather events, even when the sea rises substantially (Minnery, 2015). Actually,

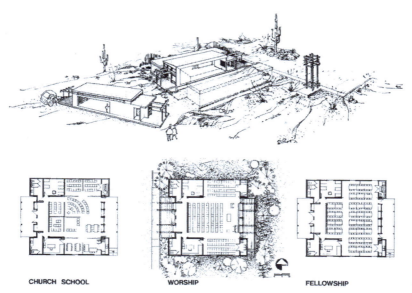

FIGURE 2.4 Relocatable church concept.
Source: Par3 Studio.

FIGURE 2.5 Horton Plaza: mall.
Source: Author – Robert Hershberger.

architects and engineers have responded to such issues for centuries, designing buildings to withstand extremely high wind, earthquakes, and heavy snow loads, none of which may occur within the useful lifetime of the building. Resilience is described here as the ability for a design to withstand physical changes of the environment and continuous wear by the users.

Current discussion of resilience is often in the context of rising ocean waters and how to deal with related storm surge in coastal locations. This, too, is not really something new. Buildings in flood zones near rivers and oceans have been elevated on stilts to allow the floodwater to pass under the usable space in the building, keeping the occupant and the livable spaces above high water. Mies van der Rohe did the same when he designed the Farnsworth House on stilts in the flood zone of the Fox River in Plano, Illinois (Shulman, 2015). This approach worked admirably until floods began to rise above the floor level and destroy surfaces and furnishings in the building. Climate change and new housing developments near the site increased such flooding, charging architects and engineers with the challenge of considering resilient alternatives to protect the historic home in the future.

Clients for major buildings in coastal cities are also re-thinking the standard practice of placing the transformers, electrical service, generators, and mechanical equipment rooms in the basements of buildings where they are likely to be flooded. The predesign planner's obligation in all cases is to inform the designers of the potential hazard. This obligation also includes finding creative ways to locate or re-locate these services, so that rising seawater or hurrican-related flooding do not put them out of service.

2.7 Redundancy

One way to be flexible is to have redundancy. Hospitals are invariably designed with gas or diesel generators to take over in case electrical service to the building goes down, protecting vulnerable patients that rely on mechanical systems. It is unimaginable to have a contemporary hospital without such safety measures. Similarly, large institutions that must stay in continuous operation have back-up systems in place, storing motors, light bulbs, and other necessities, all of which must be identified in the predesign document.

2.8 Conclusion

Flexibility in all of its manifestations is an extremely important issue to be addressed in predesign planning for urban environments, landscape architecture, architecture, and interiors, just as it has become important in all of the other areas covered in this book. It is important that predesign planners understand the importance of this issue and articulate it in the predesign phase so the designer will address it appropriately.

2.9 Acknowledgments

Much of the content and most illustrations in this chapter were first published in *Architectural Programming and Predesign Manager*, by Robert Hershberger, McGraw Hill, New York, 1999; reissued by Routledge, London, 2015.

2.10 References

Ackoff, R. L., Gupta, S. K., and Minas, J. S. (1962). *Scientific Method: Optimizing Applied Research Decisions*. New York: John Wiley & Sons, Inc.

Hershberger, R. G. (1999). *Architectural Programming and Predesign Manager*. New York: McGraw Hill; Re-issued (2015), London: Routledge.

Minnery, R. (2015). Resilience to Adaptation: The Crucible for an Ethical Practice in Architecture. *AIA Architect*, July, pp. 46-50.

Pena, W. M., *et al.* (1969–2015). *Problem Seeking: An Architectural Programming Primer*. Houston, Washington, D.C., New York: CRSS, AIA, Wiley and other publishers.

Schulman, B. (2015). Shoring Up Is Hard To Do. *AIA Architect,* December, pp. 38–42.

Smith, M. (2016) *Think Smart Planning*. http://thinksmartplan.com/wordpress/?s=flexibility. Accessed March 20, 2017.

Soanes, C., and Stevenson, A. (ed.) (2004). *Concise Oxford English Dictionary*, Eleventh Edition. Oxford: Oxford University Press, p. 544.

3

MULTI-PERFORMANCE SPACES: ASSESSING THE IMPACTS OF AN INNOVATIVE LEED™ PLATINUM EDUCATIONAL COMPLEX ON THE TRIPLE BOTTOM LINE

Ihab M. K. Elzeyadi

3.1 Introduction

This chapter reports on a longitudinal study that evaluates building performance, considering occupant comfort, health, and dynamic space use within a LEED™ platinum-rated educational complex in Eugene, Oregon, USA. The complex combines multi-functional spaces of wet and dry labs, classrooms, meeting rooms, and offices. Designed to celebrate the fusion between research, teaching, and community engagement, multi-tasking, multi-performance, and multi-user oriented spaces are integrated within the building complex and are interconnected by un-programmed public spaces as well as a multi-level day-lit and naturally ventilated atrium. The research team for this study engaged with the design team, facility managers, and building users for 24 months, from post-construction analysis to a detailed post-occupancy evaluation. This included: resource consumption assessment (both predicted and actual use of energy, water, gas, and steam), indoor environmental quality spatial analysis, and post-occupancy surveys feedback using questionnaires, interviews, and focus groups with the building users (Preiser *et al.*, 2015). This comprehensive study takes a critical look at dynamic multi-performance spaces at environmental, physical, and socio-spatial scales, aiming to provide both substantive and context-specific knowledge for the design, operation, and assessments of multi-performance/multi-tasking LEED™ environments of the future.

3.2 Adaptive architecture and building performance

Imagine riding a mountain bike on a rugged terrain with up and down slopes. The only problem is your bike does not have front or back gears, no front shocks or springs, nor disc brakes. What would your riding experience be? You would be going on a low-performance ride destined for failure! Our approaches to designing workspaces have not been very far off from this low-performance analogy. In essence, the current environmental design and practice of architecture has been one where single-performance and low-performance are the norm (Elzeyadi, 2012, 2015a). Most commercial workspaces are designed to allow limited occupants' control, lack flexibility, have limited spatial configurations, and are isolated from the outdoor elements. Usually, this is done by employing fixed perimeter windows that restrict natural ventilation, limit daylighting beyond the building perimeter zone, and feature one-size-fits all HVAC systems. These issues result in poor indoor environmental quality and are unable to adapt to occupant multi-comfort and spatial needs.

The future of adaptive architecture calls for dynamism capable of changing with the users' demands and spatial needs (see the Introduction). As Preiser, Fisher, and Hardy outline, the future trends of customizable buildings will benefit from spaces with open architecture intended to suit changing and adaptable uses and programs. To this extent, customizable spaces can be categorized based on their performance aspects, which allow for different functions and spatial requirements to take place, from multi-performing to singular and low-performing spaces. The degree of their ability to provide different indoor environmental and spatial conditions will, in turn, determine their classifications from low/singular-performing to high/multi-performing spaces.

3.3 Multi-performance spaces

A multi-performance space is a dynamic environment designed with enough flexibility to accommodate different environmental changes, sitting positions, and views, and offers an adjustable environmental control system where lighting, ventilation, heating, and cooling can be configured to accommodate different occupancy patterns and spatial requirements (Duffy, 1992). A space with these goals is designed in concert with natural energies of daylighting, natural ventilation, outdoor views, accessible controls, and universal design spatial configurations. It is acknowledged that this space performance type can accommodate multiple functions at the same time, sequentially or at periodically recurring events. Multi-performance spaces are typically high-performing in terms of their provisions for high indoor environmental quality, indoor comfort, energy efficiency, and sustainable design principles. Sustainable design strategies adopted in this space performance type include, but are not limited to, bi-directional diffused daylighting, flex space, occupant engagement controls, and other strategies outlined in Figure 3.1.

3.4 Single-performance spaces

A single-performance space is an optimized space, typically designed with limited flexibility to accommodate only common use and pre-set occupancy patterns and functions. This space will have a set-point limited range of environmental control systems where lighting, ventilation, heating, and cooling are optimized to accommodate specific occupancy patterns and spatial requirements. A space with these goals can easily be designed with energy efficiency and sustainability in mind. This type of space, however, will provide challenges to adjust to change and will be limited in accommodating different functions or variable occupancy. This space type might employ different sustainable design strategies, as highlighted in Figure 3.1, to achieve moderate performance, but in general will fail to provide a dynamic flexible environment and will result in moderate to low indoor environmental quality.

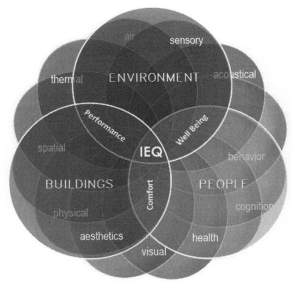

FIGURE 3.1 Design strategies of multi-performance spaces.
Source: Author.

3.5 Low-performance spaces

A low-performance space is designed with limited flexibility to accommodate both change in use and environmental requirements. This space is designed to fit a specific function by providing occupants with limited degrees of freedom to change, control, and adapt their environment. A static environmental control system where lighting, ventilation, heating, and cooling is designed to meet specific set-points and metrics, such as set temperature ranges, illumination levels, and noise-reduction coefficients, is typical for these type of spaces. These spaces are typically designed according to rigid interpretation of engineering standards and rely on active systems that lack integration with passive and sustainable strategies, such as daylighting, natural ventilation, heat-recovery systems, and occupants' intuitive controls, to name a few.

Unfortunately, this type of low-performing space, typical of the 1970s and 1980s cubicle office spaces, will have deep floor plans with under-glazed or over-glazed low-performing envelopes. These spaces are typical of 75% of corporate office spaces in North America, and today's work environments in general.

3.6 Assessing space performance of adaptive architecture – an integrated framework

Previous post-occupancy evaluation (POE) studies (e.g. Elzeyadi, 2012, 2015b) show that human comfort and building performance are multi-faceted. They are affected by the multiple components of the environment in its physical, physiological, psychological, and social attributes and properties (Preiser, 2009). An integrated framework proposed by Elzeyadi

Impacts of a LEED™ educational complex **37**

FIGURE 3.2 Adaptive architecture place experience system model.
Source: Author.

(2003) conceptualizes building performance and environmental quality in places as a complex system (Figure 3.2). The model proposes the systemic interaction of multiple parameters of people, buildings, and the indoor/outdoor environment resulting in sub-systems of building performance, occupants' productivity, comfort, and well-being. These sub-systems impact overall environmental quality and are impacted by its underlying instrumental attributes such as thermal, visual, acoustical, indoor air quality, and spatial systems. While one can assume that individuals are affected by the environment in different ways, their general perception of multi-comfort and positive perception of building performance are the result of their overall appraisal of these instrumental attributes (Elzeyadi, 2015a). This framework will guide the case study presented in this chapter by evaluating the performance of different adaptive spaces for a LEED™ platinum-rated educational building.

3.7 Case study: post-occupancy evaluation of a multi-performing LEED™ building

The Robert and Beverly Lewis Integrative Science Building (LISB) brings world-class researchers together under one roof from a range of different disciplines. The $65 million educational facility, which opened in October 2012 in Eugene, Oregon, USA, is home to strategic research clusters centered on interdisciplinary and integrative research missions that are not defined by departmental boundaries. The 103,000 sq ft (9669 m^2) facility literally unites the sciences by stitching the adjacent science buildings into one complex (Figure 3.3).

Creating a science building with sustainable features was imperative in designing the Lewis Building. Predicted to use 58% less energy than conventionally designed buildings of similar size and function, energy-saving features include natural ventilation in non-lab spaces, solar shading, daylight harvesting, night flush cooling, variable flow chemical fume hoods equipped with automatic sashes that close when not in use, and the extraction of heat from an adjacent

FIGURE 3.3 The Lewis Integrated Sciences Building (LISB).
Source: Author.

utility tunnel. To reduce usage of potable water, the building reclaims reverse-osmosis-treated water from a neighboring zebra fish research facility and uses this water to flush all urinals and toilets. All of the storm water on site is also collected and treated, and 28 solar hot water panels on the rooftop heat all domestic hot water. Operable windows with sensor-signal controls, daylighting, and access to views of nature are among the various sustainable design strategies used to earn the facility Platinum certification by the US Green Building Council (USGBC), Leadership in Energy and Environmental Design (LEED™) program.

To validate the proposed performance evaluation model (Figure 3.2), a comprehensive POE was carried out for 24 consecutive months. The POE assessed building energy and resource performance, thermal and visual comfort, and occupants' perception of comfort for a number of critical spaces in the case-study building. Spatial analysis and visualization of IEQ assessments relating the qualitative phenomenological and quantitative performance impacts of the studied spaces on both the place and the people is presented in the following sections.

3.8 Building energy performance

The building systems were extensively commissioned to ensure that they meet the design goals and predicted resource consumption. Following a two-year post-occupancy monitoring procedure and additional commissioning, results show that the building was not meeting its design goals regarding its resource consumption with a shortage of 10–15% across the various resource categories. Despite this shortage, the building is considered exemplary in its performance, exceeding most buildings in its categories with 36% energy savings over a typical code-complying building of its size and type (Figure 3.4). By analyzing the building energy metered performance without additional adjustments for any central plant efficiency, the total energy utilization index (EUI) of the building in year two was 182.63 KBTU/sq ft/year. While 10% more than the predicted performance of 165.68 KBTU/sq ft/year, it is 40% better than recent buildings of its size and type as well as 30% better than the baseline comparative of a building built to the current Oregon energy code. Additional commissioning and efficiency adjustments are being performed and its third year of operation is getting closer to its predicted energy performance (Elzeyadi, 2017).

Impacts of a LEED™ educational complex 39

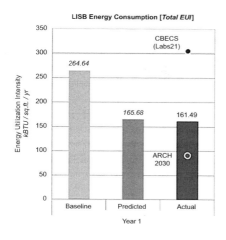 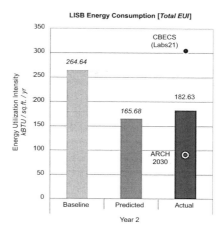

FIGURE 3.4 Energy and resource consumption in EUI of LISB.
Source: Author.

3.9 Indoor environmental quality (IEQ) assessments

Despite the importance of energy and resource savings of green buildings, proven impacts on occupants' health and performance from improved IEQ will be a game-changer in adopting green-building strategies and provide a big driver to design teams to select strategies based on proven evidence and human impacts (Elzeyadi, 2015b). These impacts could vary from reduced sick building syndrome (SBS) symptoms to increased indoor comfort of occupants due to better lighting, thermal conditions, and air quality. Evidence to support these claims has been mixed. Existing studies of occupant satisfaction and comfort in LEED™ buildings shows high variability, with some buildings rated very positively and others having modest comfort and satisfaction levels (Hwang *et al.*, 2009).

A detailed IEQ assessment procedure that evaluated visual, thermal, and spatial comfort in the building from the physical building science perspective and the latent occupants' perception of comfort using questionnaires and interviews was implemented. Multi-comfort parameters and metrics with the thermal and visual environments were assessed and analyzed for different spaces inside the building. Environmental sensors and data loggers measuring temperature, relative humidity, air velocity, and air movement stratified across the different floor levels of the buildings were deployed over the winter, spring, and summer seasons respectively. In addition, infra-red (IR) imagery was recorded over the course of sampled seasonal days for the occupants' workstations to document surface temperature and mean radiant temperature indices over the study period.

3.10 Multi-performance space

As a multi-performance space, the seminar/meeting room (Figure 3.5) provides a clear example of successful deployment of many design strategies discussed in section 3.2 of this chapter. The space has bi-directional diffused daylighting from an east-facing glazed wall as well as daylighting filtered through a west glazed wall facing the top-lit atrium. These daylighting apertures provide access to views of nature as well as opportunities for occupants' intuitive

40 Elzeyadi

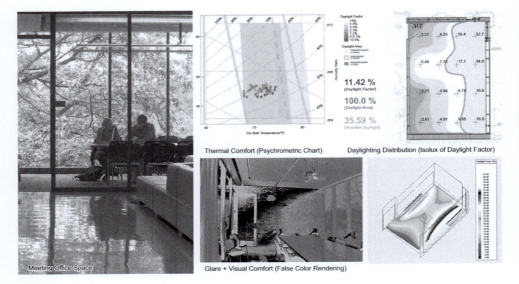

FIGURE 3.5 Multi-performance space example – meeting office space.
Source: Author.

control of light levels and glare by using drapes and blinds. The room has a flexible layout with ample opportunities to adjust seating positions and view sheds. These attributes resulted in dynamic daylighting distribution with a changing "layers-of-light" approach that gave occupants opportunities to have different levels of daylighting through the day and seasons, so as to adjust to changing needs and tasks.

The room indoor climate fits within the ASHRAE adaptive thermal comfort zone for over 90% of the yearly operating schedule. This provides a clear diversity of the indoor climate on a daily basis, as is shown in Figure 3.5. This thermal diversity, however, is still managed within the boundaries of the adaptive comfort zone. The fact that the internal climate varies within a wide bandwidth of adaptive thermal comfort will provide the occupant with thermal diversity to be able to cope with different thermal expectations and changing biological and metabolic differences among occupants (Brager and de Dear, 2016). This was a cherished quality that was explained by some occupants as a room without "thermal boredom." It resulted in a high-performance space that is able to accommodate change, adapt to different occupants' uses and needs, and provide aesthetic pleasure.

3.11 Singular performance space

An experimental laboratory space in LISB is a good example of a singular performing space (Figure 3.6). Although limited in its requirements to accommodate change to different spatial use and occupancy patterns, the space exhibits a narrow degree of variable performance indicators for thermal and visual comfort. The high performance lab space exemplifies connections to outdoor views, bi-directional daylighting, and some opportunities for adaptive comfort, however, is limited in its thermal diversity. The psychrometric charts show that for the majority of the time the space climate stays within the ASHRAE prescribed thermal

Impacts of a LEED™ educational complex 41

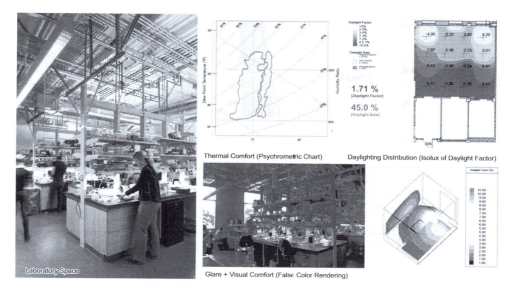

FIGURE 3.6 Singular-performance space example – laboratory space.
Source: Author.

comfort zone rather than the adaptive comfort one, i.e., the inner shade box. This tends to be fine for occupants performing tasks at the lab bench while standing or moving but it can become uncomfortably cold for seated occupants in desk spaces closer to the perimeter windows. Towards the inner walls of the space, lab equipment generating heat and activities by the occupants results in an uncomfortably warmer zone that ends up outside the ASHRAE thermal comfort zone.

Similar conclusions are drawn related to the code-driven lighting and glare performance of the space. Although abiding by prescriptive visual and thermal comfort requirements, the space provides unpleasant conditions for the occupants due to its limited ability to accommodate change in indoor climate and spatial usage (Figure 3.6). The limited degree of flexibility and employment of design strategies for multi-performance spaces in Figure 3.1 makes this a clear example of a singular-performing space.

3.12 Low-performance space

The computational office space (Figure 3.7) best demonstrates a space with good intentions, but due to underperforming visual and thermal qualities, it is low in performance. The space exhibits single-sided daylighting apertures, i.e., windows centered on the perimeter wall. The light shelves employed are separated from the ceiling plane by more than 4 ft, thus making them ineffective to provide diffused daylighting. Both the space proportions and the furniture layout result in inflexible seating positions for the occupants. Complicated occupants' controls and un-functioning control indicators result in a low-performance IEQ space, which is also poorly perceived by the building occupants (Figure 3.7). This space type is very indicative of most commercial offices, and it could be retrofitted by employing the multi-performance space strategies listed in Figure 3.1.

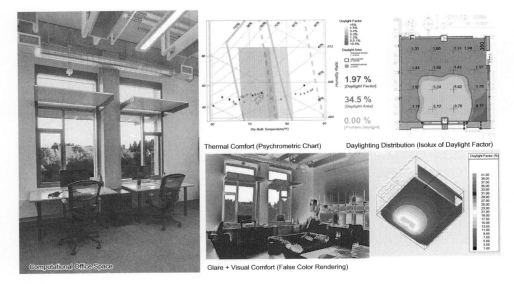

FIGURE 3.7 Low-performance space example – computational office space.
Source: Author.

3.13 Conclusion: lessons learned and future applications

Multi-performance space is a concept that proposes a different type of space adaptability and performance that is appropriate for our changing nature of space requirement and architecture. From a social perspective, adaptive spaces provide benefits at the workplace, and in many other building types, as well as environments at the urban, building, and room/setting scales. To produce an effective high multi-performance space, a designer needs to establish clear performance goals that acknowledge both the physical performance, as well as the impacts of the selected green design strategies on occupants' well-being and comfort. Establishing a process to ensure fine tuning of the systems and engaging the occupants in managing them, through feedback loops, is essential. Such feedback loops help engage the occupants in the building management, and ensure that the building as designed performs to its goals.

The main objective of this chapter is to provide detailed, as well as context-specific, information to assess IEQ inside green buildings that are designed to accommodate change and adapt to their requirements. By providing a classification framework of the various space types and their provision for levels of IEQ and comfort for the occupants, the study provides an evidence-based guide for future designs. It is important to note that green strategies should not be perceived as "one size fits all" in general, and might not be suitable in all design situations. It is clear from the findings that performance of some strategies can positively impact behavior in one condition, yet have negative implications in others. Designers will need to balance pros and cons of green building systems as they manage their goals to provide multi-performance or singular performing spaces. It is understood that low-performance spaces should be avoided at all costs. It is also of paramount importance to design spaces that combine high performance and high IEQ. The proposed IEQ model conveys the complex nature of the parameters of the indoor environment in producing a quality setting for the occupants. The hope is to aid designers in adopting this model to guide early design decisions of adaptive buildings that can embrace change and perform in a multi-dimensional manner.

3.14 References

Brager, G. and de Dear, R. (2016). Expectations of Indoor Climate Control. *Energy and Buildings*, 24, pp. 179–182.

Duffy, F. (1992). *The Changing Workplace*. London: Phiadcn Press.

Elzeyadi, I. (2003). Environmental Quality – Shaping Places for People: A Systemic Framework for Conceptualizing People and their Workplaces. In: *Shaping Places for People*, pp. 71–79. Proceedings of the Environmental Design Research Association EDRA 34th Conference, May 22–26, Minneapolis, MN.

Elzeyadi, I. (2012). Post-Occupancy Evaluation: A Design Operations and Performance Assessment of a LEED Platinum Building. *World Health Design Journal*, January 2012, pp. 60–69.

Elzeyadi, I. (2015a). A Tribute to Performance Arrows: Designing for Better Indoor Environmental Quality. In: *Thought and Leadership in Green Buildings Research*. Greenbuild 2015: Monumental Green. Washington, DC: USGBC Press.

Elzeyadi, I. (2015b). A Green Lesson: Measuring the Impacts of LEED certification credits on People, Planet and Profit of K–12 Schools. In: N. Fernando and G. Baker, *EDRA 2015 - brainSTORM: Dynamic Interactions of Environment-Behavior and Neuroscience*, Los Angeles, CA, 27–30 May 2015, pp. 48–59.

Elzeyadi, I. (2017). A Comparative Analysis of Predictive and Actual Performance of High Performance LEED Buildings. In: Preiser, W. F. E., Hardy, A. E., and Schramm, U. (eds.), *Building Performance Evaluation: From Delivery Process to Life Cycle Phases* (second edition). New York: Springer.

Hwang, R.-L., Lin, T.-P., Liang, H.-H., Yang, K.-H., and Yeh, T.-C. (2009). Additive Model for Thermal Comfort Generated by Matrix Experiment Using Orthogonal Array. *Building and Environment*, 44, pp. 1730–1739.

Preiser, W. F. E. (2009). The Triad of Programming, Post-Occupancy Evaluation (POE) and Universal Design: Toward Continuous Quality Improvement. In: Taylor, A. (ed.) *Linking Architecture and Education: Sustainable Design of Learning Environments*. Albuquerque, NM: University of New Mexico Press.

Preiser, W. F. E., Davis, A. T., Salama, A. M., and Hardy, A. E. (eds.) (2015). *Architecture Beyond Criticism: Expert Judgment and Performance Evaluation*. London: Routledge.

4

MIXED-USE DEVELOPMENT USING AIR RIGHTS ABOVE THE JR TRAIN STATION AT NAGOYA, JAPAN

Gen Taniguchi, Akikazu Kato, and Shiho Mori

4.1 Introduction

At the heart of central Japan, the Japan Rail (JR) Central Towers complex at Nagoya station circulates people, commerce, resources, and ideas. Developed by railway company JR Tokai, this transit hub links conventional lines of JR, two private railways, a metropolitan subway, a connection to Chubu International Airport, and the Shinkansen bullet train that runs between Tokyo and Osaka. One of the most heavily trafficked stations in the world, it is a huge amalgamation of commercial facilities, hotel rooms, and offices. The advantage of combining uses is the creation of additional services and a new way of experiencing city life. However, so often the result of this is a mere accumulation of functions rather than their complete integration. A group of high-rise towers may house separate functions and features without any connection or coherence to one another, as is the case with the Tokyo Metropolitan Government building by Kenzo Tange. Each of the two independent towers and annex buildings signifies the vertical dividedness of the administration. Although rejected in the design competition for the same commission, the schematic design by Arata Isozaki showed a sharp contrast to this. This chapter will review and evaluate the building performance of the JR Towers from the above perspectives, and will compare it with the horizontally-oriented Kyoto Station Building. Because the JR Central Towers complex is expected to serve as a station for the new generation of Shinkansen trains with linear magnetic propulsion motors, it could unite Tokyo and Nagoya in 40 minutes by the year 2025. The impact of this reduced travel time may result in an overall reconfiguration of the city structure and way of life in Nagoya. The chapter will discuss the future issues for the next phase of renovations.

4.2 Impact of large complex buildings on the city

Demonstrative of this mixing of transportation hub and office building is the combination of Grand Central Station and the Pan Am (Met Life) Building in New York City. The station, built in 1913 and significantly updated in 1998, and the Pan Am Building, built in 1962 and purchased by the Metropolitan Life Insurance Company in 1981, have both undergone significant changes in their lifetimes (New York Times, 1998). Emblematic of modern building technology, the complex blocks the vista of Park Avenue, showing the impact of such a building on the city landscape. From the very conception of Grand Central Station, the proposal of a high-rise building using the air rights of the site was considered, resulting in the Pan Am Building of 1962. At 292,000 square meters (3,140,000 sq ft) of office space, it was the largest skyscraper in New York City until it was surpassed in size by the World Trade Center in 1970–71.

The meaning of air rights is the unused development rights. The development rights generally refer to the maximum amount of floor area permissible on a zoning lot, and when the actual built area is less than this allotted total, the difference is referred to as unused development rights. A transfer of development rights (TDR) allows for the handover of unused square footage from one zoning lot to another in limited circumstances, usually to promote the preservation of historic buildings, open space, or unique cultural resources (New York City Planning 2016). There are various interpretations of air rights over Grand Central Station.

In Japan, the most famous air rights story is that of the JR East Japan Company selling the air rights over the Tokyo station Maruno-uchi Building. Built in 1914 and designed by legendary architect Kingo Tatsuno, these rights were sold to fund the station's renovation project. The project, running from 2007 to 2012, was reported to have cost nearly 50 billion yen (US $450 million) as funded by the purchasers of the air rights. Likewise, the JR Central Towers is another story or interpretation regarding development rights, which will be discussed in the following section.

Similar to Grand Central Station obstructing the view of Park Avenue, JR Central Towers blocks the vista of Sakura-dori Boulevard, with a subway line, next-generation bullet train, and linear motor train penetrating the building. The height of the Towers is 245 meters (805 ft) with 51 stories; comparably, the Pan Am Building is 246 meters (808 ft) or 50 stories.

Capturing the scenic landscape of Japan is the Kyoto Station Building, built in 1997. Architect Hiroshi Hara was chosen through an international design competition among seven world famous architects. His scheme lowered the building height to 60 meters (200 ft) in consideration of the expansive views of surrounding scenery, despite the allowable height of 120 meters (400 ft). Comparing the Kyoto Station Building to JR Central Towers, and the Tange designed Tokyo Metropolitan Government building to Isozaki's proposal for the same project juxtaposes horizontality to verticality, combination to integration.

4.3 Discussion of limitations of the construction site: limited or unlimited?

The late Yoshihiko Sakai, who oversaw the JR station building development, was a man of talent. In the earlier days of the Japanese National Railways Company, i.e., before privatization, he was sent to France to study railway-related real estate projects. He was determined to build a structure of competing size and quality to those in Tokyo and Osaka. Responding to the guidelines governing air rights and correspondence between a building and its site, he rationalized a train station is a piece of land where rails are laid continuing out from a city center. Thus, the allowable building volume would far exceed

FIGURE 4.1 JR Towers building site and railway platform.
Source: Authors.

those of existing buildings in the city. He proceeded to program a gigantic skyscraper, opposing the views of the controlling authority of Nagoya City. The area for platforms and rails was decided to be excluded from the building site, leaving a jagged strip of land with an awkward shape to be used for the construction site. A bonus percentage of the land was given to enlarge the allowable volume, following an extension clause for large-sized sites.

Mixed-use development using air rights **47**

4.4 Selection of architects

Mr. Sakai endeavored to select an architect who would bring elegance to the design of a railway station building. Several firms and signature architects came to visit him, and finally, Kohn Pederson Fox Associates (KPF) was chosen in collaboration with Sakakura Associates in Japan.

4.5 Limitations of the twin tower composition

This station building is a huge complex of station functions with the addition of offices, a hotel, department stores, a number of restaurants and retail shops, roof and floating gardens, and public plazas (Figure 4.2). With an organic continuity, the building was expected to function as a small city. However, in separating the major components of hotel and office blocks into asymmetric towers, the architectural design symbolized separation rather than connectivity.

The same phenomenon is found in the twin-tower design of the aforementioned Tokyo Metropolitan Government Building designed by Kenzo Tange. It could be said that to relay continuous and effective administrative services to citizens, a compact building of

FIGURE 4.2 Façade of JR twin-tower building.
Source: Public domain.

conglomerate block design might symbolize a more intricate network of various services, and that the massive design of Arata Isozaki's scheme at the time of the design competition might better symbolize and facilitate the network. Certainly, there should have been a better choice than the composition of two high rise towers standing in sublime isolation.

Mr. Sakai realized this drawback during the planning and design process; however, because it was too late to alter the major overall design composition, the development of an information system to integrate the station building as a whole was sought. A planning committee was organized with our mentor Professor Makoto Yanagisawa to create a system that enabled users to work or shop while in the hotel, or to shop and enjoy hotel services while working. The goal of the endeavor was to blend individual functions of "work, live, play, and travel," which were once defined independently by Le Corbusier and the philosophy of Congrès International d'Architecture Moderne (CIAM). While the level of information technology at the time did not meet these requirements, the current rapid progress should overcome these gaps soon.

4.6 Merits and demerits of the oval-shaped office

The typical floor plan of an office tower consists of an oval outer rim covering half of a rectangular core. Thus, the geometrical center points are not clarified as in the shape of a panopticon, an 18th-century concept of an institutional building where a single watchman can observe all at once. The majority of office layouts follow the Japanese medium of using a central island–type layout. A typical example is that of the Taisei Corporation Nagoya Branch Office (Figure 4.3). The authors' studies carried out with students clarified the activeness of communication among island groups, suggesting the overall progression of different work divisions. People were working in the space between desks, and not toward them, naturally gravitating towards each other. Moreover, the perimeter zone of the oval rim left adequate space for informal exchanges and work, rather than the inefficiency of a rectangular layout of desks and other furnishings.

4.7 Features of large Japanese offices: continuation of super deep floor plans

Early sketches of glass skyscrapers, such as those by Mies van der Rohe in 1922, harnessed greater outer surface area in complex shapes like a four-leaf clover. It seems that this was the start of deep floor plans in office buildings, setting a precedent for the Japanese offices of today (see Chapter 7). They might be workable for expansive offices of large corporations; however, because a large service core occupies the center of the floor-plate, it seems that workers migrate a lot around the office like a tuna or a bonito. The most miserable tenants tend to be small businesses who struggle to open an office at the city center. The rent is high, and the number of workers may be small, so a small portion of the rented office will have minimal frontage and deep sides that look like long strips of paper for haiku known as "Unagi-no-nedoko" ("bed for eel," meaning quite narrow). When applied to an oval floor plan the situation results in a shape like a crack in an egg shell.

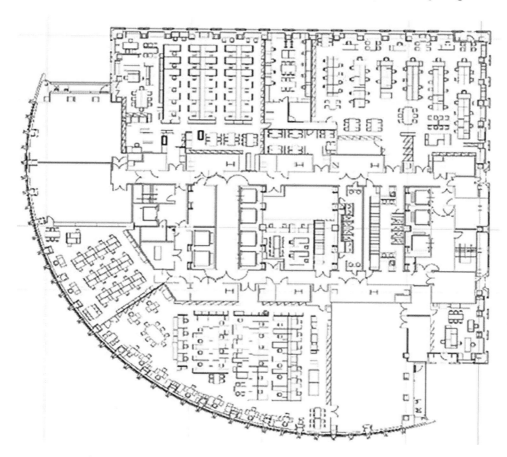

FIGURE 4.3 Office plan of Taisei Corporation Nagoya branch office.
Source: Authors.

4.8 Experimental office development

Because Nagoya is located between the mega-cities of Tokyo and Osaka, it is common for people to gather from the east and the west to hold meetings in the JR Central Towers Building. Kokuyo, one of the leading furniture providers in Japan, understood the significance of office location and space planning quite well. A glass-covered meeting room with a flexible furniture layout was placed at the entrance to be used by office staff and a number of users, acting as an open satellite office. Figure 4.5 shows the layout of the offices Kokuyo has evolved in the years from 2000 to 2013, thereby showing its different business strategies.

The office was developed in the JR Central Towers Building following the design concept of a live office. This means that it acted as a showroom for office design and furnishings as proposed by the company, representing a customer-centered and communication-oriented approach. The location above Nagoya station symbolized a meeting point from both east and west. The staffing typologies were clarified as follows: "runners" representing workers in the sales section, who spend relatively little time in the office using traditional workplaces, but

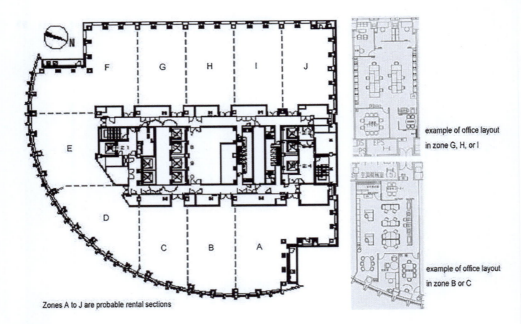

FIGURE 4.4 Office layout of smaller tenants of JR Office Tower.
Source: Authors.

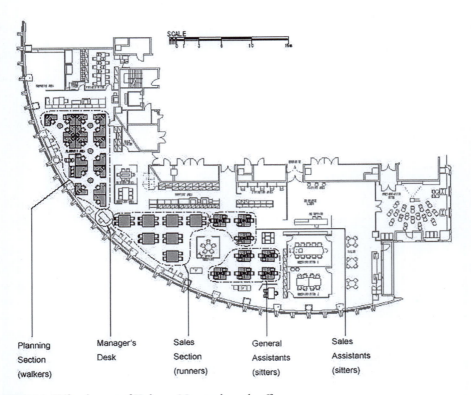

FIGURE 4.5 Office layout of Kokuyo Nagoya branch office.
Source: Authors.

rather, operating on a non-territorial or "free-address system"; "walkers" belong to those in planning and design sections, who have a certain degree of mobility with non-assigned workspaces; and finally, "sitters" are those mostly administrative personnel, using traditional desks and work spaces with a "fixed-address" system (Kato, 2015). Unfortunately, the company shifted their office to a different office building in pursuit of higher efficiency in 2008, and then to another to realize the visualization of the work process in 2013.

4.9 Form and function

Finally, the performance evaluation of the building refers to the modernist proverb "form follows function" and the antithesis "function follows form." It should be noted that the fit between "form and function" is further enlarged to an extreme in a huge facility and complex.

4.10 Acknowledgements

We would like to dedicate this chapter to the late architect Yoshihiko Sakai and the bereaved family.

4.11 References

Kato, A. (2015). Building Performance Evaluation in Japan. In: Preiser, W. F. E. and Vischer, J. C. (eds.). *Assessing Building Performance*. London: Routledge, Chapter 14.

New York City Planning (2016). Glossary of Planning Terms, www1.nyc.gov/site/planning/zoning/glossary.page. Accessed March 20, 2017.

New York Times (1998). Streetscapes / Grand Central Terminal; The 23-Story, Beaux-Arts 1913 Tower That Wasn't, www.nytimes.com/1998/10/11/realestate/streetscapes-grand-central-terminal-23-story-beaux-arts-1913-tower-that-wasn-t.html. Accessed March 20, 2017.

5

PROSPECTS FOR ADAPTIVE, INCLUSIVE DESIGN: LESSONS LEARNED FROM CHILDREN'S MUSEUMS

Korydon Smith and Beth Tauke

5.1 Introduction

"Children are not just small adults" and we cannot design services, activities, or environments for them as if they were (Lancet, 2001, p.431). Children, if given the opportunity, would likely design wildly different cities, buildings, and products than planners, architects, and designers currently make on their behalf. Children's museums are the rare exception.

Children and adults see the world differently. They see time, space, and scale differently. They see themselves differently. Their interactions with and representations of places and people are as disparate as the concepts of "play" and "speech." While adults communicate through speaking, writing, sign language, and body language, "play is the language of children" (Frost, 1998, p.10). Children express and explore anxieties and joys, realities and imaginations, and personal thoughts and interpersonal relationships through play of many forms. Scholars and practitioners commonly describe the physical and emotional development of children as psycho-motor phases on the path to adulthood. More recent discoveries, however, show important distinctions between children and adults regarding sensory processing. Though biological, cultural, and other factors play mediating roles, it is generally not until age eight, for example, that children use multiple sensory modalities to overcome uncertainty and not until age twelve that children fully integrate their senses into what is called "sensory fusion." Prior to these developmental phases, children process sensory information through single, unfused modalities (Nardini, Bedford, and Mareschal, 2010). In short, single-mode perception, multi-modal discernment, and sensory fusion are highly differing ways of taking in and interpreting the world.

The contrast between child and adult perspectives raises a wide range of philosophical questions across multiple disciplines. Since the mid-twentieth century, school teachers, pediatricians, child counselors, and other professionals who work closely with children have debated, revised, and ascribed to ethics codes specific to the population they serve. These include not only obvious statutes, such as sanctions against exploitation, but also less intuitive ones, such as the importance of facilitating autonomy or reaffirming a child's subjective views of him/herself and the present situation. Many child-centered codes of ethics align with the more general empathic and criticism-free principles of social work and other professions, i.e., seeing the world from the vantage point and lived experience of the client. It is asking the question, "What is it like to be you?" without passing judgment on his/her circumstances, beliefs, or behaviors.

Planners, architects, and other design professionals seldom confront child-related ethics so directly. Moreover, unlike the therapist, design professionals routinely make aesthetic and other judgments. It is integral to decision making in design. Yet, with the rise of inclusive design, humanitarian design, and design for health, comparisons between child-services and design professions gain utility. Advancements in neuroscience, for instance, have shed light on the fields of both child development and environmental psychology. Both areas of research converge within the spaces of children's museums, and, therefore, multiple lessons on architectural adaptation can be drawn from the research on and design of places for kids. We describe four: (1) promoting play for all, (2) balancing change and continuity, (3) enhancing therapeutic design, and (4) encouraging autonomy.

Children's museums have proliferated in recent decades, from 38 in the United States in 1975 to approximately 250 by 2015, with 70 more in the planning stages. The growth may be attributed to a variety of factors, not the least of which is economic development, demonstrated by the fact that more than a third of children's museums have been cornerstones in downtown revitalization efforts (Association of Children's Museums, 2015). The larger point here, however, focuses on what the field of architecture can gain by analyzing both the role of architects and the innovative features evident in the design and programming of children's museums. Of course, architects in an array of practices seek out the playful and imaginative architectural forms, spaces, and materials typically seen in children's museums, but, other objectives often take precedence. Children's museums are exemplary for studying both adaptive architecture and inclusive design, particularly due to the diverse populations they serve and the need for ever-changing exhibits. Several other reasons illustrate their broader applicability to architectural research and practice.

First, children's museums involve multiple scales and types of design: urban, landscape, building, exhibit, product, information/systems, and customer-service design. Second, children's museums engage the cognitive, emotional, sensory, and physical needs not only of boys and girls of all ages and abilities but also the parents and grandparents that accompany them. Third, children's museums must accommodate a wide array of subject areas and learning environments, as well as new activities and programs. Lastly, designers of children's museums must carefully attend to pragmatic issues, such as safety and security, while also appealing to the imaginations, creativity, and playfulness of visitors of all ages. Play spaces must foster enjoyment and self-confidence, while also promoting exploration and facing fears (Tierney, 2011). Children's museums, therefore, illustrate how color, texture, lighting, acoustics, and other experiential aspects not only accommodate but also inspire diverse users and activities.

5.2 Lesson 1: promoting play for all

Children's museums serve people of all ages—from infants and toddlers, to young adolescents, to teens, to parents and grandparents—and, therefore, must attend to a wide array of interests, preferences, and learning needs. Extending beyond the traditional market audience, the Children's Museum of Phoenix, for example, has been hosting "Play Date," an adult's night at the museum, for several years. Children's museums in Boston, Indianapolis, Pittsburgh, Manitoba, and elsewhere host similar events, which include adult-oriented activities—eating, drinking, and dancing—in concert with games and play forms typically associated with childhood. As evidenced on the webpages of many museums, these annual or semi-annual events frequently sell out, a tangible affirmation of the importance of play in adulthood, particularly in stress management and continued learning (Brown and Vaughan, 2009). The value of adult play is an important lesson and one that has informed workplace design in recent years, most famously exemplified in the integration of work and play in several of Google's headquarters (Stewart, 2013).

Children's museums also include a wide range of media and a variety of subjects—science, art, history, literature, etc. This includes the growing trend in services, programs, and exhibits for specific populations, such as children on the autism spectrum. A clear illustration is the Chicago Children's Museum "Play for All" initiative, which launched in 2004 (Golden and Walsh, 2013). Comprehensive in its approach, and with flexibility as a core principle, "Play for All" coordinators re-envisioned everything from customer service to exhibit design. The program emerged from a realization that disability laws and codes, such as the Americans with Disabilities Act of 1990, were insufficient in both scope and standards. Moreover, given the enormous emphasis on play-as-learning in children's museums, more creative approaches to designing for diversity were needed. As such, the team involved local disability organizations, as well as all museum departments, in the planning and design process. Particularly due to taking on a disability perspective, new interactive exhibits emerged, e.g., the chalk drawer, a drawing system connected to a wheelchair that produces large-scale floor art. The result is an art- and play-form that did not previously exist, and a way of including children who use wheelchairs daily, children who temporarily need a wheelchair, and ambulatory children.

5.3 Lesson 2: balancing change and continuity

A trait of many museums, especially illustrated in children's museums, is the wide variety of experiences that must be carefully curated to achieve cohesiveness. For museums, curating, and the educational and architectural equivalent, programming, is ongoing. Adaptability is a core principle in museum design, such that programming is not equated to an early design phase but continues throughout the life of the building. Exhibits change—yearly, weekly, or hourly—as do the staff members who develop, implement, and oversee them, along with the patrons who support a museum and the occupants who inhabit it. There are both educational and economic reasons for changing the contents, organization, and programs of a museum. Nevertheless, museum designers and administrators must "balance needed change with cohesion and continuity" (Silverman, 2010, p.107). Architects and curators must attend to the needs of the first-time visitor as well as the decades-long benefactor. For the former, spatial and thematic continuity between exhibits, and their associated rate-of-change, is critical to orchestrating the flow of movement and building incremental knowledge. Said differently, though the timeline varies, museum exhibits are constantly changing to address both market forces and emerging research, and, therefore, the experience of the repeat visitor changes.

A clear illustration of spatial continuity and change is the FlowWorks exhibit at the Children's Museum of Houston. This 5,000 square-foot (465 square-meter), outdoor showcase, which opened in 2009, leads children through a series of interactive water features. As they sequence through a series of more than 30 hands-on experiences, children follow the

Lessons from children's museums **55**

flow of the water to learn about "the forces and properties of water through waves, vortices, and rapids" as they actively change when and how the water moves (Children's Museum of Houston, 2014).

In complement to spatial continuity is the development and transformation of personal meaning over time: the resonance with one's value system, interests, life experiences, and social relationships. Museums, like the Strong Museum in Rochester, New York, often arise from the donations of personal or family collections. The degree to which those collections resonate with the life stories of museum goers can be the difference between an empty and a thriving museum. An intriguing example resides in a National Adoption Day program that Miami Children's Museum began in 2008 and remains a core annual event. In concert with a gallery display, 98 adoptions were finalized the inaugural year, and hundreds since then. This example depicts the power of museums to engage timely cultural conversations, such as foster care and adoption, in a manner that connects with the personal experiences of families and broader society. Miami's adoption program also illustrates a primary role of children's museums: facilitating children-to-children and family-to-family connections, "museums as places to meet and connect with other families for interaction, information, and friendship" (Silverman, 2010, p.109).

5.4 Lesson 3: enhancing therapeutic design

While the emergence of environmental psychology in the mid-twentieth century demonstrated the influences of the built environment on human behavior—e.g., worker productivity—studies on environmental risk factors to physical health and the roles of design in mental health are more recent. Many architects and physicians of the 19th and 20th centuries did engage building types and principles akin to the contemporary focus on design for health, e.g., Alvar Aalto's Paimio Sanatorium of the early 1930s or Dr. Thomas Story Kirkbride's asylum plans nearly a century earlier, but they were based largely on speculation and rhetoric, not on research evidence. More recently, the rise in humanitarian architecture, exemplified in the 2006 *Design Like You Give a Damn: Architectural Responses to Humanitarian Crises* (Architecture for Humanity, 2006) and other publications, demonstrates the integration of social and scientific research with a practical-yet-passionate value system. This mindset has extended into a wide variety of building types for vulnerable populations, e.g., therapeutic residential environments for people with Alzheimer's disease, supportive school design for autism spectrum disorders, and healing community spaces for refugees or victims of torture.

For instance, the Children's Museum of East End, outside of New York City, delivers programs for local children and their parents, especially a large community of immigrants in the area. Designed through stakeholder input, the museum provides art and play therapy to children while adults attend sessions on parenting, career planning, and other topics. Of note, over a 5-year period, starting with the launch of the community-based program in 2008, museum attendance grew 40% (Long, 2013).

Building on the Play for All program and partnering with occupational therapists from the Belle Center of Chicago, the Chicago Children's Museum, which serves more than 400,000 visitors and community members annually, created the "Therapy Play Guide" (Chicago Children's Museum, 2011). It provides prompts for integrating various forms of learning—gross motor skills, fine motor skills, visual-motor skills, multi-sensory abilities, communication, literacy, social skills, reasoning, and life skills—into each exhibit area. This strategy links the specific design features of each exhibit with somewhat unexpected learning prompts, such as listening to the flow of water in the Water Ways exhibit.

5.5 Lesson 4: encouraging autonomy

Whether talking about the relationship between mother and child, teacher and child, therapist and child, or architect and child, issues of paternalism come into play. Children are vulnerable to manipulation of all kinds: physical, emotional, and cognitive. The reasons that many professions exist, in fact, is to protect children from manipulation and harm. With these responsibilities, however, come the ethical questions raised at the beginning of this chapter. In a museum context, the debate is brought to light by comparing the agendas of different museum stakeholders: children, parents, and non-parental adults; curators, program staff, and benefactors; out-of-town guests and the local community (Anderson, Piscitelli, and Everett, 2008).

Adult imaginations and agendas, generally speaking, do not align with those of children. Yet adults make most of the design and programming decisions that affect the museum experience and, ultimately, affect the learning outcomes of young museum goers. Soliciting the input of children is one strategy that can be done throughout the lifecycle of a museum—from pre-planning to programming and design, to educational program development, to post-occupancy and program evaluation. Additionally, architects and museum administrators must consider the culture and medium of the end user from the end-user's perspective (Anderson *et al.*, 2002). What are the norms, values, behaviors, and expectations of the unique "culture" a museum serves: children?

Children's museums are, first, about education. Play is simply a method of promoting self-discovery over authoritarian learning. Self-monitored learning, by contrast to authoritative assessment, is a core aspiration in child education (Mazza and Tufte, 1972). Children's museums promote self-regulated learning through interactive exhibits that provide direct feedback. This is especially powerful when hands-on learning, common to nearly all children's museums, is integrated with staff-led storytelling and the active engagement of the child's imagination and life experiences (Munley, 2012; Piscitelli and Anderson, 2001). Research shows that not only do children have an overwhelmingly positive attitude toward museums of many kinds but children also have remarkable accuracy in their recall of past museum experiences and exhibits (Piscitelli and Anderson, 2001). Educators and architects both have much to gain from the educational settings and methods common in children's museums. Likewise, children's museums have, themselves, incorporated lessons learned from the research, practical experiences, and innovations of their peers.

In the mid-1990s, the Children's Museum of Indianapolis, for instance, challenged the dominant paradigm of designing science exhibits. The museum's science division recognized that science learning, which requires a "long-term developmental process," was at odds with conventional museum design, which tends to shepherd people quickly from one exhibit to the next. The planning and design team for the Children's Museum of Indianapolis, by contrast, developed a "funnel approach" to gallery design. This concept utilizes the main level for browsing, providing an array of options for brief learning and play experiences, while more distant galleries, quieter and more intimate, facilitate deeper and more focused learning experiences. In other words, the entry level provides "entry-level" learning, while upper levels advance the learning (Schauble and Bartlett, 1997). This strategy promotes user independence and individually paced learning.

5.6 Conclusion

Rarely do architects design buildings for themselves. They design for others. Empathy, therefore, is essential, and doubly so when designing children's museums. Undoubtedly, architects, as well as museum administrators and staff, must ensure the health, safety, and welfare of children. Preventing injuries, minimizing health risks, and averting security threats are core concerns. These paternalistic roles, and that of organizing the educational objectives of each museum experience, nonetheless, need to be combined with autonomy-focused values.

While we might not intuitively think of children as wise, parents and people who work with children will often cite the profound lessons they learn about themselves and the human condition from the wisdom of children. As architects, we might ask: what are children's views of the world and what can we gain in designing environments for them and with them? How might we improve all built environments—such as hospitals, banks, shopping centers, and transit hubs, even prisons—by applying these lessons? How can the boundaries of already humanitarian-minded fields, such as inclusive design, i.e., design-for-all, universal design, etc., also gain from these lessons?

Through children's museums, we see the capacity of architecture to invent new forms of play and learning for all members of society. We see the capacity of architecture to promote emotional continuity and cognitive transformation. We see the capacity of architecture to enhance or deliver therapeutic interventions. We see the capacity of architecture to foster independence. "Museums and galleries of all kinds have both the potential to contribute towards the combating of social inequality and a responsibility to do so" (Sandell, 2002, p.3), and the same may be said of architecture more broadly. This is what inclusive architectural practices do; they facilitate social equity and self-actualization.

As outlined in the introductory chapter, the impetuses for this book were many, not the least of which is a human-centered, rather than technologically centered, Third Industrial Revolution. Evidenced in everything from the "Arab Spring" to the "farm-to-table" movement, it is a revolution earmarked with the need for adaptability. The discipline and practice of architecture has, arguably, remained in an economically, technologically, and spatially conservative position since the mid-twentieth century. During previous eras of rapid change, however, architecture has been at the center of society's philosophical questioning, serving as the medium through which to explore and concretize emergent societal values.

Adaptive architecture is much more than spatial, material, formal, or technological adaptation. Adaptive, inclusive design moderates and mediates individual emotion and cognition, as well as the health, well-being, and worldviews of the public, including its youngest members. A genuinely adaptive architecture, therefore, transforms the minds of future architects.

5.7 References

Anderson, D., Piscitelli, B., & Everett, M. (2008). Competing agendas: Young children's museum field trips. *Curator, 51*(3), 253–273.

Anderson, D., Piscitelli, B., Weier, K., Everett, M., & Tayler, C. (2002). Children's museum experiences: Identifying powerful mediators of learning. *Curator, 45*(3), 213–231.

Architecture for Humanity. (2006). *Design like you give a damn: Architectural responses to humanitarian crises*. New York: Metropolis Books.

Association of Children's Museums. (2015). About children's museums. Retrieved from www.childrensmuseums.org/childrens-museums/about-childrens-museums. Accessed March 20, 2017.

Brown, S., & Vaughan, C. (2009). *Play: How it shapes the brain, opens the imagination, and invigorates the soul*. New York: Avery.

Chicago Children's Museum. (2011). Chicago Children's Museum therapy play guide. Retrieved from www.chicagochildrensmuseum.org/CCM_Therapy_Play_Guide.pdf. Accessed March 20, 2017.

Children's Museum of Houston. (2014). FlowWorks. Retrieved from www.cmhouston.org/flowworks. Accessed March 20, 2017.

Frost, J. (1998). Neuroscience, play, and child development. Paper presented at the IPA/USA Triennial National Conference. Longmont, CO.

Golden, T., & Walsh, L. (2013). Play for all at Chicago Children's Museum: A history and overview. *Curator, 56*(3), 337–347.

Lancet. (2001). Time to be serious about children's health care. *The Lancet, 358*, 431.

Long, S. (2013). Practicing civic engagement: Making your museum into a community living room. *Journal of Museum Education, 38*(2), 141–153.

Mazza, P., & Tufte, C. (1972). Children see themselves as others see them. *Peabody Journal of Education, 49*(3), 235–238.

Munley, M. E. (2012). Early learning in museums: A review of literature. Retrieved from https://www.si.edu/Content/SEEC/docs/mem%20literature%20review%20early%20learning%20in%20museums%20final%204%2012%202012.pdf. Accessed March 20, 2017.

Nardini, M., Bedford, R., & Mareschal, D. (2010). Fusion of visual cues is not mandatory in children. *Proceedings of the National Academy of Sciences, 107*(39), 17041–17046.

Piscitelli, B., & Anderson, D. (2001). Young children's perspectives of museum settings and experiences. *Museum Management and Curatorship, 19*(3), 269–282.

Sandell, R. (2002). *Museums, Society, Inequality*. London: Routledge.

Schauble, L., & Bartlett, K. (1997). Constructing a science gallery for children and families: The role of research in an innovative design process. *Science Education, 81*(6), 781–793.

Silverman, L. (2010). *The Social Work of Museums*. London: Routledge.

Stewart, J. B. (2013, March 15). Looking for a lesson in Google's perks. *The New York Times*. Retrieved from www.nytimes.com/2013/03/16/business/at-google-a-place-to-work-and-play.html?_r=0. Accessed March 20, 2017.

Tierney, J. (2011, July 18). Can a playground be too safe? *The New York Times*. Retrieved from www.nytimes.com/2011/07/19/science/19tierney.html?_r=2. Accessed March 20, 2017.

REFLECTIONS ON PART II

Michael J. Crosbie, Ph.D., FAIA

"Challenging preconceived ideas with adaptability"

Part II is about the concepts and processes of adaptability: companies providing adaptability, programming for adaptability, adaptability within building development, and learning from the scale of children. It also considers how adaptability and multi-functional space—whether at the scale of a single room or an urban precinct—is manifested in a variety of projects around the world. The comparison of these individual efforts reveals that the very achievement of adaptive, multi-functional architecture rests upon the adaptability of our own preconceived ideas about how space functions and evolves.

Magley presents the work of Habitat for Humanity International (HFHI) as a case study for us to understand how intercultural exchange is essential in making space for cultural identity to take place. In the case of HFHI, adaptability is aided through world-wide interdisciplinary collaboration. As a model for how this can happen across national and cultural boundaries, HFHI's work stands in contrast to more conventional aid, which relies on the distribution of funds to communities in need. Instead, HFHI works to empower existing community groups where they are already working. The Global Village project in Ethiopia is HFHI's largest in the world. The work is highly managed, monitored, and directed by HFHI staff that stay with a single project, while volunteer workers rotate in for a few weeks at a time, collaborating with different local trades and community members. These workers are expected to engage culturally, and are trained to recognize a range of detailed cultural issues and be cognizant of social customs. They follow locally grown design principles and values that shape the houses equitably, such as equal access to infrastructure, space, and services. Visiting volunteers build alongside community members to facilitate adaptability. Such exchange between volunteers and community members is not possible with a direct funding model, which tends to prefer solutions that are flown in and installed, conceived far from the places in which they will "land." The larger message here is that design and planning should also be approached with this level of cultural exchange and on-site immersion. Design professionals should operate in similarly structured experiences. This encourages a shared commitment of time and skill, which can change people on both sides of the equation, opening a wider world to them. Practices such as Mass Design Group in Boston offer a similarly unique practice model of design, research, and advocacy in the creation of adaptable environments—incorporating locals in other countries into building design, Mass's buildings are carefully tuned to the culture and climate, and try to give back to the community. Mass is set up as a non-profit entity—a model that allows the firm to practice architecture and design in a very broad way.

Hershberger and Smith note that a pre-designer can best serve if the design problem is not manipulated or squeezed from a method of problem solving that is itself the product of a certain cultural reflex to solution formulation, such as those born out of a Western industrialized context. The particular characteristics of the planning problem must be appreciated, perceived, and engaged on their own terms, without a problem solver's prejudiced view of what will work best for people of another culture. A multidisciplinary team, which must include users, has to reach consensus and definition of the most important issues to be addressed in the pre-design planning. One of the biggest challenges of pre-planning is to help a client or user see into the future. Across cultural landscapes, the pre-planning process itself needs to be adaptable, even multifunctional.

Elzeyadi's helpful insight that "single-performance" space is also "low performance" space prods us to reconsider our value systems in assessing the design of the built environment. Multi-performance spaces result in high performance, and this translates into value. Multiple layers of performance can "charge" a space with potential levels of utility. The changes that different people enact on a space lend it a certain dynamism that can engage its users, as functions might adapt from hour to hour, day to day, week to week—veritably any time frame. In a certain way, such spatial dynamism is like the presence of natural light, natural ventilation, or views, which give a space its own character and identity on a temporal plane. Not surprisingly, multi-use space has a higher quotient of sustainability, as a variety of functions are served over time. But human comfort and building performance are multifaceted. Multi-use spaces can combat "thermal boredom," as some users describe it. Lack of boredom, thermal and otherwise, is key to spatial dynamism.

The JR Towers project profiled by Taniguchi, Kato, and Mori seems the epitome of architecture that results from the conceptual silos we create in our own minds when it comes to spatial use. The challenge is to integrate both vertical and horizontal spaces in a new experience of urban life, outside of common urban places that have little spatial overlap. The JR Towers site contains mixed uses, but they were literally "siloed" in the towers, which drastically limited horizontal integration and connectivity. From a city and regional planning perspective, the design of JR Towers was ironic in that many of the visitors to the project travel long distances east and west on the country's horizontal datum, only to be denied a multi-spatial experience once they arrive at the complex.

"Play is the language of children," Smith and Tauke quote professor and child development expert Joe L. Frost in his description of how we learn to communicate. Might this translate into a design language for architecture? Can we engage children in the design of the built environment through play, and how might this be absorbed by adults who have unlearned their playful behavior? And finally, can it be applied in other kinds of environments outside of children's museums? Children's museums are a perfect building type to study for adaptability, because they have to respond to different children with different backgrounds and age groups, all experiencing the world in different ways. Such museums also have to accommodate a number of simultaneous activities. Interestingly, Smith and Tauke show that play emerged as a critical piece of the design puzzle when consideration of disability was emphasized. It seems that connecting the two—play and accommodating those with pronounced disability—is an effective aid in the design process. Children's museums at their heart are places for children and families to bond and to address contemporary social issues, always through multi-faceted play. These environments promote social equity and self-actualization, which could be (I would argue "should" be) a multi-functional dimension of all architecture, no matter what its purpose.

The acceleration of digital communication, knowledge sharing, and the erosion of disciplinary boundaries demands that we evolve in the way we think about space—its creation and its continuing modification—and the role of professionals in this endeavor. The subtext of these chapters asks us to examine and be critical of our own cultural and professional norms, and "be present" with the others with whom we work. We need to be open to the problem, not bend the problem to fit a predetermined idea of how best it might be solved based solely on our past history.

PART III
Rooms/settings scale

Preamble

William Fawcett

The chapters in this part address a number of issues that apply to the adaptive use of rooms and spatial settings within buildings. Each chapter is based on a case study of a particular setting or context, but the approaches and techniques are generally transferable to many other types of setting.

The introductory chapter, Chapter 6, is concerned with the challenge of adaptive design when there is uncertainty about future activities. The ultimate test of an adaptive strategy is how it will work in use, but this information cannot be available at the time of design. Using a healthcare-based example, it is argued that activity simulation provides a practical resource for evaluating the adaptive performance of design strategies.

Following the discoveries made in the previous chapter, Morgan's chapter (Chapter 7) is concerned with the design of environments that will be suitable for diverse users. His case study is about multi-storey office buildings where the size and shape of floor plans are fixed in advance of tenant occupation. To explore the potential for accommodating a wide variety of tenant requirements, he constructs a typology of floor plans and analyses their performance with respect to several factors, identifying better performing solution types.

Hodulak, in Chapter 8, reviews the pros and cons of changing from an established activity setting to one that offers potential benefits but also risks. The specific context is German office interiors, where the cellular office is still widely used and open planning is under scrutiny. Open planning offers greater flexibility and adaptability but has functional drawbacks, and it conflicts with the long-established expectations of German office workers.

Hibbs, in Chapter 9, studies the adaptation of existing institutional buildings for evolving requirements, specifically that of museums. She reviews the evolution of the activities and buildings of the Science Museum in London since its opening in 1928, and shows how a comprehensive analysis of current requirements has led to a new masterplan to support on-going change, including the adaptation of inherited buildings.

In Chapter 10, Fay proposes that investigating the performance in use of facilities is a way of guiding adaptive improvements. Her case study describes a diagnostic post-occupancy evaluation of the emergency department in Kentucky University Hospital, which opened in

2010. Observations, monitoring, interviews, questionnaires, and focus groups were used to gather information, which was fed into collaborative charrettes to identify improvements to both the setting and work patterns.

Roessel, in Chapter 11, focuses on the conventions that sustain the harmonious use of multi-activity environments. The case study shows the connection between the culture and beliefs of the Navajo community and their traditional dwelling form, the Hogan. It is a multi-use environment, but with strong conventions about both the physical form and the ways that particular activities take place in the Hogan. Many of these conventions were adopted on a larger scale in the planning of a Navajo community college.

6

THE MEASUREMENT AND EFFICIENCY OF ADAPTIVE DESIGN STRATEGIES

William Fawcett

6.1 Synopsis

The arguments in favour of adaptive architecture will be stronger if its adaptive performance can be measured. This is difficult because of uncertainty about future activities, but assuming that activities will change radically in unforeseeable ways can lead to excessive investment in over-complex adaptive designs. An example shows a systematic approach to forecasting a range of possible future activities and using this data to evaluate alternative adaptive strategies. It can be seen as an application of the real options approach to decision-making under uncertainty. A key component is the use of computer-based Monte Carlo simulation of possible activities. Some people object to forecasting because adaptive design allows for uncertainty about activities, but every adaptive design strategy makes an implicit forecast of future activities. It is preferable to make explicit activity forecasts so that adaptive designs can be tested and the best performing ones identified.

6.2 Evaluation of adaptive environments

Most chapters in this book are concerned with the challenge of designing new kinds of environments for human activities, now that the digital revolution has made old design conventions based on functional determinism obsolete. Innovative and creative thinking has led to solutions that function well for activities that are variable in the short term or changing in the longer term. This chapter investigates whether the performance of these and other proposals for adaptive environments can be quantified, in terms of their adaptive functionality as well as their resource demands.

Quantification is especially relevant if an adaptive strategy requires additional costs or other resources compared to less adaptive or non-adaptive alternatives. This is not always the case – a skilled designer may produce designs that are both more adaptive and more economical than those of a less-skilled designer. However, there are many situations where the ability to provide for a wider range of possible activities does require additional resources. Consider floor loading as a simple example: different activities have different floor loading

68 Fawcett

requirements, and the stronger a structure is the greater the range of activities that can use it. What is a reasonable design loading to use? In the UK the design loading for office floors has been set at 2.5 kN/m^2 (52 lb/ft^2), based on research into actual loadings, which are often less than 1.0 kN/m^2. But until the 1990s, design loadings followed:

> the mantra 'four plus one', 5 kN/m^2 (104 lb/ft^2), being 'four' for medium-term variable occupancy and 'one' for long-term variable action of demountable partitions. This was specified in the supposed cause of flexibility. The direct cost was overdesign and increased cost of new buildings. (Hume and Miller, 2015)

Without debating whether the 2.5 kN/m^2 floor loading standard strikes the right balance between cost and flexibility, the existence of a trade-off is clear.

Advocates for adaptive architecture would argue that extra investment is justified by the opportunities for a wider range of different activities during the service life. Less committed decision-makers would prefer to see evidence that the future benefits are at least as great as the present investment. This evidence is difficult to provide: although the extra up-front costs are relatively easy to quantify, the benefits of adaptive strategies occur in the future and are therefore subject to uncertainty.

6.3 Present knowledge and future activities

When the architect Eberhard Zeidler of Craig Zeidler & Strong was designing the McMaster University Health Sciences Centre (MHSC) in Hamilton, Canada, in the late 1960s, he believed that uncertainty about future activities was so great that the design:

> required cellular growth and independent cellular change: a universal 'plug-in' space that could accommodate any function, ranging from factory use, living or hospital spaces, to complex uses such as nuclear research. Each use had to be interchangeable, as nobody could predict where each should be located or what size it should be five or ten years from now. (Zeidler, 1973)

The building is a heroic example of design for adaptation (Figure 6.1). The 16,400 m^2 (176,000 ft^2) complex opened in 1972 and continues in hospital use. It has four floors with intermediate service floors and projecting lift shafts for the addition of a fifth floor. The grid of 21 m (69 ft) square column-free bays can be extended in any direction and the cladding can be demounted and modified.

Even before it opened, the maximalist McMaster approach was questioned by John Weeks, an architect who had made extensive studies of growth and change in hospitals:

> It is arguable that the degree of flexibility provided by the use of very wide spans and inter-floor service space is unnecessarily high. The ability to provide services at every point over the whole area of a building is a luxury which is needed in very few areas of the health sciences complex. But the notion is attractive, and further study of the benefits of its adoption in increasing the useful life-span of a high cost building fabric is necessary. A balance between increased efficiencies and economies in maintenance costs to offset increased capital cost might be found. (Weeks, 1969)

The 'further study' of the McMaster approach that Weeks recommended can now be carried out, since we know the activity change that actually occurred. Such a study has to compare (i) the additional cost of the adaptive strategy, and (ii) the service life benefits in accommodating activity change. On the first point, Weeks estimated that the initial cost of a hospital built using the McMasters approach was about 85% higher than a conventional hospital of the period (Llewelyn-Davies *et al.*, 1973, 14). On the second point, a study of the first 30 years of its life found that:

> MHSC, which was designed never to be finished, did not change in accordance with the original vision. The building did not follow its intended master plan. The expansion possibilities were not fulfilled, and the interior redevelopment was limited in scope. In this way, the vision that had intended to create an infinitely flexible and dynamic structure resulted in a static monument. (Pilosof, 2005)

The fact that there was less exploitation of the adaptive features of MHSC than originally expected may be due to the preferences of later managers, not any technical inadequacy. For

FIGURE 6.1 The McMaster University Health Sciences Centre (MHSC) at Hamilton, Canada, was designed by Eberhard Zeidler of Craig Zeidler & Strong and opened in 1972. It took a high-cost, maximalist approach to adaptive design, but many of the provisions for growth and change have never been used.
Source: Ian Elllingham, 2016

70 Fawcett

example, a costed proposal for adding the fifth floor was developed in the late 1980s, but it was rejected in favour of constructing a new building on a nearby site (Pilosof, 2003).

The designer's justification for the highly adaptive strategy at MHSC was uncertainty about the future, but the strategy actually reveals an implicit belief about the future, namely that there would be extensive and radical activity change requiring substantial reconfiguration of the MHSC's physical environment. It is hard to escape the conclusion that this belief was mistaken and that there was over-investment in the complex and expensive adaptive features of the building.

The designers of adaptive environments should seek to minimize the risk of over-investment in adaptive features, and also minimize the risk of under-investment in adaptive features, which may be a more common shortcoming. This requires measurement of costs and benefits – at the time of design, not 30 years later.

6.4 Worked example

An approach to quantification is explored in the following worked example. Like MHSC it is in a healthcare setting, but it relates to short-term adaptive use at the scale of the room (see Introduction) rather than long-term adaptive use at the scale of the building as a whole. The data is hypothetical.

An adaptive design strategy is sought for a healthcare clinic with variable patient demand. Although exact prediction of patient demand is impossible, suppose that some statistical properties can be established:

1. Five patients arrive per time period (perhaps an hour or a day).
2. The length of stay varies with an average of four periods.
3. Patients can be of four types: Type S ('simple'), Type A, Type B, and Type C ('complex'). The patient types have equal frequencies in the long term but the mix of arrivals in any given time period is unknown.

Over time patients of the various types arrive seeking treatment and stay for varying periods. The demand profile, i.e., the number of patients of each type currently requiring treatment, is continually changing, as shown for a sample of 20 time periods in Table 6.1. On average, there are five patients of each type and an overall total of 20 patients, but in any particular time period the number of each type varies considerably, as does the overall total but to a lesser extent. Given this variability of patient demand it is evident that the clinic needs a set of treatment rooms that is adaptive for varying patient demand.

To quantify the variability of patient demand a computer model using Monte Carlo simulation was programmed to step though a sequence of 10,000 time periods: in each period new patients are randomly assigned to the four types and their duration of stay is also randomly generated. The model keeps an updated count of the number of new and existing patients of the four types seeking treatment; as the patients' duration of stay is completed they drop out of the count. The model generates 10,000 simulated demand profiles, equivalent to many years of in-use experience. Some basic statistics for the simulated demand profiles are shown in Table 6.2.

Turning from patient demand to the treatment rooms, they can also be of four types, with varying provision of equipment and facilities and varying costs: Type S ('simple', 4 cost

Adaptive design strategies **71**

TABLE 6.1 A sample of 20 simulated demand profiles for consecutive time periods. The highest values are marked with upward flashes and the lowest values by downward flashes.

	NUMBER OF PATIENTS BY TYPE				
SAMPLE	**S**	**A**	**B**	**C**	**TOTAL**
1	7	5	2	6	20
2	8↗	5	1↘	7↗	21
3	7	6	1↘	6	20
4	5	5	3	4	17↘
5	5	4	5	5	19
6	4	2↘	8	5	19
7	5	2↘	7	5	19
8	5	2↘	4	6	17↘
9	6	3	3	6	18
10	5	4	7	4	20
11	4	4	8	5	21
12	3↘	5	7	5	20
13	4	5	9	4	22
14	5	4	9	4	22
15	4	7↗	11↗	2	24↗
16	4	5	9	2	20
17	7	3	8	2	20
18	5	5	7	3	20
19	5	7↗	7	1↘	20
20	4	6	9	3	22
AVERAGE	4.87	5.13	4.97	5.01	**19.99**

Source: Author.

TABLE 6.2 Summary statistics for the 10,000 simulated demand profiles. The minimum and maximum values occur rarely: the number of times they occur in the 10,000 simulated demand profiles is given in square brackets.

	Patients of Type S	*Patients of Type A*	*Patients of Type B*	*Patients of Type C*	*Total patients*
Minimum	0 [21]	0 [38]	0 [38]	0 [41]	13 [4]
Average	5.00	5.04	5.01	4.98	20.03
Maximum	14 [1]	13 [5]	14 [1]	13 [4]	28 [1]

Source: Author.

units per room), Type A (6 cost units), Type B (6 cost units), and Type C ('complex', 8 cost units). Patients do not always have to be treated in a room of matching type; the range of possibilities is shown in the feasibility matrix (Figure 6.2): where there is a '1' in the matrix, it indicates that the patient of the row type can be treated in a room of the column type; a '0'

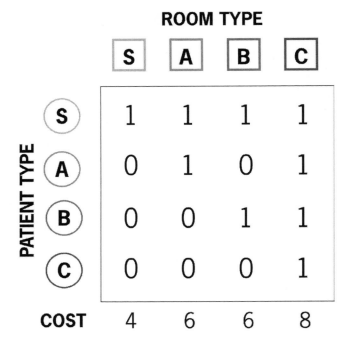

FIGURE 6.2 The feasibility matrix for the healthcare clinic worked example. There are four patient types and four room types. '1' indicates that treatment is feasible, '0' that it is not. The relative cost of the four room types is also indicated.
Source: Author.

indicates that this is not possible. Type S ('simple') patients can be treated in any room type, but Type C ('complex') patients can only be treated in Type C rooms. Type C 'complex' rooms, being best equipped and most flexible, are suitable for all patients, but they are the most expensive.

The design challenge is to provide a set of treatment rooms of the four types (S, A, B, C) with adaptive potential to cope with varying patient demand. Many possible strategies could be considered. The cost of a strategy is determined by the number and type of treatment rooms, and its adaptive performance is measured by the percentage of the 10,000 simulated demand profiles that it can accommodate. Thus, each design strategy is measured by two values: its cost and its adaptive performance.

The cost and adaptive performance for 50 different strategies are shown in a scattergram (Figure 6.3). It shows a clear trade-off between cost and adaptive performance: at the bottom end of the cost range the strategies have low adaptive performance (< 10%), but adaptive performance rises rapidly with increasing cost, up to a plateau where additional costs give no further benefits.

Some of the design strategies are highlighted on the scattergram (see Table 6.3 for data about these design strategies):

A. The average demand is five patients in each of the four types, and design strategy A has five rooms of each type; it has a low cost of 120 units. However, patient demand

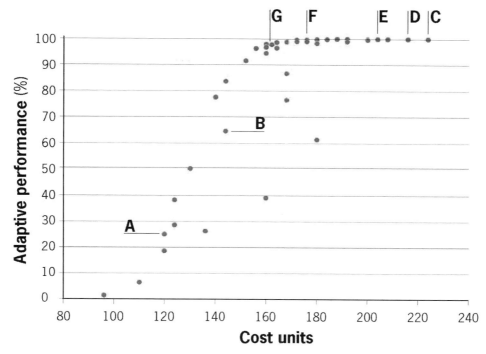

FIGURE 6.3 Scattergram showing the cost and adaptive performance (% of the 10,000 simulated demand profiles that can be accommodated) for fifty design strategies. Data for the highlighted strategies is given in Table 6.3 and they are discussed in the text.
Source: Author.

virtually always varies from the average and this strategy has poor adaptive performance, accommodating only 25% of the 10,000 simulated demand profiles.

B. Strategy B has six rooms of each type instead of five in strategy A, which increases the cost to 144 units and the success rate to 65% – still a low figure.

C. At the other extreme, the maximum number of patients requiring treatment in the 10,000 simulated demand profiles is 28, so a strategy with 28 type C rooms is certain to accommodate 100% of the profiles. This strategy C provides adaptive performance to meet the varying patient demand, but at a high cost of 224 units.

D. The 28 treatment rooms in strategy C cope with the maximum number of patients requiring treatment, but this maximum occurs in only one of the 10,000 simulated demand profiles (see Table 6.2). Strategy D with 27 type C rooms achieves 99.99% success rate and gives a saving of 8 cost units (3.5%) compared to strategy C – a compelling trade-off between cost and adaptive performance.

E. A little experimentation shows that alternative strategies achieve 100% success rate, if this is required; for example, strategy E costs 200 units, saving 24 cost units (11%) compared to strategy C.

F. A small relaxation of the adaptive performance target allows substantial cost savings; for example, strategy F achieves 99.88% success rate and costs 176 units, saving 48 cost units (21%) compared to strategy C.

74 Fawcett

TABLE 6.3 Data for the design strategies highlighted in the scattergram (Figure 6.3).

Design strategy	Rooms of Type S	Rooms of Type A	Rooms of Type B	Rooms of Type C	Total rooms	Cost units	Success rate
A	5	5	5	5	20	120	25.03%
B	6	6	6	6	24	144	64.66%
C	0	0	0	28	28	224	100.00%
D	0	0	0	27	27	216	99.99%
E	4	2	2	20	28	200	100.00%
F	2	6	6	12	26	176	99.88%
G1	4	5	5	11	25	164	98.74%
G2	2	6	6	10	24	160	97.95%
G3	4	5	5	10	24	156	96.23%

Source: Author.

G. There are a number of strategies costing around 160 units that can accommodate over 95% of the 10,000 demand profiles, saving around 64 cost units (30%) compared to strategy C. Three examples are included in Table 6.3.

A factor that has not been explored is the consequence of failing to accommodate a demand profile: would this simply lead to queueing for treatment, or have more serious consequences? The simulation model could be extended to include queueing.

In this example, the trade-off between cost and adaptive performance is evident and can be quantified, but it is still not obvious which of the 50 design strategies, or an alternative design strategy, should be chosen. What sacrifice of adaptive performance should be accepted in exchange for what cost saving? This is not a design question but depends on the building owners' or users' value system. In cases where the value system is itself quantifiable, the optimum strategy can be determined (Fawcett, 2009).

In almost all architectural projects, there is competition for scarce resources, and investment in adaptive performance is likely to be scrutinized for efficiency. This suggests two principles of efficient design for adaptation:

• for a given adaptive performance target, seek the strategy with the lowest cost;
• for a given budget, seek the strategy with the highest adaptive performance.

The healthcare clinic example is simpler than most real-world situations, but the principle that both adaptive performance and resource demand should be analysed and compared is widely applicable. The temptation to over-complicate the simulation should be resisted; effective modelling always requires simplification, so long as the key features of the system are captured. Simulation modelling allows designers and managers to explore the trade-off between adaptive performance and cost in many alternative scenarios. In a healthcare setting the choice between the alternatives is the province of healthcare managers who may, or may not, feel that some loss of adaptive performance is justified by cost savings.

As the great Victorian civil engineer Sir Benjamin Baker said in another context, occasional failures have to be accepted: 'The attempt to guard against every contingency in all cases would lead to ruinous and unjustifiable extravagance' (Rolt, 1962).

6.5 Systematic approach

The McMaster University Health Sciences Centre and the simulated healthcare example exhibit contrasting approaches to designing adaptive strategies for variable or uncertain activities. The first approach asserts that future activities are uncertain and uses this lack of data to justify high expenditure on adaptive strategies; the second simulates the range of possible future activities and uses this data to quantify the trade-off between the adaptive performance and cost of alternative strategies. The second approach is preferable; it can be called a systematic approach to adaptive design.

Systematic approaches to decision making under uncertainty are encountered in other disciplines. A useful precedent is the concept of real options (Mun, 2008), which was, in turn, derived from financial options. Options are only exercised if the option-holder benefits; otherwise they are left unexercised. Real options apply these ideas in non-financial situations, and in the architectural context an adaptive design can be interpreted as providing the owner or user of a building with options that allow for changes in use or changes to the fabric; they will be exercised if and when future circumstances make it advantageous (Ellingham and Fawcett, 2006; Fawcett, 2011). It is normal for only some of a building's options to be exercised with others left unexercised. In the case of the MHSC, the designers created a plethora of options, most of which have remained unexercised.

It is always good to hold options, but they generally have to be paid for – never turn down a free option! Although the future cannot be predicted, the real options approach simulates the range of future possibilities, and uses this data to establish the value of an option. Values can be compared with the cost of acquiring the option, to assess whether it represents a good investment. The second healthcare example followed the real options-type approach.

How widely can this systematic approach be applied to adaptive design strategies? It is necessary to forecast future activities – not deterministically, but probabilistically. This can be based on real observations, as might apply in the healthcare clinic worked example; this is more appropriate for short-term cyclic activity change than long-term evolutionary change. Alternatively, forecasts may simply be based on beliefs about the future, as applies in many practical situations. When the beliefs are made explicit they can be used to simulate possible activities and test adaptive strategies.

6.6 Conclusion

The concept of adaptive architecture has an elusive charm, but it would be of far greater practical value if it could be subject to the same tests of efficiency as other design attributes. These tests would identify and hopefully eliminate strategies that are over-designed or under-designed in relation to the need for adaptation. Defining the need for adaptation is equivalent to answering the question: 'what range of activities should the adaptive strategy provide for?' Some people might argue that this is in conflict with the purpose of adaptive design, which is to allow for uncertainty about activities. But the universally flexible design is a myth and, like it or not, any adaptive design strategy is tied to an implicit range of possible activities. Far better that it should be well-researched range than a stab in the dark.

6.7 Acknowledgements

I would like to thank Ian Ellingham for many stimulating discussions and comments that have contributed greatly to this chapter; and Martin Hughes for programming the simulation model for the example.

6.8 References

Ellingham, I. and Fawcett, W. (2006). *New Generation Whole-life Costing: Property and construction decision-making under uncertainty*. Oxford: Taylor & Francis.

Fawcett, W. (2009). 'Optimum capacity of shared accommodation: yield management analysis.' *Facilities,* 27, 339–356.

Fawcett, W. (2011). 'Investing in flexibility: the lifecycle options synthesis.' *Projections: The MIT Journal of Planning*, 10, 13–29.

Hume, I. and Miller, J. (2015). 'Imposed loads in historic buildings: assessing what is real.' *The Structural Engineer*, June, 40–43.

Llewelyn-Davies, Weeks, Forestier-Walker & Bor (1973). *Long-Life Loose-Fit: A comparative study of change in hospital buildings*. Unpublished report, London.

Mun, J. (2008). *Real Options Analysis* (2nd edn). Hoboken, NJ: Wiley.

Pilosof, N. P. (2003). 'Planning for change: Hospital design theories in practice.' Dissertation for Master of Architecture, McGill University, Montreal.

Pilosof, N. P. (2005). 'Planning for change: Hospital design theories in practice.' *AIA Academy of Healthcare Journal*, 8, 13–20.

Rolt, L. T. C. (1962). 'Benjamin Baker.' *Great Engineers*. London: Bell.

Weeks, J. (1969). 'Multi-strategy buildings.' *Architectural Design*, 39, 536–540.

Zeidler, T. H. (1973). 'Designing for the unknown future.' *Business Quarterly*, 37.3, 28.

7

FINDING THE BALANCE: A MODEL OF ASSESSMENT FOR COMMERCIAL FLOOR-PLATE PERFORMANCE

Jeffrey L. Morgan

7.1 Introduction

Commercial tower floor-plates epitomise adaptive spaces as tenants regularly churn or update their own premises within a 'shell-and-core' leased space. Different types of organisations have a need for a multiplicity of environments within the workplace. In commercial office fit-outs, the latest trend of an activity-based workplace (ABW) allows occupants to choose the type of working environment that best suits the task they have at any given time.

However, well before the internal fit-out of an office is conceived, the design of a commercial floor-plate undergoes extensive development and refinement resulting in the fundamental spatial arrangements and environments within which any workplace must be realised. Within the earliest stages of a commercial tower design lie the moments when critical decisions are made that have the most enduring and profound impact upon the nature and quality of the eventual workplace. Much of the focus and discussion currently revolves around ABW environments and their benefits for today's agile workplace. However, internal fit-outs regularly change and can be created in any given space. This chapter seeks to provide discussion around how the design of a floor-plate, which caters to numerous programs throughout its duration, impacts the latent qualities of visibility, connectivity, daylight, and proximity to the façade, and therefore the internal physical and psychological environment.

7.2 Design overview

The design of a commercial tower floor-plate and its core is invariably an exercise in evaluating a myriad of different influences including client aspirations, site opportunities and constraints, financial realities, and construction methodologies. During the concept development stages when initial floor-plate configurations are explored and evaluated by their response to the site and client brief, justifications are made by architects to promote the direction of a preferred solution. The process of developing an architectural proposition is never black and white. Design proposals are the culmination of a carefully considered balance of influences set within a hierarchical decision making framework that leads to the proposition. Often that framework is highly subjective, as is the nature of design.

However, developers, leasing agents, and tenants typically respond more comfortably to numbers and data generated through more objective assessments rather than perceived subjective viewpoints of a building's character or qualities. Anecdotally, these types of approaches to evaluate floor-plate performance are utilised and adapted by academics, architects, and developers to evaluate various assessment criteria. The aim of this chapter is to explore what trends or relationships may emerge through a typological analysis of floor-plate design.

This is not to say that architecture is, or should be purely an empirical exercise, as clearly it is not. However, some measure of objectivity in the decision-making framework is certainly beneficial during the design process. The intent of this study and model development is not to suggest that the resultant statistics of a particular floor-plate 'prove' its superiority over another. Rather, when overlaid with our subjective points of view, these more objective considerations help generate a more robust and rigorous design discourse to better inform the decisions we make.

This chapter will provide a greater understanding and measure of the decisions that are made at the inception of the design process for commercial office towers through the development of parametric assessment algorithms that generate a typological study of various floor-plate shapes and sizes. Beyond this initial exercise is the potential to develop a benchmarking database of commercial tower developments against the given criteria, and create a parametric design tool to simultaneously drive and assess the performance floor-plates during the design stages of commercial buildings.

The development of this parametric model intends to analyse commercial floor-plates against six common criteria used to evaluate office floor-plates including: net-to-gross ratios; wall-to-floor ratios; day lighting coverage; average distance from façade; floor-plate connectivity; and floor-plate visibility (Figure 7.1). Some of the assessment categories are simple, commercial development-driven criteria whilst others relate to the physical and psychological environment of the floor-plate. When these criteria are considered as part of a complex framework, value judgements can be made on a more well-informed basis.

7.3 Typological analysis

7.3.1 Criteria and method of assessment

Net-to-gross ratio and the wall-to-floor ratio provide the best measure of the typical floor-plate's relative construction costs and therefore its viability as a commercial development (Barton & Watts, 2013). Whilst these indicators of financial efficiency will inevitably be highly weighed in any discussion, the remaining four criteria consider the qualities of the floor-plate that impact upon its internal physical environment and workplace characteristics. Although these criteria may not provide the objective clarity that the financial metrics offer, they do present a means to communicate the benefits and relative performance of a floor plate's more intangible qualities, which influence its occupation and workplace quality.

Parametrically, assessing the net-to-gross and wall-to-floor ratios are straightforward calculations based on the area and perimeter length of a given floor-plate shape, its proportion of core to overall floor-plate area, and typical storey height.

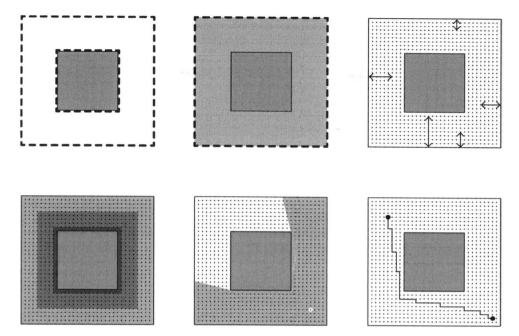

FIGURE 7.1 Floor-plate assessment criteria: Top-left: net-to-gross ratio. Top center: wall-to-floor ratio. Top right: average distance to façade. Bottom left: daylight penetration. Bottom center: floor-plate visibility. Bottom right: floor-plate connectivity.
Source: Author.

To assess the floor-plate's internal environmental characteristics, more complicated algorithms were developed to create an 'assessment grid' for any floor-plate configuration. This grid is established by offsets from the façade at 1.5 m (5 ft) intervals to locate a field of evenly spaced points, which are used as the basis for examination (Figure 7.2). Once the grid of field of points is established, comparative analysis of different floor-plate typologies and scales is possible. The same algorithm can be used to benchmark existing buildings to develop metrics on their floor plates. Ultimately, the base algorithms can be used to drive a parametric model in the simultaneous design, evaluation, and iteration of not only a typical floor-plate, but an entire building form.

Using the algorithms developed to assess each of the outlined criteria, a typological study of floor-plate shapes, sizes, and core locations was undertaken. Square, rectangular, circular, elliptical, and triangular floor-plates ranging in size from 750 m^2 (8,073 ft^2) to 2,500 m^2 (26,910 ft^2) with variations of central, engaged, and remote cores were assessed. From this typological analysis, patterns and influences on performance emerged, which help build a base understanding of typology (Figure 7.3).

7.3.2 Net-to-gross area efficiencies

Though terminology may vary in different regions, the most common criteria considered when evaluating floor-plates is the ratio between net leasable area (NLA) to gross floor area (GFA). This ratio is dependent on a number of factors including the shape and size of the

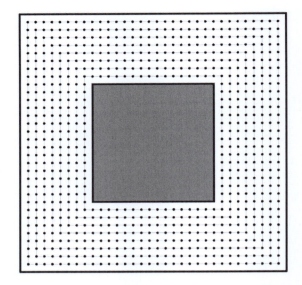

FIGURE 7.2 Assessment grid of points generated for square floor-plate with central core.
Source: Author.

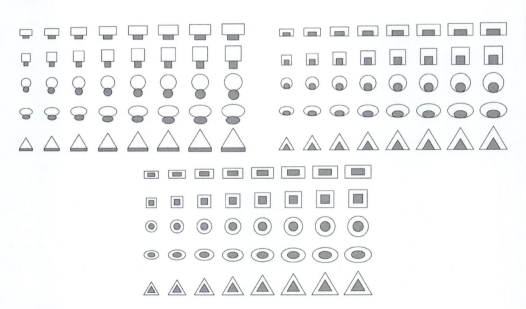

FIGURE 7.3 Generic floor-plate analysis typologies.
Source: Author.

floor-plates, the building height, and the level to which the design seeks innovative solutions to incorporate the core components. Often, the size and shape of a typical floor-plate is strongly influenced by the site constraints, with the height of the building commonly influenced by local planning regulations that set maximum development area allowances and height controls.

Commercial floor-plate performance **81**

The British Council for Offices has published as a guide typical floor-plate efficiencies for different building heights, with the most efficient floor-plates achievable on low–rise developments where the impacts of the core are far less than a high–rise tower. Efficiencies of greater than 85% can typically be achieved on low-rise developments between 2–4 storeys, whereas efficiencies may range between 65–75% for developments greater than 40 storeys (British Council for Offices, 2009).

For the purposes of typological assessment, the net-to-gross ratio remained a constant 75% within the equation and therefore was not assessed. In a benchmarking analysis, the net-to-gross ratio component would be included as evaluation criteria, or as a parameter control inside a generative parametric model.

7.3.3 Wall-to-floor ratio

The wall-to-floor ratio is an indicator of geometric shape efficiency calculated as the gross amount of external façade area divided by the gross floor area. This ratio is commonly used as a gauge to evaluate the impact of the façade costs, which can typically represent up to 20% or more of the overall construction value (Watts, 2010). A ratio of 0.40:1 or better is considered to be a well-performing ratio, whilst ratios above 0.50:1 are 'considered to need some compensating benefit for the loss of efficiency of enclosure' (Battle, 2003).

Additionally, research published by the Council for Tall Buildings and Urban Habitat (CTBUH) notes that these ratios can vary significantly across different geographic regions. For instance, average wall-to-floor ratios for Asia's tallest towers can range between 0.30–0.36 whereas in London, the tallest towers average a ratio of 0.51 (Watts, 2010).

As a measure of compactness of a particular floor-plate or shape, the wall-to-floor ratio not only provides an indication of potential relative façade costs, but also predicted thermal performance (Ashworth & Perera, 2010). As a geometric function to enclose a given area with the least perimeter, the typological assessment returned expected results with circular floor-plates being the most efficient, followed by square, rectangular, and triangular as the least efficient.

Whilst the results for this criterion are as expected with the 750 m^2 (8,073 ft^2) triangular central core returning the highest ratio of 0.62:1 and the circular floor-plate returning the optimum ratio of 0.49:1, the percentage differences between the various shapes converge with an increase in floor-plate size, reducing to 0.34:1 and 0.27:1 respectively for a 2,500 m^2 (26,910 ft^2) floor plate, thus making the choice or distinction of floor-plate shape less important as its area increases. Conversely, the differences in wall-to-floor ratio among the various shapes are exacerbated as the floor-plate area decreases.

7.3.4 Average distance to façade

Developed by Ermal Shpuza, the 'average perimeter distance' (Shpuza, 2003) assesses a floor-plate's configuration to determine the average level of environmental comfort as considered by the average distance from a set of all given points on a floor-plate to the perimeter façade. Higher averages result from buildings with deeper spans, whereas more slender buildings offer closer proximity to the perimeter. The measurement concludes that a shorter average distance to the façade is beneficial, as occupants who are closer to the façade benefit from greater levels of daylight and view amenity.

Conceptually, the algorithm developed in this study returns a similar value, although it deviates from the formulaic approach proposed by Shpuza. Here, the assessment grid previously outlined provides the set of points from which the average distance to the façade is calculated. Each point is multiplied by a corresponding 1.5 m (5 ft) incremental offset distances from the façade. The summation of total distance from each point are divided by the total number of points to return an average distance to the façade.

The typological study reported in this chapter found that the average distance to the façade was affected by both a floor-plate's shape as well as its area. Triangular floor plates, with a higher wall-to-floor ratio, position a higher proportion of assessment grid points along the parallel lengths of a façade, thus resulting in closer average distances of 5.28 m (+/− 17 ft) on a 2,500 m² (26,910 ft²) floor-plate and 2.70 m (+/− 9 ft) on a 750 m² (8,073 ft²) floor-plate. Conversely, the more compact circular shapes generate deeper portions of the floor-plate, thereby delivering higher average values ranging from 6.77 m (+/− 22 ft) to 4.09 m (+/− 13ft) for the 2,500 m² (26,910 ft²) and 750 m² (8,073 ft²) floor-plates respectively. Logically, an increase in floor-plate area produces a corresponding increase in the number of assessment grid points further from the façade, and therefore higher average distances.

7.3.5 Daylight coverage

When assessing daylight penetration into commercial office buildings, a commonly used guideline originally established by the British Council for Offices proposes that daylight can effectively reach 2–2.5 times the height of the window or façade. Assuming window height of 2.7 m (+/− 9 ft), this produces a range between 5.4–6.75 m (+/− 18–22 ft) in which adequate daylight extends internally. From this, a nominal distance of 6 m (+/− 20 ft) from the façade has been commonly classified as 'Grade A' space. 'Grade B' office space falls within the 6–12 m (+/− 20–39 ft) band, whilst 'Grade C' space lies beyond 12 m (+/− 39 ft) from the façade where no effective daylight falls. The study uses a simple offset from the façade perimeter to quantify the area of each of these bands and determine the percentage of floor-plate that exists within them.

The typological studies demonstrated that the triangular floor-plate, which produced the highest wall-to-floor ratio, also returned the highest percentage of floor area within the first 6 m (+/− 20 ft) of the façade for both the 2,500 m² (26,910 ft²) (62.95%) and the 750 m² (8,073 ft²) (99.89%) floor-plates. A greater perimeter length may lead to increased façade area, but it also provides greater proximity to the façade with improved daylight and view amenity afforded by it.

7.3.6 Floor-plate visibility

Floor-plate visibility has a profound impact on the workplace. Unobstructed floor-plates promote visibility and awareness among co-workers, fostering communication and interaction. The assessment of floor-plate visibility considers the area of floor plate visible from each point within the assessment grid to determine an average floor-plate visibility percentage. The algorithm calculates this for each point within the assessment grid to provide a more robust and true measure of the criteria.

The typological study found the primary factor impacting floor-plate visibility is the location of the core. Central core buildings perform the worst due to the core's visual obstruction

Commercial floor-plate performance **83**

across the floor-plate whilst engaged and remote core buildings perform substantially better with remote core buildings providing up to 100% floor-plate visibility.

Looking more closely at the central core floor-plate shapes, the analysis showed that circular and triangular floor-plates offered greater average visibility, approximately 40% across the floor-plate compared to the square and rectangular typologies providing approximately 35%. Interestingly, variations in floor-plate sizes had a negligible impact on the average visibility.

7.3.7 Floor-plate connectivity

This measure calculates a floor-plate's degree of horizontal connectivity by determining the distance between each point on the assessment grid to every other point on the grid. An average distance between all points is generated and through comparison, performance ranges are able to be established to determine how a particular floor plate performs by this measure. Floor-plate connectivity is strongly impacted by two variables: its size and the location of the core within the floor-plate. As a floor-plate's area increases, its connectivity performance decreases. On floor-plates of the same size, a centrally positioned core negatively impacts on connectivity as it forces occupants to walk further around it to reach the opposite side of the floor-plate. By contrast, floor-plates with remote or side core arrangements return better connectivity values as they facilitate more direct routes from different points within the office floor.

Like wall-to-floor ratio, floor-plate connectivity is also a measurement of compactness, but related to the physical distances between any two points on a floor-plate rather than the comparison of its perimeter to internal area. As observed with the wall-to-floor ratio analysis, the more compact circular and triangular shapes also offer smaller average distances between any two given points on the floor-plate. Even in today's workplace, with the extensive use of messaging services to communicate among employees, it is critical that people still have a physical presence and engage with one another. With more highly connected floor-plates, it is more likely that employees may walk to meet one another, rather than message, email, or phone one another.

7.4 Benchmarking and parametric generation

A benchmarking study is currently under way that will provide a wealth of knowledge regarding commercial office floor-plates from around the world. Results of the floor-plate analysis are able to be filtered by country, city, year (decade), floor-plate shape, floor-plate gross area, core typology, and height. This information will allow the comparison of similar floor-plate typologies against a given design proposal.

It may also uncover design trends revealing not only how previous decades may have approached office tower design, but also how the commercial office has evolved across different parts of the world. As referenced in Chapter 8, the German office typology is still dominated by the cellular office 'for reasons originating in local traditions, cultural values and customary expectations' (Chapter 8), whereas other parts of the world are predominantly moving to more open environments. An understanding of whether a cellular or open office approach will be implemented could impact the choice of floor-plate shape.

All of this knowledge will be beneficial in the formulation, presentation, and justification of commercial office-tower proposals. The ultimate use of the algorithms generated for the

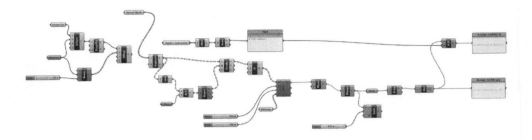

FIGURE 7.4 Grasshopper parametric algorithm.
Source: Author.

typological and benchmarking studies embeds them within a parametric model for the design of a commercial office tower. Parametric models have been used to develop and document complex building geometries for the past 15 to 20 years. However, in many instances, the parametric models are only 'geometry driven' as they seek to produce a seductive or complex building.

The proposed integration of the floor-plate assessment criteria within a generative parametric model seeks to move beyond the common, form-based initiatives towards a model that both sets and returns values in a broader application of the technology. Feedback on the criteria can be readily generated on a particular iteration, helping to value and judge the suitability of that particular outcome. Inversely, parameters can be set within target ranges to ensure a particular criteria is met, letting other criteria fluctuate as required.

7.5 Conclusion

Whilst in some respects they may be considered singular-purpose buildings, commercial office buildings do embody the essence of adaptive architecture, as they aim to cater to the different needs of tenants across single and multiple floors and over time as needs change and tenants come and go. The constant in the equation of change is the adaptability of the shell and core office typology.

It is important to remain aware of the purpose and application of this floor-plate typology and benchmarking research. The intention is to provide a greater depth of information about a design proposal to assist in the complex decision-making hierarchy. The typological study does not suggest that one floor-plate shape is better than another. Simply put, with a wider range of information available, more informed and hopefully better decisions can be made.

7.6 References

Ashworth, A., & Perera, S. (2010). *Cost Studies of Buildings*. London: Prentice-Hall.
Barton, J., & Watts, S. (2013). Office vs. Residential: The Economics of Building Tall. (D. Safarik, Ed.) *CTBUH Journal*, Issue II, 10–12. Retrieved from http://global.ctbuh.org/resources/papers/download/255-office-vs-residentialthe-economics-of-building-tall.pdf. Accessed 22 March 2017.
Battle, T. (Ed.). (2003). *The Commercial Offices Handbook*. London: RIBA Publishing.

British Council for Offices. (2009). *BCO Guide to Office Specification 2009*. London: British Council for Offices.

Shpuza, E. (2003). Light, Views and Money: Average Perimeter Distance and its Relation to Floor Plate Geometry. Fourth International Space Syntax Symposium, London.

Watts, S. (2010). The Economics of High Rise (as per 2nd Quarter 2010). *CTBUH Journal*, Issue III, 44–45. Retrieved from CTBUH – Council for Tall Buildings and Urban Habitat: https://store.ctbuh.org/p-73-2010-issue-iibriout-of-printi.aspx. Accessed 22 March 2017.

8

BEYOND THE CELLULAR OFFICE: ADAPTABLE OFFICES FOR MEDIUM-SIZED COMPANIES

Martin Hodulak

8.1 Introduction

Taking the German-built stock of office buildings into consideration, it can be argued that Germany has a long and lasting tradition of cellular offices. Admittedly, multi-national corporations have started implementing more open office concepts in the past years. These are widely acknowledged and publicized, but currently remain a side issue in the overall picture of the market.

Cellular offices in Germany are popular for reasons originating in local traditions, cultural values, and customary expectations (Hodulak, 2016). However, their widespread utilization might also be due to their simplicity, additive modularity, and robustness, and thus their ability to fit most requirements and situations. Just the fact that this office type has been around for decades, and even centuries, suggests a high degree of adaptability.

The need to optimize in terms of efficiency as well as effectiveness necessitates that German companies review their office concepts. "In commercial office fit-outs, the latest trends of Activity based workplace (ABW) allow occupants to choose the type of working environment that best suits the task they have at any given time" (Chapter 7). Open-space ABW offices are more space-efficient, effective in terms of process support, and appear to be more flexible and adaptable compared to cellular offices. As a result, medium-sized companies are starting to adopt open ABW office concepts. The switch from time-tested cellular offices to new open ABW concepts is a major strategic decision, an experiment, and a challenge. Accordingly, companies want to be certain that their planned approach is right for decades to come. Addressing the company's existing needs and the adaptability to their future requirements is one of their major concerns.

In this chapter, two questions are examined: what are the key characteristics of German cellular office concepts that have kept them adaptable and thus attractive for decades? And, can new open-space ABW office concepts match the qualities and adaptability of traditional cellular offices?

8.2 German cellular offices tradition

German experts on workplace consulting, as well as current literature, regard four office concepts as being characteristic of the German office tradition of recent decades: the cellular office, the group office, the combination office, and the open-plan office (Kelter, 2003; Staniek, 2005; Congena, 1990). The cellular office, with its perfect conditions for concentrated and solitary work, can be regarded as the opposite of an open-plan office. An open plan offers excellent conditions for teamwork, communication, information flow, and ad-hoc meetings, which are more difficult to achieve in cellular offices. Group offices and combination offices represent the middle ground between these two concepts, aiming to achieve a balance of good conditions for concentration and communication. In recent years, these four types were complemented by further open-office concepts, often called a business club, reversible office, flexible office, or open-space office. Contrary to all previous concepts, these open and often activity-based office layouts are not about balancing support for communication or concentration but are providing full and unconditional support for both.

Figure 8.1 depicts the market demand, i.e., new buildings, for different office concepts in Germany, in relation to one another over a period of the past 60 years. Taking the evolution of the various concepts into consideration, the traditional and still-predominant workplace concepts in Germany are the single and double occupancy cellular offices. The most common type is the double occupancy cellular office, believed to provide a good balance of space efficiency and functionality. It is not as space-consuming as a single occupancy cellular office, and yet offers a relatively high amount of privacy and environmental control since it is shared with just one fellow worker. An empirical survey conducted by the Fraunhofer IAO (Institut für Arbeitswirtschaft und Organisation) in 2002, however, comes to a different conclusion (Spath & Kern, 2003). When asked about their motivation and perceived productivity within their office space, employees working in double-occupancy cellular offices ranked their environment as particularly unproductive and, in relation to all other established office types, as the least motivating.

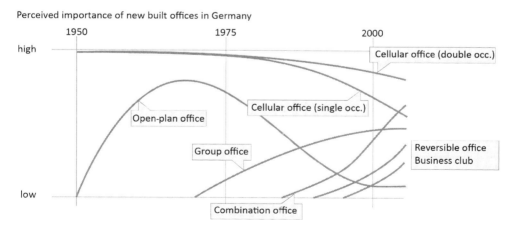

FIGURE 8.1 Cycles of demand for office concepts.
Source: Martin Hodulak based on Beyerle (2003).

8.3 The cellular office concept

Origins of cellular offices and the underlying principle can be traced back as far as the 14th century. The town hall of Plauen in central Germany, which was erected around 1380, the Uffizi in Florence built in 1560, and today's 21st-century office buildings all rely on the same precept and contain similar properties and qualities. Characteristic of all cellular office concepts are narrow and often small floor-plates, a linear array of cellular offices along the building façade, and an inner circulation axis. The majority of tasks are performed within the individual cells. Therefore, few additional spaces, such as meeting rooms or break areas, are provided.

The array of small rooms, separated by load-bearing walls, has its origins in construction materials and building principles from the past, which limited the floor spans and relied on the use of daylight and natural ventilation. While new technologies such as steel beams, fireproof materials, and artificial sources of light and ventilation initiated North American deep and open floor plans (Muschiol, 2007), these developments never had a substantial influence on office concepts in central Europe. Office buildings in European city centers remain low up to this day and building depths and floor spans still remain narrow. This might have its origins in the tight urban fabric of German cities and local construction practices, but it is staying popular as it keeps the building and operational costs low. Offices and workplaces along the façades don't need any artificial lighting in the daytime, nor do they need any mechanical ventilation or air conditioning. Fire protection is kept low tech by dividing floor plans into small, independent zones.

Information and communication technologies change the way we work, but have not had any effect on cellular offices so far. The potential for enhanced mobility, digital information access, and shared documents has little impact on them. As user interviews show, the cellular office workspace still remains the focal point of work, and files and documents are still stacked and kept in offices for individual use.

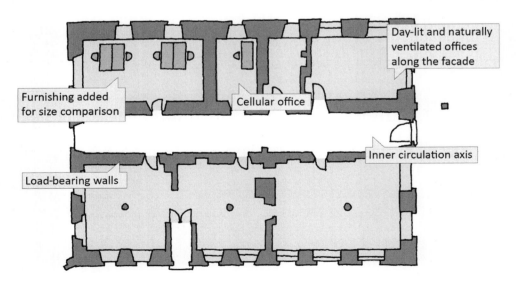

FIGURE 8.2 Town hall, Plauen.
Source: Martin Hodulak based on Kleibrink (2005).

Cellular offices are efficient to run as technical services are kept basic. However, the workspaces themselves need more floor area. A reduced desk space or file storage will not necessarily result in a reduced overall area as the dividing walls are fixed and the workplace perimeter remains unchanged. Moreover, workspaces cannot be rearranged in new layout, as would be the case in more open office concepts.

8.3.1 Adaptability of cellular offices

Depending on single and joint occupancy, the cells are assigned to either one or two persons for their individual use. Being dedicated as well as enclosed, the cellular office provides a very high degree of autonomy and control and it can be treated more or less independently as far as function and appearance are concerned. Tools, equipment, and furnishing can be altered individually and without any effect on neighboring office spaces. It is common to decorate or personalize offices to the user's individual needs, taste, and preference. Workers are also used to adjusting lighting, temperature, and ventilation individually. Having a territory of their own puts them in control of the physical environment. Moreover, it provides a way of displaying rank and position within an organization.

The aforementioned features have accounted for a high degree of flexibility and adaptability through the decades. Changing organizations, new work patterns, evolving tools, technologies, and workers' expectations all have been accommodated within cellular office concepts. It could be argued that it is the simplicity and robustness that make them highly adaptable to individual needs, work patterns, and personal taste.

8.4 The open-space ABW office concept

As stated in the Introduction, the invention and explosion of the digital revolution has changed the world dramatically in the past few decades. Until then, most of the basic aims,

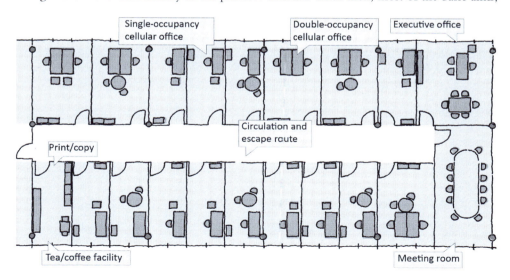

FIGURE 8.3 Typical cellular office plan.
Source: Martin Hodulak.

goals, and concepts for offices were more or less similar to those of the Uffizi in 16th-century Florence. At that time, Cosimo I "probably built the earliest purpose built offices in western culture." "Cosimo placed clerical workers performing essential services for the public together in 'the offices' to increase their efficiency by being close to each other, and to have them where he could see them and the public could find them" (Vischer, 2005). Since the digital revolution, major parameters of work have shifted as the office is no longer bound to a place. Communication, information, and collaboration can now take place anywhere, and workers do not necessarily need to be in the office to be productive or be accessible. This has resulted in new work styles, thus challenging established office concepts.

Thanks to the digital revolution, activity-based working and open-space office concepts became popular in the past decade, in particular among large global corporations. Expansive open-floor layouts without any or with only marginal partitioning were introduced in order to achieve higher space efficiency, flexibility, and standardization of workplaces. However, in addition to open-plan concepts from the fifties and sixties, elements for informal communication, collaboration, or as a retreat were included. Unlike traditional workplaces, where assigned desks would be the single location of work, staff in open-space concepts could move and choose among various work settings during the course of a day. "The basis of the traditional office has been that most work activities can take place at the desk. More innovative work environments aim to relate work activities – such as research, writing, telephoning, video and teleconferencing, project team or solitary modes of working – to differently designed worksettings" (Hardy *et al.*, 2008).

8.4.1 Adaptability of open-space offices

The need to respond to changing business, corporate organization, processes, work patterns, and culture is ranked highly among corporations. In a survey conducted in 2012,

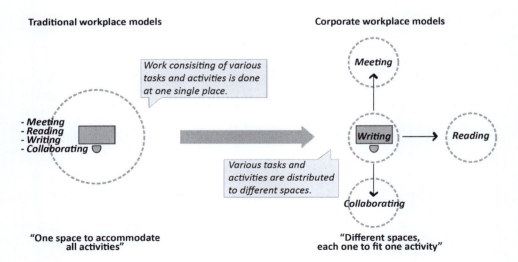

FIGURE 8.4 Traditional versus open-space principle.
Source: Martin Hodulak.

"adaptability for change" was among the top three goals of one third of corporations, the other two being "efficiency of workflow" and "attractiveness for staff" (Hodulak, 2016). Most corporate open-space office layouts reflect this desire for adaptability. Office floors are repetitive, regardless of the different departments they accommodate. Floor layouts are open and zoned according to activities, and are equipped with highly standardized workspaces and work settings, arranged along generic layout patterns.

8.4.2 Functional adaptability

By linking different work activities to specific work settings, individual workspaces can be kept basic and can follow a single standard, yet the office as a whole can still accommodate a range of different, and even changing work styles. Workspaces are used, then, as a "home base" and mostly for basic activities, such as reading or writing. All other activities are relegated to additional designated work settings. Employees engaged in long or confidential telephone calls no longer need private offices, but can use enclosed spaces nearby. Members of project groups can use project spaces, while retaining their individual workspaces within their departments. For management workspaces, where meetings are frequent, no additional space or seating is required within their office, since they can gather in a range of open or closed meeting spaces nearby.

Abandoning the traditional principle of assigning a worker to one workspace only, but rather offering a range of different work settings (ABW), results in a highly flexible and adaptable work environment. Ultimately, this appears to be the solution to the never-ending search for the all enabling workplace. Until now, neither the cellular office nor the open–plan arrangement has been able to accommodate office workers' need for both concentration and communication. Both are now achieved in open-space ABW concepts. Workers can simply choose and move to the appropriate setting according to the task at hand.

Utilizing different work settings also facilitates project work, where team sizes change over the course of projects. As floor layouts are undivided, and work settings are standardized, teams can expand and downsize without any necessary alterations to the floor layout.

8.4.3 Formal adaptability

In traditional office concepts, it is common for workers to adapt and personalize their individual workspaces. They often provide their own additional equipment or gadgets for work, grow their own plants, and decorate their workspaces with photographs, awards, and degree certificates. Work-related items such as books, calendars, or posters are further means of personalizing and adapting the workplace to individual needs and tastes, and other means of distinguishing it from the workspaces of colleagues. Among the most important reasons for differentiating workspaces is the need to showcase the employee's rank, position, and function within the organization. "It communicates how important the employees are and with whom they are expected to interact" (Vischer, 2005).

Since standardization is an underlying principle of most open-space office concepts, there is little leeway for personalizing the workspace. Employees may be allowed to set up personal items on their desks. Dividers or acoustic screens may be used to hang pictures, calendars, or posters. However, the workspaces are open and, to maintain a coherent corporate appearance, personalization has to be minimized.

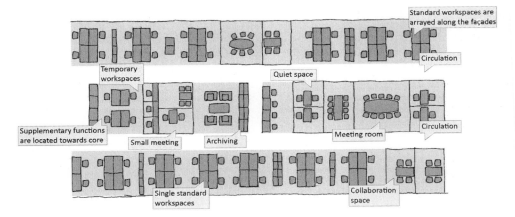

FIGURE 8.5 Typical open-space floor layout.
Source: Martin Hodulak.

The highly standardized, non-personalized workplaces contribute substantially to the corporate or company needs for office adaptability. However, it should be noted that it is not only the office that is adaptable but also, or perhaps rather, the users who need to become adaptable. In open-space concepts, workers abandon personalization of their workplace, give up personal control of light, air, and temperature, and leave their traditional, rank-related offices behind. The principle of the individual office is no longer valid as "a powerful and deeply rooted symbol of the individual's and the organization's mutual rights, responsibilities, expectations and commitment" (Vischer, 2005).

8.5 Adaptable offices for medium-sized companies

From project experience, German medium-sized companies' attitude toward new workplace concepts are cautious. Generally speaking, medium-sized companies are highly competitive, agile, and inventive, although, at the same time, they are locally rooted and base their success on a moderate yet steady development and growth. They need convincing reasons for abandoning tried-and-tested paths and solutions, such as cellular offices, for something new. However, changing work patterns, new information and communication technologies, and evolving workers' expectations have led medium-sized companies to review their workplace concepts. The following diagram depicts frequent aims and goals of new workplace concepts, as stated by medium-sized companies. In order to keep client data confidential, the diagram combines the content of several programming workshops conducted between 2010 and 2015.

Open-space offices are based on the principle of abandoning individually dedicated workspaces in favor of a range of shared task-specific work settings. This implies workers' mobility and also a certain degree of non-territoriality within the office. It implies highly standardized workplaces in an open-floor layout, which facilitate and encourage work at different work settings. It implies information and communication technologies and devices, such as laptops, smart phones, and a digital infrastructure, which enable mobility within and outside of the office for the entire staff. However, these characteristics and attitudes are not common among medium-sized companies.

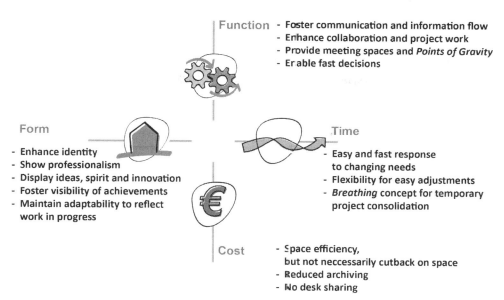

FIGURE 8.6 Aims and goals referring to new office concepts.
Source: Martin Hodulak.

In past projects, establishing open-space concepts and ensuring their acceptance and success in medium-sized companies needed introduction, support, and tradeoffs to a far greater extent than in the corporate world, where cultures of different countries mix and various work styles co-exist. The loss of personalization, control, and territoriality needed compensation through more autonomy such as the choice of location and time of work. The loss of hierarchy-related offices needed to be traded off by small but enclosed spaces or dedicated management meeting rooms.

Practical experience shows that open-space concepts in medium-sized companies depend first and foremost on the workers' ability to cope with and adapt to new work styles, as well as to make use of new technologies. The inability to achieve either of these resulted in the loss of former workplace qualities such as private space, personalization, and territoriality without benefitting from the enhanced quality of work environments with open-space concepts.

8.6 Conclusion

The digital revolution has changed many aspects of our lives and our work style, and is the foundation for new office concepts, such as open-space ABW offices. New concepts support different processes, work patterns, and changes very efficiently, since a specific work pattern can be matched easily with the corresponding work environment. In the case of an organizational change, the traditional rearrangement of different rank-related workplaces becomes redundant, as ideally all employees use the same workplace standard. In terms of flexibility and adaptability, open-space concepts are undoubtedly superior to cellular offices.

However, open-space offices are complex to develop, challenging to implement, and demanding in their day-to-day operation. They lack the simplicity, modular adaptability, and robustness of their traditional counterparts. They depend on well-balanced environmental systems to keep the open floor plates well tempered, well lit, and acoustically comfortable. They depend on infrastructure and technical devices to enable staff to work mobile, on and off site. They also rely on carefully negotiated rules and etiquette to lower the potential of conflicts in open spaces. And last but not least, they rely on workers' willingness and ability to adapt to new situations and to embrace new potential opportunities.

8.7 References

Beyerle, T. (2003). *Immobilienwirtschaftliche Trends – Zukunftsorientierte Bürokonzepte*. Frankfurt: Deutsche Geselschaft für Immobilienfonds mbH.

Congena. (1990). *Kombi Büro*. Baden–Baden: FBO.

Hardy, B. *et al.* (2008). *Working Beyond Walls*. London: Office of Government Commerce.

Hodulak, M. (2016). *Feasibility of Standardized Global Workplace Models*. Stuttgart: Fraunhofer Verlag.

Kelter, J. (2003). *Entwicklung einer Planungssystematik zur Gestaltung der räumlich-organisatorischen Büroumwelt*. Heimsheim: Jost Jetter Verlag.

Kleibrink, M. (2005). Effizienz von Bürogebäuden. In J. Eisele, and B. Staniek, *Bürobau Atlas* (pp. 76–85). München: Callwey.

Muschiol, R. (2007). Bewegungsqualität in Bürogebäuden: Ergebnisse einer empirischen Studie. Aachen: Technical Universität Dresden.

Spath, D., & Kern, P. (eds.). (2003). *Office 21 – Push for the Future*. Köln: Egmonts vgs.

Staniek, B. (2005). Büroorganisationsformen. In J. Eisele, and B. Staniek, *Bürobauatlas*. München: Callwey.

Vischer, J. C. (2005). *Space Meets Status: Designing Workplace Performance*. New York: Routledge.

9

ADAPTIVE ARCHITECTURE OF THE LONDON SCIENCE MUSEUM: A NEEDS ASSESSMENT

Kristin E. Hibbs

9.1 Introduction

This chapter explores and evaluates the programmatic and spatial needs of the Science Museum in London. There is, and has always been, an inevitable requirement for change over time as the museum's position within wider contexts shifts. Planning for this change requires a long-term strategy, or masterplan. The museum masterplan maintains the focus on the visitor experience and provides a framework for decision-making, prioritization for capital invest-ment, and support for fundraising activities.

The Science Museum is an eminent institution responsible for an internationally impor-tant collection documenting the history of science, technology, and medicine. As the "Home of Human Ingenuity," the museum's mission is to make sense of the science that shapes our lives, to help create a scientifically literate society, and inspire the curiosity of the next generation.

The UK government introduced free admission to national museums in 2001. This marked a turning point for the Science Museum and other national museums. In 2014, the National Museum Directors' Council published a set of figures on their website from the first ten years of free admission that showed visitor numbers increased dramatically (National Museum Directors' Council 2014). The Science Museum Group (the parent body for the Science Museum, formerly known as the National Museum of Science and Industry) pub-lished its Annual Accounts for 1999–2000 and reported the Science Museum received just over 1.4 million visitors (National Museum of Science and Industry 2000). A press release from 13th April 2016 reported the museum's highest recorded visitor attendance at more than 3.4 million visitors (http://sciencemuseum.org.uk/about-us/press/april-2016, accessed March 22, 2017). The Science Museum continues to find new ways to support its visitors by adjusting the activities and facilities offered. Today the museum hosts not only the permanent galleries and temporary exhibitions where the collection is displayed and interpreted, but also multiple cafes and shops, an IMAX cinema, lecture theater, learning spaces, live drama per-formances, corporate hire and events spaces, simulator rides, play areas, offices, workshops, and a research library.

9.2 Planning for change in the museum

The Science Museum developed its current masterplan in 2010–2011. The masterplan is a live document used to guide redevelopment in a multi-layered format, with each layer representing a key part of the business of the museum. Masterplanning is a methodology that takes a holistic view to find a good balance across these layers, which can often be in tension with each other. Setting out the strategic plan in physical space, the Science Museum masterplan looks across the following layers:

- The collection. The collection gives the museum identity. Researching and interpreting the collection provides a focus for the museum's narrative and the visitor experience.
- The visitors. The visitor profile can shift over time, but the museum also actively tries to adjust this profile by targeting key visitor groups through content and programming. The Science Museum has always been a popular destination for school groups, 5 to 16 year olds, and it works hard to provide exciting and memorable experiences for them with the hope that they will return to the museum with their families. Looking forward, the museum aims to broaden its focus to include a more diverse adult audience.
- The building infrastructure. The museum building requires investment in its infrastructure, i.e., lifts, ventilation, heating, security, etc., with multiple building systems coming to end of life. The general decoration and maintenance of the building has fallen behind, leaving large areas of the public realm looking tired and drab. This investment is an opportunity to find energy-efficient solutions, to establish a new maintenance program, and to reset the standards of quality and performance specification for the building.
- The architectural space. The museum wants to make the most of its architecture. Post-occupancy evaluations identify what works well and where there are inefficiencies. Research is also conducted with our visitors to understand how they navigate through the building and what they find difficult during their visit. This research is carried out through vox pops, exit surveys, and small focus groups. Analysis of the back-of-house areas, the workshops, kitchens, offices, and storage spaces is also undertaken. Taken together, the museum works to ensure that the building provides a safe and healthy environment that is accessible, legible, and efficient. Through design, the ambition is to create a beautiful, engaging, and memorable place that visitors return to and that people enjoy working within.
- The funding. The museum is always working to develop new funding streams. In addition to government funding, the Science Museum receives financial support through corporate sponsorship, philanthropic donations, visitor donations, grants, partnerships, and revenue-earning activities such as shops, cafes, and private events.

The challenge in adapting the existing museum is to conceive of one holistic, integrated vision for the visitor experience. Visiting an exhibition to look at objects, having a coffee, buying a book, seeing a film, sitting down for a rest, stopping to use the toilet, collecting your coat from the cloakroom, etc., should be seamless and immersive. The quality of design, material and color palette, lighting, wayfinding signage, and tone of voice must all work together across the whole building.

The Science Museum works with many different designers and architects to implement the masterplan. This approach builds pacing and variety to the visitor experience.

9.3 Looking back to move forward

Part of the masterplanning process is to look back at the museum's history, the original architectural brief, and the original architectural spaces for inspiration and guidance. The Science Museum project was born out of the 1851 Great Exhibition, held in Joseph Paxton's Crystal Palace, which presented cutting-edge technology, design, and manufacturing from around the world. It was a success and the profits earned were re-invested to purchase land in South Kensington. Prince Albert's vision was to create a center to promote the understanding of technology of the day through the establishment of libraries, colleges, museums, and a great meeting room (Bud, 2010).

In 1910, Parliament appointed Sir Hugh Bell to chair a Committee establishing recommendations for the design and intellectual structure for the new Science Museum building. The Bell Committee took a very practical view to site constraints and set out a calculated yet grand vision that could be constructed in phases. The site allocated was a long, thin sliver of land stretching from Exhibition Road to Queens Gate (see Figure 9.1).

9.3.1 A place for learning

> Special encouragement to teachers to utilize the objects in the Collections more fully for educational purposes, and ... to instruct their students by direct reference to the apparatus and models should be maintained and extended. (Report of the Departmental Committee on the Science Museum and the Geological Museum [Bell Report] 1911, p.11)

The new Science Museum was to be a place for learning, understanding, and examination, providing inspiration for both a general public and a specialist/academic audience. The brief called for demonstration rooms, ample space around object displays to allow for on-gallery talks and demonstrations, and the introduction of a handling collection to give visitors the opportunity to touch the objects. This, alongside visits to the galleries and independent observation of the collection, informed much of how the museum was originally laid out and still influences decisions today.

9.3.2 Strategic positioning

> The Museum to maintain as close touch as possible with societies whose members are actively interested in the advance of knowledge or in the progress of invention in the departments to which the collections relate. (Bell Report 1911, p.11)

The museum was to be positioned at the heart of ' live science" to strategically build support from professional organizations that would help promote or otherwise benefit the museum. In order to support this aim, the brief called for a conference room where these groups could meet.

In addition to the conference room, a lecture theater was described. Demonstrations and public lectures from experts were prioritized as core activities as a way to strengthen the general public's understanding and interest in science.

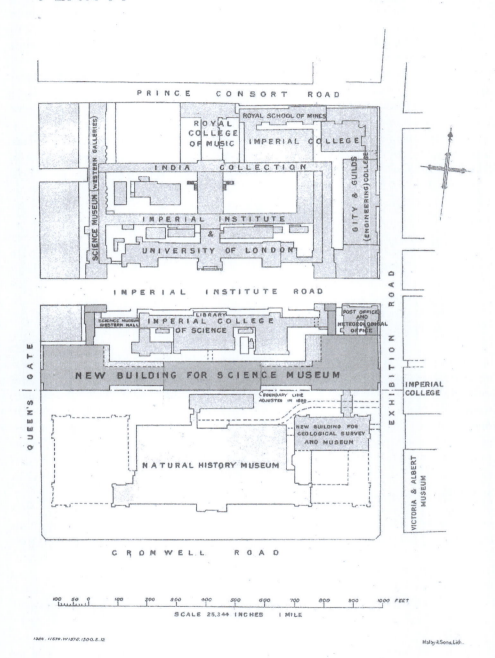

FIGURE 9.1 Site plan for the new building of the Science Museum.
Source: Crown copyright (1911).

9.3.3 Grandeur and economy

> The new building may be designed on lines that will give every freedom both in the initial allocation of place … and in future modifications of arrangement. This is a matter of no little importance, for the progress of science and invention quickly varies.
> (Bell Report 1911, p.13)

The new building would house the national collections, and thus must be worthy of such important, one-of-a-kind objects. Therefore, large open halls would provide the scale and drama, not to mention the right amount of space to display great steam engines and locomotives. But the halls also served another purpose, to create places for orientation for the visitors. The Science Museum was to have two or three large open halls, arranged along the east/west axis of the site (see Figure 9.2).

Beautiful as they are, large halls are naturally less efficient in terms of usable floor area, so a balance was found whereby each large hall would be surrounded by side-lit galleries. Each side gallery was to maximize windows at a high level to allow natural light to flood inside, but more importantly, windows were not to come down too low so that wall space could be best utilized for large graphics, information, or the display of objects. Side galleries needed to work very hard, maximizing all usable surfaces.

9.4 Step-by-step: phasing the masterplan

The first phase for the Science Museum masterplan will see more than half of the museum redeveloped, one project at a time, creating six major galleries by the end of 2019. Media Space opened in 2013, providing the museum with two new temporary exhibition galleries on the second floor. A further temporary exhibition gallery was refurbished on the first floor to host a blockbuster exhibition program, with the inaugural show being "Cosmonauts: Birth of the Space Age" (see Figure 9.3). Her Majesty The Queen opened the Information Age gallery in 2014 by sending her first tweet (see Figure 9.4). The new mathematics gallery, designed by Zaha Hadid Architects, opened at the end of 2016 (see Figure 9.5), alongside a new hands-on interactive gallery designed by Muf Architecture – Art. The largest single project at the Science Museum will be the new suite of Medicine galleries, designed by Wilkinson Eyre Architects. In addition to these collaborations, the museum will also refurbish its original lecture theater. All of this work will take place whilst the museum remains in operation for the public. The impact of this work is constantly monitored and one of the main challenges is maintaining well-signed circulation routes for the visitors to find their way around. While this level of disruption does affect the visitors' experience, it also demonstrates to the public the museum's ambition and commitment to improve the museum for the future.

9.4.1 Opportunities to improve public spaces

The museum's main entrance creates the visitors' first impression and sets the tone for their visit. Getting it right is important, and getting it wrong is rather easy. A museum visit starts well before arriving at the building through the website, marketing, and even word of mouth. The Science Museum will redesign its entrance as part of the masterplan work

FIGURE 9.2 The Jubilee exhibition in the East Hall of the Science Museum.
Source: Science Museum, London / Science and Society Picture Library (1935).

(see Figure 9.6). Visitors should see and recognize the building from a block away and as they get closer, the entrance should be clearly marked. Organized queuing outside, moving visitors inside quickly, and managing security checks are important tasks for the museum. This project will enable the museum to greet its visitors, ask for donations, sell tickets, and provide information and maps. Transitioning from the outside world into the magical world

FIGURE 9.3 Gallery view of "Cosmonauts: Birth of the Space Age" exhibition.
Source: Science Museum, London / Science and Society Picture Library (2015).

FIGURE 9.4 Gallery view from the mezzanine toward the Rugby Tuning Coil at the center of the Information Age gallery.
Source: Science Museum, London / Science and Society Picture Library (2014).

FIGURE 9.5 Gallery view during construction for the new mathematics gallery designed by Zaha Hadid Architects.
Source: Science Museum, London / Science and Society Picture Library (2016).

FIGURE 9.6 The bicycle tour was installed in 2012 to inspire delight and nostalgia in visitors upon entry.
Source: Science Museum, London / Science and Society Picture Library (2012).

FIGURE 9.7 The Making the Modern World gallery is one of the Science Museum's most popular spaces for dinners and parties.
Source: Science Museum, London / Science and Society Picture Library (2013).

of the museum, the entrance should evoke a sense of delight and anticipation for the visitors' upcoming experience.

The Science Museum is hired out for conferences, product launches, birthday parties, corporate dinners, cocktail parties, and even the wrap parties for blockbuster films. Attending an event in a space that was clearly not made for that event is potentially thrilling. Sitting down for dinner surrounded by spacecraft, rockets, trains and airplanes can make for memorable experiences (see Figure 9.7). As this business grows, the demand on space and support facilities increases. The Science Museum has decided to undertake a number of projects to better support the events business, namely the creation of a new dedicated-event suite. A possibly surprising challenge for this project will be to design the visitor journey through the museum to and from these new spaces. Choreographing this journey so that guests pass through galleries and view the collection on their way helps to set the museum as a venue apart from hotels or conference centers.

9.5 Conclusion

Museums are in a constant state of slow flux. Mature museums, like the Science Museum, have a century's worth of experience behind them. In that time, the museum has developed an understanding of its building and knows that it cannot be treated too preciously. Learning to adapt within its constraints can often result in serendipitous moments. It is near impossible to go anywhere within the Science Museum without walking past and seeing the collection.

There is satisfaction that comes from making a space work well in a different way from how it was originally conceived.

Since the Science Museum was established, the institution and its business has grown and developed, and like all businesses, managing growth and change requires strong strategic planning. The masterplanning process is proving a successful method for the Science Museum to plan for its future, enabling positive discussions about the tensions, demands, and opportunities within each layer of the organization. It defines constraints and guidelines against which the museum can respond creatively with new solutions, provides focus for decision-making, and promotes pro-active, balanced, coordinated development. Being in a position to plan further ahead has also meant that the museum has time to think about how to structure the delivery teams for each project, resulting in implementing multiple projects in parallel. The increased speed and efficiency has built momentum and brought positive attention to the Science Museum, which in turn helps to build support for the funding of future projects and ensure the livelihood of one of London's oldest cultural institutions.

9.6 References

Bud, R. (2010). Infected by the Bacillus of Science. In Peter J. T. Morris (Ed.), *Science for the Nation: Perspectives on the History of the Science Museum* (pp. 14–15). Basingstoke: Palgrave Macmillan.

National Museum Directors' Council. (2014). Tenth anniversary of free admission to national museums. Retrieved from www.nationalmuseums.org.uk/what-we-do/encouraging_investment/free-admission/. Accessed March 22, 2017.

National Museum of Science and Industry. (2000). Accounts for 1999–2000. Retrieved from http://group.sciencemuseum.org.uk/wp-content/uploads/2015/09/NMSI-accounts-1999-2000.pdf. Accessed March 22, 2017.

Report of the Departmental Committee on the Science Museum and the Geological Museum, Part 1 (also known as the Bell Report). (1911). (pp. 11–13). London: His Majesty's Stationery Office.

10

POST-OCCUPANCY EVALUATION OF A MULTI-TASKING ENVIRONMENT: THE UNIVERSITY OF KENTUCKY MEDICAL CENTER'S EMERGENCY DEPARTMENT

Lindsey L. Fay

10.1 Introduction

The healthcare industry is experiencing one of the largest rises in building design in history due to aging hospitals, population shifts, emerging technology, and an increased demand for healthcare services. A key member of the healthcare system is the emergency department (ED), acting as a gateway to the hospital for about half of all admissions. Emergency departments are often described as fast-paced and unpredictable environments staffed by multi-disciplinary teams of physicians, nurses, patient-care technicians, therapists, and non-clinicians such as housekeeping, security, and patient relations assistants that work as a team to deliver care to the acutely ill.

A significant rise in ED volume and construction is expected over the next decade due to the implementation of the Affordable Care Act. This requires evidence for the effective design of emergency departments that can support efficient workflow processes, integrated technology, ease of communication, and optimal patient outcomes. To improve upon these issues, the field of healthcare design has moved toward "evidence-based design," which bases design decisions on credible research to achieve the best possible outcomes. The evidence-based design process identifies the use of post-occupancy evaluation (POE) as the ideal method for "systematically evaluating the performance of buildings after they have been built and occupied for some time" (Preiser, Rabinowitz, and White, 2015).

10.2 Background

In response to increased demand for medical services, the University of Kentucky developed a plan for phased replacement of the original Chandler Hospital, which was constructed in 1955. The new ten-floor medical center includes an emergency department, two towers of private patient rooms, operating, imaging and surgery centers, and public spaces including a cafeteria, gift shop, and waiting areas. The guiding principles for design were focused on patient access and care, the academic mission of the university, an integration of clinical services, efficiency, flexibility, and image.

FIGURE 10.1 University of Kentucky Medical Center and emergency department entrance. *Source*: Scott Pease.

The emergency department was the first unit to move to the new medical center and opened its doors in 2010. The design response placed emphasis on creating a comforting and welcoming environment that was easy to navigate with increased quality and safety for patients and staff, and incorporated patient-centered and multidisciplinary care, technological flexibility, and amenities for patients and their families (Christmann 2011). The 40,000 square foot (3,715 square meters) space utilizes a linear configuration with a central core, and includes separate treatment areas for pediatric and adult patients. The adult side encompasses 46 treatment areas organized around five pods: triage, acute care, critical care, express care, and trauma. The pediatric unit includes a separate waiting room, 12 treatment rooms, and two triage rooms. Four additional treatment areas, which are centrally located, are designated as "swing" rooms for pediatric or adult patients and can be used as needed based on patient volume.

Researchers at the University of Kentucky were contacted by GBBN Architects of Cincinnati, OH to conduct a post-occupancy evaluation of the newly completed emergency department. The multi-disciplinary approach to the POE resulted in unique benefits for the academic researchers, students, and designers, as well as the healthcare organization. Bosch and Nanda (2011) state "Collaborations between firms, healthcare providers, and universities can create a perfect nexus for research where resources can be combined to develop a feasible and affordable research plan, with returns for each sector" (p. xi).

FIGURE 10.2 University of Kentucky emergency department's linear configuration with a central core.
Source: Scott Pease.

10.3 POE methodology

Preiser (2001) defined three levels of investigation that comprise a POE, as well as a three-phase cyclical process for carrying out the research that involves planning, conducting, and applying. The first level, an *indicative* POE, leads to an awareness of strengths and weaknesses of a particular building's performance. The second level, an *investigative* POE, yields "a thorough understanding of the causes and effects of issues in building performance" (Preiser *et al.* 2015). The third level, a *diagnostic* POE, aligns built environment measures with occupant responses, and can often result in the creation of new knowledge.

The study design for the UK Hospital POE employed a comprehensive framework to examine built environment variables, user experience, and operational outcomes through the use of a *diagnostic* POE. Core areas of evaluation for the POE included:

- assess the detailed environmental quality of spaces or places and their impact on care delivery;
- determine the design's impact on family, patients, and caregivers; and
- analyze the design layout and its impact on delivering efficient, dependable, and safe care.

The team agreed that spaces such as reception, registration, waiting, triage, treatment rooms, trauma rooms, and nurse stations would be included in the study.

Planning for the research study first began with a literature review. The review included an extensive search for existing literature and an inspection of each study's methodologies and tools. Literature assessed topics such as healthcare design, evidence-based design, post-occupancy evaluations, emergency departments, as well as staff and patient issues relative to efficiency, safety, and privacy and confidentiality. The review found a growing body of research on these topics, but only one pilot post-occupancy evaluation of an emergency department.

A multi-phased and multi-method research plan was employed based on the breadth of spaces and issues to be measured and to gain a deeper understanding of the environment and occupants. Data for the study was collected over the course of 18 months and yielded both quantitative and qualitative results. Data collection occurred in two separate phases, with data analysis occurring after each phase. Ten researchers including two faculty members, two graduate students, and six undergraduates collected data. Through the research, students were able to more personally understand the complexities of this formerly unfamiliar environment.

Prior to data collection, approval from the Institutional Review Board of the University of Kentucky was obtained. Students were involved in the data collection, so human subject certification and training in the use of the research instruments was completed to ensure validity and reliability. For Phase 1, team members were divided into pairs and observed in four-hour shifts over a range of days and times for a period of ten weeks, yielding more than 200 hours of observation. Specific methods included behavioral mapping, communication documentation, distance traveled by staff, acoustic measurements, and occupancy counts.

10.3.1 Behavioral mapping

Behavioral mapping occurred in four primary areas of the emergency department including pediatrics, acute care, critical care, and trauma. Observations were completed over the course of four-hour shifts during all hours of the day. Mapping was completed by hand on instruments that included a floor plan, a key indicating color codes, instructions, and additional space to document impromptu observations or relevant staff comments. Color-coding was used to record the movement of physicians, nurses, and technicians in 15-minute intervals. Physicians' walking patterns were recorded in cool colors, nurses' in warm colors, and technicians' in neutral colors, such as grey.

10.3.2 Communication documentation

Observations of verbal interactions among various user groups were concurrently documented with the behavioral mapping. The method again utilized the developed instruments to record where and with whom conversations were occurring in the core of the emergency department. Conversations were indicated on the maps by a red circle with letters noted inside indicating if a patient (P), doctor (D), nurse (N), technician (T), family member (F), or housekeeping (H) personnel was participating in face-to-face communication.

10.3.3 Distance traveled

Walking distances of doctors and nurses were collected using pedometers. The data collection periods aligned with the four-hour observational periods. The staff members were given a pedometer at the beginning of the observational period and were instructed to wear it until later approached by a researcher. The data collected was later converted to one-hour shift durations to enable comparison with other studies.

10.3.4 Acoustic measurements

Acoustic measurements were taken throughout the entirety of the adult and pediatric treatment and waiting areas. In the treatment areas, measurements were taken every 30 minutes during each four-hour observational period. Data was collected over the course of five weeks. Acoustic measurements in the waiting areas were taken every 15 minutes during each four-hour observational period over the course of one week.

10.3.5 Occupancy counts

Occupancy levels within the emergency department were counted in all treatment areas of the ED over the course of one week. To collect this data, researchers utilized a floor-plan instrument to record the number of patient and/or visitors occupying each treatment room. Each researcher recorded data in 30-minute intervals by traveling an identical path that began in the waiting room.

To give meaning to the observational data, Phase 2 focused on patients' and providers' views of what was working well, and identified changes needed in the current design. Phase 2 took place one year after the initiation of Phase 1. The Phase 2 methodology used questionnaires, focus groups, and interviews to gain input from patients, their families, and caregivers. Data collection again occurred over a period of ten weeks.

10.3.6 Questionnaires

Questionnaires were developed and administered to patients, visitors, and staff of the emergency department. The patient questionnaire included 44 questions in total presented in seven categories and the visitor questionnaire included 49 questions presented in the same seven categories, each completed during the discharge process. The categories included questions related to the participants' assessment of arrival and waiting experience, treatment rooms, the physical environment, safety and staff support, environmental variables, and overall emergency department experience. Responses were based on a five-point Likert scale and opportunities for open-ended comments at the end of each category were provided.

The staff surveys were administered in both electronic and paper formats and included 68 questions presented in ten categories. These categories included participant demographics, unit configuration, efficiency, furnishings, equipment and storage, the physical environment, ambient environment variables, treatment rooms, privacy and safety, staff satisfaction, and overall emergency department design. Again, space was provided for open-ended comments. Three additional questions were provided for comparison by staff that had also worked in the old ED.

10.3.7 Focus groups

In order to understand and further clarify the findings from the first phase and questionnaires, eight focus groups were conducted; two with nurses and one group each from housekeeping, security, physicians, paramedics, technicians, and patient relations assistants. A total of seven core questions were asked of all focus groups addressing the overall layout of the emergency department, treatment rooms, communication, safety and security, efficiency, and

110 Fay

environmental factors within the environment. The average number of participants was five per group with each session lasting an hour. Responses were audio recorded and transcribed.

10.3.8 Interviews

Several interviews were conducted with emergency department supervisors and key hospital administrators as the final step in the post-occupancy evaluation. To maintain consistency among methods, the core questions developed for the focus groups were again utilized for the interviews with additional questions being tailored to address the unique aspects of each interview participant. Each session was an hour in length, audio recorded, and transcribed.

10.4 Outcomes

One of the most important aspects of post-occupancy evaluations is the ability to measure outcomes and share the knowledge gained. The unpredictable environment of the ED and complex web of multi-disciplinary healthcare providers required that outcomes from this POE be countered against one another. This reinforces the importance of a multi-methodological approach. While much evidence gathered from the research suggests that many attributes of the UK ED are contributing to a positive patient, visitor, and staff experience and demonstrate ways the design has successfully responded to the guiding principles, other outcomes have revealed design attributes that should be further assessed by the designers to ensure a deeper understanding of environmental and operational factors shaping the ED experience.

10.4.1 Behavioral mapping

Outcomes from the behavioral mapping indicate that the central core of the emergency department impacted observed staff differently. It was found that nurse movement remained primarily within their assigned pods, moving from their central workstations to treatment rooms, medicine rooms, and supply rooms, while technician and physician movement remained primarily along the periphery of each pod. It was also found that the centrally located pod, which houses the charge nurse and is adjacent to the physician workstation, received the highest levels of staff traffic and occasionally led to congestion.

10.4.2 Communication documentation

The documentation of communication groups seems to support that the overall configuration positively impacts face-to-face social interaction and efficiency. In particular, the location of the central core, which is comprised of nursing workstations, successfully contains the majority of social interactions, which most commonly comprise two to three people.

10.4.3 Distance traveled

The pedometer data revealed that physician, nurse, and technician travel distances aligned with national averages (Pati and Lee, 2011). Physicians were reported as walking an average

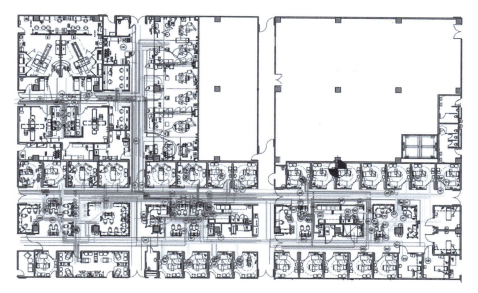

FIGURE 10.3 Behavioral mapping and communication documentation.
Source: Author.

of 3.2 miles (5.15 kilometers) per 10-hour shift, nurses walking 3.38 miles (5.44 kilometers), and technicians walking 4.99 miles (8.03 kilometers).

10.4.4 Acoustic measurements

The findings from the acoustic measurements confirm that the goal of creating a quiet emergency department was achieved. The mean of the sound level in the waiting areas was reported at 56.56 dB, which is comparable to conversation in a restaurant. All other locations within the ED where acoustic measures were taken reported sound levels ranging from 54.75 dB to 59.86 dB. Specific design attributes that contributed to a quiet ED include single patient rooms with solid wood core doors, solid partitions, and acoustic tiles.

10.4.5 Occupancy counts

The observations of visitor and patient use of rooms revealed that individual units of the emergency department varied in capacity levels. Overall, adult room usage reached maximum capacity more frequently than the pediatrics unit. The pediatric unit was at full capacity 7.5% of the time; acute care 12.5%; express care 55%, and the critical care and trauma units were at full capacity 10% of the time. Additional analysis of the data revealed that due to proximity, the swing rooms were utilized for pediatric purposes more so than adult.

10.4.6 Questionnaires

A total of 117 patient questionnaires, 111 visitor questionnaires, and 87 pediatric visitor questionnaires were completed and eligible for analysis. Overall, data revealed that patients

112 Fay

and visitors were more satisfied with the design of the emergency department than staff. Patient satisfaction with the design was strongly associated with patient room and the overall ED environment. Additionally, issues related to privacy and confidentiality were highly effective in shaping both the visitor and patient experiences. Staff satisfaction with the design was most strongly associated with sufficient storage, efficiency, and feelings of safety and security.

10.4.7 Focus groups

The focus group data offered a robust reporting on the thoughts and feelings of the staff in regards to the emergency department design. Content analysis of the focus group transcripts was conducted and revealed several themes across participant groups. The first was that proximity of the staff to one another within the central core and the treatment rooms leads to good face-to-face and team communication. Regarding the issue of privacy and confidentiality, the staff felt that while private patient rooms contribute to a decrease in privacy breaches, the overall openness of the linear core layout offered minimal areas for private conversations outside the patient room. Efficiency within the emergency department was thought to improve, but the increased size of the overall footprint was viewed as a barrier to this. Additional areas of concern as expressed through the focus groups included limited storage, number of access doors, and wayfinding issues.

10.4.8 Interviews

Similarly, the administrative interviews offered important pointers for further interpreting the observational outcomes and echoed issues brought to light by the focus groups. In particular, participants believed the location of the central workstations promoted staff interactions, while still being accessible to patients and visitors of the emergency department. Additionally, factors such as operations, processes, and staffing frequently emerged as important considerations for effectively understanding the ED design.

10.5 Application

Taking the POE process full cycle is critical in bridging the gap between research and practice. Recommended actions for improvements to the ED and future designs were developed through a collaborative design charrette hosted by the design firm. At the charrette, outcomes were presented and two teams of researchers and practitioners were asked to utilize the research findings to complete exercises from a human-centered perspective. Outcomes from the charrette considered not only physical improvements to the space, but suggestions for intake and processes that could impact throughput, efficiency, and satisfaction. The engagement of interdisciplinary participants in this process brought a shared vision to the design process and resulted in more thoughtful designs.

10.6 Conclusions

The complex environment and web of occupants making up the ED environment can shift from order to chaos within a very short period of time. The implementation of a post-occupancy evaluation offers useful insight for improving patient care processes, work-flow efficiencies, and the delivery of efficient, safe, and satisfactory care with the ultimate goal of improving future ED designs. As such, systems for conducting POEs have grown, offering an array of diverse methodologies for assessing the technical and functional performance of the built environment.

The findings from this study indicate that a systematic, multi-methodological approach is critical for effectively examining multi-disciplinary, multi-tasking spaces such as emergency departments. Information gained from both project phases described above allowed for a more thorough analysis of the design layout and its impact on functional outcomes. Assessing the effectiveness of design decisions is a benefit for not only the design firm, but is also effective in the healthcare organization and university researchers and students involved in the study.

10.7 References

Bosch, S., & Nanda, U. (2011). Outside the ivory tower: The role of healthcare design researchers in practice. *Journal of Interior Design*, 36(2), v–xii.

Christmann, J. A. (2011, November). A new design in Kentucky's emergency care. *Healthcare Design*, 11, 32–40.

Pati, D., & Lee, A. (2011, February). Designing smart. *Healthcare Design*, 11(2), 32-38.

Preiser, W. F. E. (2001). The evolution of post-occupancy evaluation: Toward building performance and universal design evaluation. In Federal Facilities Council (Ed.). *Learning from our buildings: A state-of-the-practice summary of post-occupancy evaluation* (Technical Report No. 145, pp. 9–22). Washington, D.C.: National Academy Press.

Preiser, W. F. E., Rabinowitz, H. Z., & White, E. T. (2015). *Post-occupancy evaluation*. London: Routledge.

11

A CONSTRUCT OF GENEROSITY IN NAVAJO CULTURE: THE HOGAN

Jaclyn M. Roessel

11.1 Introduction

"Everything begins in the home" – Ruth Roessel, Navajo educator (1981)

Navajo people are by nature an inclusive people. Often calling themselves an "open-arms" people, Navajos exist today as arguably the largest American Indian community in North America because of this historic inclusivity. This culturally adaptive community traces its existence in their oral traditions from four original clans that began their people's history to a kinship system today that has over 60 different clans, many of which come from the adopting of new people and cultures (Iverson and Roessel, 2002). Ability to adapt is also seen in the Navajo's acceleration and savviness in art forms like the integration of weaving and silver-smithing. These two crafts were introduced by the Spanish but were turned into art by the Navajo because of their ability to increase the technical and artistic skill needed to create pieces (Marshall, 2005).

As with all parts of Navajo culture and life, there exist many oral traditions and stories that trace the importance of practices carried out by the people. This is especially relevant to the stories relating to the origins of Navajo homes. Navajo traditionally lived in dwellings called "hooghan," a word in the Navajo language that translates to the "home or place of dwelling." The term "Hogan" is an anglicized version of the Navajo word "hooghan." For this chapter, the modern term "Hogan" will be used most.

11.2 Philosophy of Hozhó

This chapter concentrates on the importance of the design of the Navajo Hogan in Navajo society and culture. This traditional multi-use space not only serves the function of a dwelling but, according to Navajo belief, provides an opportunity for Navajo people to learn about themselves and where they come from. Through various interactions with the home – from conception, building, and living in the structure – the Hogan is an extension of clan values and cultural practices, meaning this "structure" provides, what architectural historian Bernard

Rudovsky calls, "a tangible expression of a way of life." Much of this expression rests on the themes of the base character, virtue, and value of living in a generous way.

The basis of Navajo religion is the concept of Hozhó. Hozhó is a philosophy that notes everything has a life essence and lives in harmony with each other; from animals, to the five-fingered people, to rocks, water, and air. Navajo believe they are in constant dialogue with the world around them, and that everything they engage with has a life force that is impacted by their existence. It is a reciprocal relationship they hold with everything from the animals they care for to the homes – hogans, they live in (Wyman and Haile, 1970).

Central to Navajo religion is the Hozhójí ceremony, also known as the Beauty Way or Blessingway Ceremony. Separate from healing rituals held by the community, the purpose of this ceremony is often held as restorative, meant to regenerate Hozhó within a person throughout their life. Fundamental to the Hozhójí ceremony is a set of "Hogan songs" that begins the proceedings. This set of twelve songs is very significant in the process of the ceremony as these are songs executed by a medicine person with utmost precision (Roessel, 1981). It is believed that these songs are the same songs that came from the start of the creation, when the Diyin Diné first started the Hozhójí (Mitchell et al., 2001). The meaning of the songs is recited with the intention of restoring balance within the Hogan, which in turn aids in restoring harmony to the patient's life. In this thinking, the Hogan helps generate a positive tone in the person's life, establishing a reciprocal dialogue between the people who live in the home and the Hogan itself.

11.3 Creation of the Hogan

The formation of the Navajo Hogan is first mentioned in the oral history of the community, passed from generation to generation. While anthropologists can share aspects of Native cultures, Native communities turn to these foundational oral histories as a reference to their people's past and traditions.

The first Hogan was created during the period of time when the Diyin Diné, i.e., the Holy People, first inhabited the earth. The Holy People are considered to be spiritual guiders in traditional practice. During this period, Coyote, a mischievous character, created the first Hogan with the help of the Beaver People (Zolbrod, 1987). This new type of dwelling was known as a male Hogan, or fork-stick Hogan. Placed in the ground with the sacred stones of each cardinal direction, structural posts on the East, South, West, and North served as a way to bless the home and begin its existence in beauty and harmony.

Within the philosophy of Hozhó there always exists a dichotomy. Navajo believe within every individual is both a male and female essence, a belief represented in the Hogan as well. The secondary type of dwelling occupied by Navajo is the female Hogan, noted by its rounded shape (Schwarz, 1997). With the advent of the railroad into the Southwest and the greater availability of lumber, the female Hogan became the most widely used today. For this reason, this is the version of the Hogan we will reference most.

11.4 Hogan discipline and values

Since the traditional Hogan is an open floor plan, all of the teaching, ceremonies, and general daily activities occur within plain sight of everyone in the dwelling. This ability to share stories and perform ceremonies with both the family and the community able to witness and

116 Roessel

participate creates great accountability amongst everyone. In this model, teachings are shared generously with everyone.

The Navajos' concept of kinship is very complex, and the health of this system is dependent on oral teachings being shared with entire family units. The ceremonies performed in Navajo religion occur in the open room of the Hogan, thus allowing for the sharing of cultural practices to be passed on inter-generationally. This involves not only the nuclear family unit, but also the community attending the ceremony in support of the family that is holding the ceremony (Schwarz, 1997).

As noted in the Introduction, adaptive architecture can accommodate multiple uses at the same time. The Navajo Hogan is the epitome of this type of structure, since from the beginning of its existence it was meant to serve different purposes. Initially, the male Hogan was the structure where ceremonies were held, planning for events occurred, and praying took place. In contrast, the female Hogan was the structure used for cooking, resting, and often sleeping (Schwarz, 1997). Changes in the Southwest impacted this arrangement, eventually making the female Hogan the dwelling used for all activities of the Navajo people. Despite these changes, core principles and building techniques were able to be preserved because of the adaptive nature of the Navajo. As noted by Ames *et al.* (1978), Navajo builders aimed to "not conquer nature (but) work steadily to adapt to the region, climate, and topography of their surroundings." This occurred physically in the shape and materials of the Hogan using railroad ties and dirt, absorbing new materials without Anglo influence on the design.

11.5 Cultural responsiveness

The orientation of the Hogan provides many opportunities for people to understand their relationship and roles within the familial unit and community. From the beginning of Navajo existence, the world view of the home is seen as the start of how a Navajo person is meant to be and even the cycles of life they will travel through. Each direction holds teachings about the growth a person reaches: East (infancy), South (adolescence), West (adulthood) and North (old age) (Roessel, 1981). This expands into the roles and activities a Navajo person is meant to engage in different areas of the home. As this transformation began to occur so did the general evolution of the discipline of the Hogan's orientation. Essential to its existence is the doorway that faces the East (Roessel, 1981). The East is the beginning of the day, so being able to look at the sun's rise from the doorway is critical for the Navajos' desire for the vivacity of life. As noted by Harry Walters, the south side of the Hogan is associated with things needed to make a living – weaving, silver-smithing, or crafting – so along the south side production tools are located. The West, as defined by one of the Holy People "Changing Woman," is associated with social relations, housing space to visit and sleep. The North is for reverence: you prepare the Nightway mask and anything used in ceremonies on the north side. The fireplace and cooking area is in the center of the Hogan and accessible to all (Griffin-Pierce, 1992). In this sense, the structure is seen as an entity itself. Through the Navajo perspective, the Hogan becomes didactic in nature, and not solely an inanimate shelter.

One of the earliest models of asserting the Hogan design in the planning of spaces is seen in the construction of Navajo Community College (now known as Diné College) in 1973. The campus was created to evoke the philosophical orientation of the Hogan at a campus level by creating many polygon structured buildings across the campus. From dormitories that occupy the west side of campus to the kitchens and cafeteria being located near the fire or center of the Hogan, structure is prevalent in making stark reference to marking a space with cultural relevancy. As the most integrative example of Navajo architecture used in a public space in the Navajo Nation, the model of the Navajo Community College created a way for the Navajo community to display layers of pride in culture and history. In this aspect, the Hogan becomes a new type of adaptive structure. Used as a symbolic gesture of the new phase of American Indian education, history and culture coalesce to allow the students to feel at home at the first tribal community college.

Further use of Navajo ideals in architecture is seen in a second study facilitated as part of the planning surrounding the Navajo Mission Academy in New Mexico. Preiser (personal communication, 2015) notes the community's congruous desire to develop an architecture that was reflective of cultural values. This study focused on identifying the cultural criteria necessary for building on the reservation, with the user group noting "harmony," "cooperation and responsibility," and "modesty" as paramount to building a structure that was culturally responsive.

In this case, the development of a culturally responsive design that incorporated the noted criteria is what separated the building from other educational facilities. The development of the Navajo Mission Academy was created with reciprocal involvement from community members who valued the importance of having educational facilities that integrate Navajo world view (Preiser, 1985).

11.6 Conclusion

Navajo people believe the energy of the home frames the activities that occur within a dwelling at one time. For the Hogan, the ability of its floorplan to be a visual prayer and affirmation of the Navajo way of life is a testament to a different type of multi-use building. Archetypal of didacticism in architecture, the multi-faceted structures not only provide safety from the outside elements but truly become a vessel of connecting Navajo to their core beliefs of respect, cooperation, and generosity.

The history of the Navajo Hogan has continuously been one that has adapted with the people it has housed since their creation. The Hogan, in the psyche of the people, is one of them, a living being with which they have a continuous relationship. With the changing landscape of Navajo development, the Hogan is often used as a very public way to display pride in culture and the history of a people that is dynamic and vibrant. The Hogan will continue to adapt to the people's habitability and spiritual needs as the Navajo develop new needs as well.

11.7 Acknowledgments

In an exchange with co-editor Wolfgang F. E. Preiser, the author was made aware of a study funded by the National Science Foundation, with a focus on culture-responsive design: Navajo Mission Academy Student Residencies – An Experiment in Cross-cultural Research and Programming by Wolfgang F. E. Preiser, Ph D., the project report was published in 1985 by the Center for Environmental Education, School of Architecture and Planning, University of New Mexico, as part of their monograph series.

118 Roessel

11.8 References

Ames, W. J., Bartlett, D. C., Gaspar, M. J., James, E., Lowell, D. J., Pioche, N., & Pratt, B. C. (1978). *User participation and requirements in planning Navajo school facilities in New Mexico*. Albuquerque, NM: University of New Mexico Press.

Griffin-Pierce, T. (1992). *Earth is my mother, sky is my father: Space, time, and astronomy in Navajo sandpainting*. Albuquerque, NM: University of New Mexico Press.

Iverson, P., & Roessel, M. (2002). *Diné: A history of the Navajos*. Albuquerque, NM: University of New Mexico Press.

Marshall, A. E. (2005). *Home: Native people in the Southwest*. Phoenix, AZ: Heard Museum.

Mitchell, M., Redhair, D. R., Mitchell, A., & Nez, A. (2001). *Origin of the Diné*. Rough Rock, AZ: Navajo Studies and Curriculum Center, Rough Rock Community School.

Preiser, W. F. E. (1985). Navajo Mission Academy student residences: an experiment in cross-cultural research and programming. In Preiser, W. F. E. (ed.), *Programming the built environment*, (136–148). New York, NY: Routledge Revivals.

Roessel, R. (1981). *Women in Navajo society*. Rough Rock, AZ: Navajo Resource Center, Rough Rock Demonstration School.

Schwarz, M. T. (1997). *Molded in the image of changing woman: Navajo views on the human body and personhood*. Tucson, AZ: University of Arizona Press.

Wyman, L. C., & Haile, B. (1970). *Blessingway*. Tucson, AZ: University of Arizona Press.

Zolbrod, P. G. (1987). *Diné bahane': The Navajo creation story*. Albuquerque, NM: University of New Mexico Press.

REFLECTIONS ON PART III

Michael J. Crosbie, Ph.D., FAIA

"A room with a view to adaptability"

A room or a small setting within a larger building is the most human of spaces we can create. The adaptability of such intimate enclosures would seem the most challenging, in that the quantity of area to work with is modest. The potential to adapt rooms and settings for a variety of uses lends them vitality, a "charge" of spatial energy. For example, who has not experienced the wonder and ingenuity of multi-use spaces on boats, where several tasks can be successfully performed at a scale that is within an arm's reach?

The big challenge of planning rooms and settings for adaptability is the fact that we do not know for certain what the future holds for a particular human activity, especially one supported by science and technology in constant flux. Hospitals and other healthcare facilities are perhaps the chief example, and this part considers a number of them. Fawcett's approach to this problem is to employ more technology—computers and software such as Monte Carlo (I love the sly irony in the software name that design is often a gamble). Such tools allow us to create complex scenarios that can be played out over time in an effort to extend the design problem far into the future, long after our design work is done. Such "activity simulation," as he calls it, allows us to reveal the variations of use with multiple iterations. Most helpful is the graphic presentation of the simulations in a "scattergram" on which we can instantly see the upper and lower limits of the variables and their impact on the design performance and cost. Such a tool is valuable in helping clients to understand the parameters of possible choices, and allowing them to make informed decisions that balance adaptability with project budget. Fawcett reminds us that universally flexible design is a myth. Designing for any eventuality is not possible. His case study of the McMaster University Health Sciences Centre reveals that the range of possible futures designed for rarely come to pass. In defense of the Centre's architects, when the building was designed nearly a half-century ago such simulation tools didn't exist. Fawcett demonstrates that it is possible to create an alternative reality in time that may be very close to what such rooms and settings will need to respond to in the future. The fly in the ointment is the unpredictability of changes in the administrative staff of such facilities, and the choices they make that will take the building in a completely different direction.

Another healthcare case study, Fay's analysis of what can be learned through the POE of a hospital emergency department, is thorough and the results are interesting, but it raises some additional questions that should be considered. Did the architects who designed this new facility commission the POE, and if so what was the motivation? Did the architects consult past POEs of emergency departments in developing their design (a literature search turned up little in terms of past POEs of this facility type)? And did the new POE consider the design goals of the architects and whether they were met? Emergency rooms are particularly complex environments for adaptability, because they can go very quickly from being underutilized to extremely busy, with staff, patients, and family members sharing a space that must accommodate fast thinking and fast action, along with the need for some measure of privacy. Fay's analysis of ER function, particularly the recording of pathways used by staff and health professionals, gives a glimpse of how these high-impact spaces can be calibrated to fluctuate between low and high use.

Morgan's examination of the factors involved in the design of office floor-plates is particularly helpful to those of us who do not operate in the world of speculative commercial construction. Floor-plate design of an office tower will be affected by such measurable factors as visibility, connectivity, and daylighting, which in turn influence the internal physicality of the office and its psychological impacts. The six measures presented remind us of the tale of an elephant described by six blind men: all are accurate according to a very limited amount of information. In the case of Morgan's taxonomy, floor-plate designs are quantified according to: net-to-gross ratio, wall-to-floor ratio, average distance to the façade, daylight penetration, floor-plate visibility, and floor-plate connectivity. Each measure has its own optimal values from an economic standpoint, compared to benchmarks in the speculative office market. When we morph the office tower form, pushing and pulling it here and there (as parametric software allows us to do), the values across these six measures change. But what if we push and pull the values instead of the form? This would result in a floor-plate design and tower form that responds to the values that a potential tenant might have for the office space. Unfortunately, once the building is designed and constructed, the values across those six measures are pretty much set in stone (or steel). Morgan's idea is intriguing, however, in that the power of parametric software in design is only partially used if we do not incorporate more variables than aesthetic form making. Such tools allow us to project a range of adaptions to the design of floor plates in ways akin to that described by Fawcett. It would be interesting to study how this tool might be applied differently for a client who will occupy the space. In the case of speculative office towers, the actual tenants aren't known beyond an average for the market one wishes to attract.

Hodulak asks some provocative questions: Why do Germans prefer cellular offices to open-plan offices? What are the local traditions, cultural influences, and expectations that drive this preference? Cellular offices seem counter to flexibility, but Hodulak maintains that they are highly adaptable to the individual needs of the person occupying the office. One space with one person can serve a variety of functions, but a shared space among two or three people turns a private office into contested territory with little possibility of expansion. Here, and as we see elsewhere in Part III, adaptability and multi-function design is not driven just by what is most efficient. Like architecture in total, cultures (personal, corporate, ethnic, national) play a pivotal role in what is possible in design. In this case, history is a factor. The cellular office space is very old and part of the European tradition. In contrast, office environments for global corporate entities transcend national/cultural values more common in mid-size companies, and corporate history and values have a bigger impact on design. The culture needs to match the design, and vice versa.

Roessel's consideration of history and culture is central to her analysis of the Navajo Hogan. She describes Navajos as "culturally adaptive," which has helped make them one of the largest Native American groups. The Hogan is a beautiful example of how people build themselves into their houses. In this case, the Navajo values of adaptability and flexibility are manifested in the Hogan with its single, multi-functional space, oriented on the cardinal points (representing the four stages of life), in which all family activities transpire across generations. The Hogan embodies the Navajo's history, culture, and values and is didactic in nature. One wonders, did the people create the architecture, or did the architecture create the people?

These case studies of rooms with a view toward adaptability and flexibility rest on a bedrock of history and culture, and demonstrate that design decisions can be made more confidently with the aid of computer simulations and such tools as POEs and BPE. However, they also prove the (sometimes irrational) human component is also a design driver. In our own society we are seeing people opt for smaller spaces (such as the "tiny house" movement of people living in a few hundred square foot units that can be hooked up to car, towed to a new location, and sited elsewhere). A few years ago architect Sarah Susanka's work in the realm of "not-so-big" houses signaled a change in people wanting to live in less space (the Great Recession also reversed the decades-long trend of houses getting larger). Shared room-sized space can also be seen in the whole Airbnb industry where people are turning individual rooms in private homes into rented space, or even the inside of private cars into shared spaces through the Uber phenomenon. Adaptable room-sized spaces appear to be responding to cultural shifts that reflect the new "Sharing Economy," changing the way we think about occupied space.

PART IV
Building scale

Preamble

Wolfgang F. E. Preiser and Jacob J. Wilhelm

Compiling the rooms and settings that make up a building, Part IV will look at how the architect or planner approaches adaptability in projects ranging from educational and residential facilities to massive museum centers and office complexes. From new builds to later interventions, adaptive architecture gives clients, operators, and users the opportunity to experience the built environment in a way that is cohesive and synergetic. Contributions will present specification, reuse, prediction, preservation, and personalization in buildings representative of the direction adaptive architecture is headed.

To introduce these concepts and explore their possibilities at the building scale, in Chapter 12 a school for blind and multi-handicapped children in Israel poses the question of what adaptability means in the operation and development of a highly specialized building for a specific user group. Using the results of a post-occupancy evaluation to increase flexibility, design interventions are made that allow continued use of the mixed residential and educational facility to meet today's standards.

Adaptively reusing existing structures not originally designed for new users poses the opposite question: how can architecture improve user experience by being non-specific? Liljegren and Kish, in Chapter 13, explore the ongoing shift back to an urban core and the adaptive reuse projects it necessitates. Through the lens of two comparable case studies, flexibility under the definition of generic, open-ended, or non-conclusive is used in design strategies that transform projects topping 1,000,000 square feet from vacated shells to lively cultural hubs. This transformation requires challenging the role of the architect, all while operating under the constraints of historic preservation.

In Chapter 14, Petronis, Whittemore, and Aguilar consider adaptability when it is incorporated in each stage of the design process. Flexibility can be introduced early on in the development of a project, as seen in the office buildings and educational facilities studied, in order to avoid costly physical modifications later in time. Both private and public-sector clients showcase strategies used from the facility planning, to construction, and onward to future expansion and adaptation, through studying both design processes and operational concerns.

The standardized designs often associated with adaptable architecture can also remain culturally sensitive and visually intriguing by including local artisans and traditional building practices. Jones, in Chapter 15, begins with indigenous building techniques rooted in climate, materials, available technologies, and tradition, and reveals what they teach us today about multi-tasking spaces. Embodying the past made present, the Soboleff Heritage Center in Alaska interprets adaptability as translating historical precedence in a way that asks more of a building's participation in a city's cultural landscape.

In Chapter 16, Anfield focuses on similar questions of personal identity in a residential complex for children in Johannesburg, South Africa. How a building adapts to, or reflects, the personality and ambitions of its user is a requirement of any successful residence, particularly in the context of childhood. Using a modular framework of salvaged shipping containers, adaptability in the form of customization and personalization takes place to relate the power of adaptiveness from the perspective of the designer as well as the inhabitant.

Each understanding of adaptability, regardless of location or scale, looks to unpack the ideals set in previous parts of this book at a level experienced by the common user and operator, relating clear design strategies to how a project will be developed in real time. As multi-tasking spaces are assembled into the projects that are increasingly needed today, successfully adaptive buildings set themselves up to be active participants in the human experience.

12

KEREN OR CENTER FOR BLIND CHILDREN WITH MULTIPLE DISABILITIES IN ISRAEL

Wolfgang F. E. Preiser and Jacob J. Wilhelm

12.1 Introduction

Keren Or (Hebrew for "Ray of Light"), a New York Foundation, built the Jerusalem Center for Blind Children with Multiple Disabilities in 1991 in Ramot, Israel. Located in a suburb of Jerusalem, the 35,000 square foot facility (see Figure 12.1) houses 40 residential children, and serves 25 other children who are brought to the Center on a daily basis. Twenty full-time and 12 part-time staff work at the Center, in addition to seven volunteers. At night time, two staff members supervise the residential children.

12.2 Keren Or history

The Keren Or Jerusalem Center came into existence 40 years ago with the mission of providing individualized, comprehensive, and nurturing educational, social, and rehabilitative programs to serve the unique needs of children in Israel who were both blind or visually impaired and also suffered from additional serious physical and/or cognitive deficits. The program blossomed into a prestigious, innovative institution, now caring for over 80 students. The development of the building and organization is outlined below:

- 1976 – Keren Or program is founded with four multi-disabled blind students.
- 1987 – The government of Israel grants Keren Or a tract of land in the Ramot suburb of Jerusalem for the construction of a new and expanded facility.
- 1991 – A 35,500 square foot state-of-the-art building is completed and moved in to, initially housing a student body of 45 children ranging from infants to age 18. The facility includes a dormitory, classrooms, therapy areas, and expansive outdoor spaces with an adapted playground and gardens. Among the services provided are vision training, hydrotherapy, music, art, speech, and physical therapies. Drama, dance, gardening, and small animal therapy are introduced. Computers, horseback riding, class and school trips, summer camp retreats, and holiday celebrations become staples of the Keren Or program.

FIGURE 12.1 Street view of the Keren Or Center for Blind Children with Multiple Disabilities. *Source*: Keren Or.

- 1995 – A section of the building is renovated to exclusively serve young adults ages 18–21, enabling them to transition toward adulthood while still being integrated in the Keren Or program. This was the precursor to the expansion of services offered by Keren Or to include adult care through off-campus apartments and Avukat Or, a comprehensive day center for adults.
- 2004 – A capital campaign is launched to build a new, high-tech hydrotherapy center, additional classrooms, and a multi-purpose auditorium. The original hydrotherapy area is to be converted into a fully functioning synagogue.
- 2009 – The expansion project is completed. Hydrotherapy becomes the hallmark of Keren Or's program. The synagogue hosts weekly Sabbath services conducted jointly with members of the local community. The auditorium provides an upscale venue for hosting professional seminars to groups from Israel and abroad, including in-house special education training.
- 2012 – A cooperative partnership program is instituted with the Perkins School for the Blind of Boston, Massachusetts.
- 2014 – Keren Or adult graduates are integrated into other programs in Israel designated specifically to help them maintain the high level of functioning they attained over many years at Keren Or.
- Today, Keren Or devotes its resources exclusively to the mission it has faithfully and successfully pursued over the past 40 years: providing the tools that allow multiply disabled blind youth in Israel to overcome overwhelming challenges and maximize their potential for happiness, personal growth, and independence.

12.3 Keren Or Center design

After hiring project architect Adina Darvasi, Keren Or decided to add to the team the co-author of this chapter, environment–behavior consultant and researcher Wolfgang F. E. Preiser, to develop design and planning guidelines for the project. Darvasi had local architectural expertise but limited experience in designing for people with disabilities. The full project team also included liaison persons from the client organization, New York-based Keren Or. The consultant's task was to develop design performance criteria guidelines for the building. Research included analysis of archives to identify critical issues related to blindness in children with multiple disabilities; site visits to precedent buildings from which exemplary design solutions could be distilled and adapted for the present project; on-site focused interviews with key informants about therapy and care of blind children in Israel; post-occupancy evaluation walk-throughs in existing facilities in Jerusalem serving blind children; focus group interviews with representatives of the client organization and the architect to troubleshoot and modify plans for the proposed future facility; finally, several post-occupancy evaluations of the completed facility were undertaken, starting on the opening day of the facility in 1991.

12.4 Multi-method data-gathering approach

Eight environment–behavior (E&B) research methodologies were employed to develop the project's design performance criteria:

- Literature research. Relevant literature co-author Preiser had accumulated over the years (Preiser 1983, 1988), and data he had previously collected while field-testing guidance

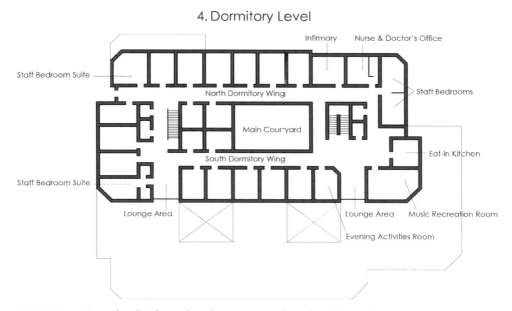

FIGURE 12.2 Upper level 4 floor plan: dormitories and residential activities.
Source: Keren Or.

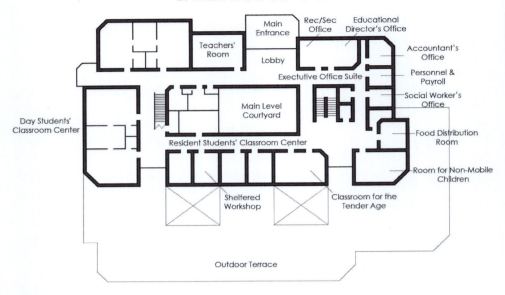

FIGURE 12.3 Main entry level 3 floor plan: administration and classrooms.
Source: Keren Or.

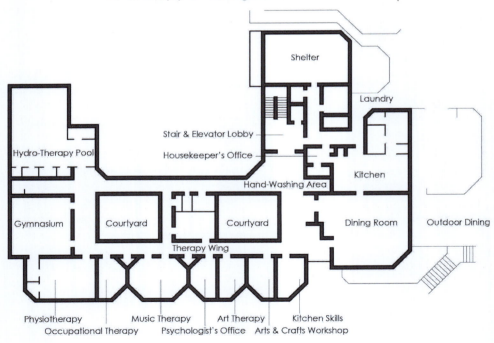

FIGURE 12.4 Lower level 2 floor plan: therapy rooms, kitchen, and dining.
Source: Keren Or.

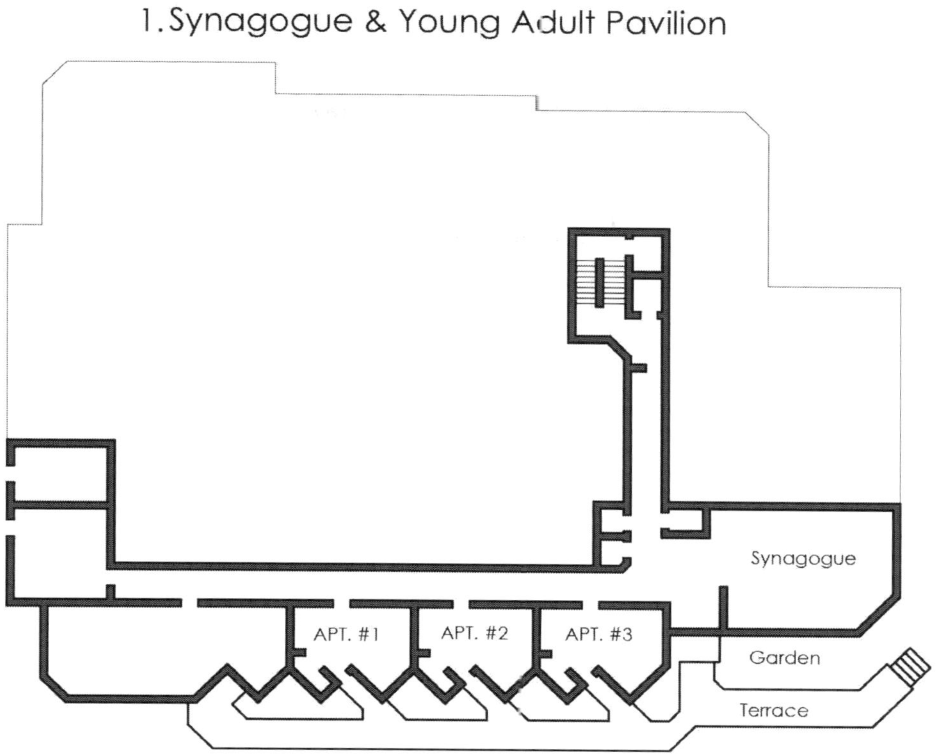

1.Synagogue & Young Adult Pavilion

FIGURE 12.5 Synagogue and young adult pavilion with attached staff apartments.
Source: Keren Or.

systems for people with visual impairments, proved invaluable in distilling key design features and guidelines. The archive, ranging in scale from product design and interior design to architecture and site design, helped develop design criteria for surface characteristics, dimensions, and color-coding, as well as general criteria for residential and training facilities for people with visual impairments.

- Walk-through probes. Systematic observation and site visits to facilities serving persons with visual impairments in Hannover, Germany and Lausanne, Switzerland permitted observation of successful and unsuccessful design features in use, documented by still photography.
- Focus interviews. Observation-based walk-through evaluations included individual and group focused interviews with facility directors, key personnel, and departmental supervisors.
- Plan annotation. Environment–behavior annotations based on the site visit observations and interviews were recorded on plans of the visited facilities. These critiques, linked to the photographic documentation, included both successful and unsuccessful design features.
- On-site observations. In Jerusalem, three strategic planning activities evaluated Keren Or's existing facility, housed in a large converted residential building. Included was systematic data on the operation through direct observation, still photography, and focused

interviews with staff and parents. This was followed by a walk-through post-occupancy evaluation (POE), and finally interviews with the Director of the Jewish Institute for the Blind in Jerusalem.

- Focus Design recommendation sessions. Based on the research, specific short- and long-term strategic recommendations to Keren Or's Board of Directors, the project team, and the architect were made. Intense political and time pressure to proceed with the project limited certain design modifications. For example, the decision was made to build on an extremely steep site originally intended for a park, which the City of Jerusalem had donated to the project. This resulted in significant difficulties moving the children throughout four levels of the building.
- Post-construction evaluation. On opening day in 1991, co-author Preiser conducted a walk-through evaluation that identified serious fire code violations and other potential safety threats to be addressed.
- Post-occupancy evaluations. At one and three years after occupancy, post-occupancy evaluations were carried out, resulting in numerous recommendations that were implemented. The conceptual framework and methodology for such evaluations can be found in Preiser and Vischer (2005), Preiser and Smith (2010), as well as Preiser *et al.* (2015).

12.5 Planning and design criteria and guidelines

The environment–behavior research by Preiser resulted in general planning and design criteria for residential/training/educational facilities for blind persons with multiple disabilities (Grosbois, 2015), many of which were included in the building as designed and built.

The guidelines presented below in tabular format are self-explanatory, and they demonstrate how many design concepts that are taken for granted by persons without disabilities change drastically for blind persons and children with multiple disabilities (Figure 12.6). The related issues are ranging from the scale of site design and building design, to layout and adjacencies of floor-plates, to rooms and their behavior settings for working, teaching, and playing.

TABLE 12.1 Evidence-based design guidelines for blind persons with multiple disabilities

Site Criteria	Proximity to schooling, training, shopping, restaurants, cultural facilities, and recreational activity space appropriate to the user group should be within walking distance, with traffic and congestion-free access to public transportation. Although this particular student population is not expected to venture outside the Center on their own, these amenities and a residential appearance helps such a facility fit into the suburban neighborhood.
25% Space Premium	Visually impaired users require 25% more space to orient themselves to objects, furniture, and other built-in contextual elements. In addition, they tend to require a larger "space bubble" around them—a zone where they feel intruded upon by others.
Safety Codes	Fire, IBC, and life-safety codes and ADA standards result in wider doorways, additional exits, and obstacle-free emergency evacuation paths for users.
Residential Scale	Because it is home to students and staff, spaces should be planned for training and educational activities apart from living areas, with a variety of forms, materials, and textures used. Daylighting, residential spatial relationships, and regional architectural features add to the residential appearance.

Bedrooms	Bedrooms large enough to accommodate flexible residential furniture, special equipment, circulation, and personal space increase the feeling of control a blind student may have.
Common Living Rooms	"Open-plan" common area design provides ease of supervision and a feeling of togetherness.
Bathrooms	In addition to ADA requirements, increased student control can be supported by hard and smooth floor materials for wheelchair users and the choice between roll-in showers and bathtubs.
Loop Guidance Handrails for Outdoor Spaces	Loop configurations of handrails that guide the user from one point in the system, through the outdoor spaces, and back to the beginning support independence. Where pathways intersect, a crossbar mounted on the handrail indicates that the guidance system is interrupted ahead and the user will soon have a choice of direction.
Touch and Smell Gardens in Raised Planters for Way Finding	Visually impaired users can easily navigate touch and smell gardens in raised planters with Braille labels, which help students identify plants and independently experience the outdoors.
Hallways	An unambiguous single main hallway with secondary hallways branching off in a clear, hierarchical fashion helps the visually impaired find their way. A narrower hallway, no more than six feet wide, provides more directional cues than one that is wider, as wider hallways feel more like a place than a pathway.
Community Plan	Single-level group living spaces of 4–6 students, a resident teacher or counselor, and an outdoor garden create community in such situations.
Window Safety	Using window stops and safety glass rather than fixed steel grates helps maintain a residential image, while still providing necessary safety measures.
Fence Safety by Planting	Planting thick, thorny shrubbery in front of perimeter fences and ledges naturally discourages getting too close to potential hazards.
Stair Safety	Lockable gates that indicate where a staircase begins can avoid accidents while still allowing able-bodied, blind residents to use staircases safely on their own.
Differential and Adjustable Height Fixtures	With residents of different ages, different amenity heights are required. As such, differentiated and adjustable height fixtures can enable each person to adapt the height of the amenities to his or her needs.
Split Handrails	A second handrail, installed at half-height below all regular height handrails, is particularly helpful for smaller children.
Handrail Orientation Device	Handrails mounted on wall services can have embedded navigation devices, such as Braille or indicators of room numbers, to support wayfinding and independence.
Colors for Residents with Residual Vision	Bright and cheerful colors and distinctly color-coded floors contribute to sensory stimulation and wayfinding for residents with residual vision.
Tactile Flooring Cues	Changing flooring material and texture near doorways, stairways, and other potentially dangerous areas remind residents they should remain cautious at such places.
Differentiated Door Hardware	Changing doorknob texture and shape can help students differentiate indoor, outdoor, and specialty room doors.
Tactile Art and Decor	Unique pieces of artwork in hallway and activity areas present a friendly image for residents, staff, and visitors, and are especially beneficial when they are tactile or sculptural.
Talking Elevator and Safety Keypads	The first Hebrew-speaking elevator in the world was installed by Otis to provide orientation to students moving between floors. A coded keypad that only staff could use to operate the controls resolved safety concerns of children playing in the elevator.

(*Continued*)

TABLE 12.1 continued

Orienting Interior Spaces	In open-plan interior spaces, such as dining halls or assembly areas, bookshelves and other space-defining elements can help create smaller, more manageable spaces. These "shoreline" guidance devices can allow the student to proceed to his/her assigned seat at the dining table on their own, without a white cane or assistance.
Hanging Napping Baskets	A basket-like device suspended from a single point in the ceiling was devised by Center staff, and has been found to be an ideal relaxation/napping place for small children while in the classroom.
Raised Doorknobs	Via staff recommendation, door hardware moved from normal height to approximately six feet off the floor helps prevent children from escaping classrooms unattended during unsupervised moments.
Dutch Half-Doors	Dutch doors in bedrooms allow teachers to acoustically and visually supervise children's bedrooms, while also allowing for cross ventilation to passively cool the building.
Time-Out Room	A space with padded walls prevents self-inflicted injury to disruptive children.
Storage	Storage for bulk goods of frequent use near the food preparation area and equipment storage for larger, specially-designed gadgets must be provided.

Source: Authors.

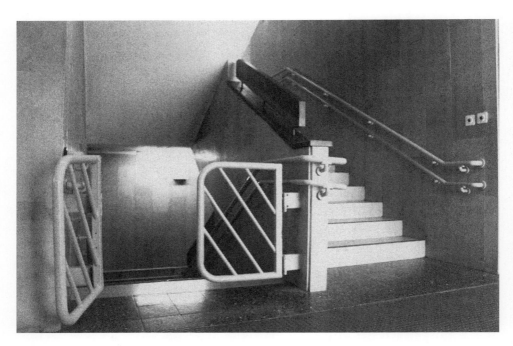

FIGURE 12.6 Special, double handrails in staircase, color coded in yellow for better visibility.
Source: Keren Or.

12.6 Conclusions

The evidence-based guidelines below reflect a unique and humane philosophy of caring for blind children with multiple disabilities. The focused E&B research carried out in similar facilities around the world, together with the knowledge of the "resident experts" who operate the Center, ultimately led to a high-quality environment. A series of ongoing follow-up POE visits identified additional inadequately addressed operational, functional, and psychological issues that were resolved through modifications. A "cottage concept" for housing the population of the Center would have allowed four to six children to live in one cohesive unit with a counselor, more akin to a family home. Although a flat site with direct access to the outside might have made a "cottage concept" design more possible, the present Center Director reports that the similarity of floor plans on each floor helps occupants orient themselves and find their way. The Center's mission and therapeutic philosophy is to encourage improved planning at future, similar facilities elsewhere. For this reason, it encourages post-occupancy evaluation and comparative analysis of similar facilities in a never ending quest to continually improve planning and design guidelines.

12.7 Acknowledgments

Keren Or exists thanks to the vision and efforts of its founder and first director, Dr. Jacob Igra, the oversight, dedication, and perseverance of Dr. Edward L. Steinberg, Chairman of the organization's Board of Directors, and the dedicated staff and directors. Extended information on the Keren Or Center and its donors can be found at www.keren-or.org/ (accessed March 22, 2017).

12.8 References

Grosbois, L.-P. (2015). *Handicap et Construction: Conception Universelle de L'accessibilite* (10th edition). Paris: Edition Le Moniteur.

Preiser, W. F. E. (1983). A Combined Tactile/Electronic Guidance System for the Visually Handicapped. *Proceedings of the First International Symposium on Maps and Graphics for the Visually Handicapped*. Washington, D.C.: Association of American Geographers.

Preiser, W. F. E. (1988). A Combined Tactile-Electronic Guidance System for Visually Impaired Persons in Indoor and Outdoor Spaces. In: Chigier, E. (ed.). *Design for Disabled Persons*. Tel Aviv, Israel: Freund Publishing House.

Preiser, W. F. E., and Smith, K. H. (eds.). (2010). *Universal Design Handbook* (second edition). New York: McGraw-Hill.

Preiser, W. F. E., and Vischer, J. C. (2005). *Assessing Building Performance*. London: Routledge.

Preiser, W. F. E., Rabinowitz, H. Z., and White, E. T. (2015). *Post-Occupancy Evaluation*. London: Routledge.

13

OMGIVNING: TRANSFORMING HISTORIC ICONS THROUGH ADAPTIVE REUSE

Karin Liljegren and Kelly J. Kish

13.1 Introduction

As a cultural hub for southern California, downtown Los Angeles saw its peak in the 1920s and 1930s. During this period the area saw a frenzy of construction consisting of high rises and office buildings constructed chiefly of steel and cast in place concrete. These technologically modern cores were embellished with details borrowing from nearly every historical phase of architecture, from Moorish to Gothic to Neoclassical. As the city became increasingly de-centralized after the introduction of the freeway system, downtown Los Angeles became more or less irrelevant. The former city center was vacated. As a result, the stately buildings of downtown Los Angeles gave up their original functions, and they were left either vacant or to house a myriad of new purposes, ranging from garment industry sweat shops to swap meets. Journeys to downtown LA were thought only for the brave at heart.

13.2 Background

The past 15 years have seen a significant shift in the makeup of DTLA (downtown Los Angeles). With a city wide shortage of housing coupled with a new embracing of things urban, downtown LA has been experiencing a resurgence and a redevelopment. Part of this new interest in urbanism is the salvaging and restoration of many of DTLA's historic, landmark buildings. These buildings are being transformed to serve a purpose unlike that of their original design and function. Two such examples of this phenomenon are the Broadway Trade Building and the Sears Roebuck Distribution Center.

The Broadway building is located in what is known as "the historic core" of downtown Los Angeles on Broadway while the Sears building is located just east of downtown in the neighborhood of Boyle Heights. Both buildings consist of floor areas of over 1,000,000 square feet. Both buildings are also considered historic landmarks, presenting unique challenges to re-development.

Three key elements came into play when considering the adaptive reuse of these two buildings. These elements begin with the notion of flexible spaces, which result from "generic

FIGURE 13.1 1951 – historic exterior view of the May Company Department Store (called Broadway Building hereafter).
Source: USC Whittington Archive, public domain.

design." As these developments are essentially "shell-and-core" projects with no specific end user, spaces needed to be designed for a multitude of user scenarios, thus providing future operators with spaces that allow maximum customization. This is coupled with the notion of an "ego-less" design approach. In this approach, rather than the form of the building taking design precedence, the emphasis is on the use and attributes of the spaces created by the intersection of the building's historic and newly constructed architectural elements. Additionally, there is the idea of these buildings evolving as "culture hubs." That is to say, each of these buildings will have a distinct identity as the result of conscientious branding that will bring together, under one roof, like-minded users. This notion relies on the force of the collective in lieu of the force of the corporate.

13.3 The Broadway Building

The Broadway Trade Building is situated between Broadway, Hill, and 8th Streets in downtown Los Angeles. The building known originally as the "Great White Store" served as the flagship store for the May Company and was, at the time, the largest department store west of Chicago.

FIGURE 13.2 Historic exterior view of Sears Roebuck Distribution Center (called Sears Building hereafter).
Source: Los Angeles Public Library, public domain.

FIGURE 13.3 The Broadway Building main floor.
Source: Los Angeles Public Library, public domain.

FIGURE 13.4 The Broadway Building typical floor today.
Source: Authors.

Built in four phases beginning in 1908, the structure consists of concrete columns and slabs reaching a height of ten stories. Since the store's demise in the 1970s, the building has sat largely under-utilized and for the most part vacant with the exception of a swap meet on the ground floor.

Omgivning was tasked with transforming this former retail giant into a wholly new entity, i.e., an entity having multiple new functions and attributes different from the original building. The basement level is to be occupied by parking. The first floor is to house retail, multiple restaurants, a food hall, and a lobby/lounge/bar for a hotel located on upper floors. The second floor is to house retail as well as office spaces. The third, fourth, and fifth floors are to be used for office space for either single or multiple tenants. On the sixth floor will be a social club, restaurant, bar, gym, and hammam, i.e., Turkish spa. Levels seven through ten are to be occupied by a hotel. The roof of the seventh floor is to be programmed with expansive outdoor amenities accessible to the general public. Similarly, the roof of the tenth floor is to provide outdoor amenities operated by the hotel. Approximately half of the new roof bars/restaurants will be housed in existing, former mechanical penthouse structures.

A building that underwent a similar transformation is the Knappe Center in Michigan by Quinn Evans Architects. As with the Broadway Building, the Knappe Center began its life as a large department store. This large, historic structure, after its life as a retail center expired, was in turn converted into retail, offices, and residences.

The Broadway building's existing building envelope is in the Neoclassical style and adorned with elaborate entablatures and a heavy pediment. These elements are left chiefly untouched with the exception of work required for restoration and preservation.

FIGURE 13.5 Broadway Building existing penthouse.
Source: Authors.

The building's prominent orientation at the corner of Broadway and 8th Street makes it a key piece of the new restoration movement 'Bringing Back Broadway.' A key part of this movement is to re-establish the role of the pedestrian along Broadway, accomplished by removing a lane of traffic along the roadway and allowing buildings such as the Broadway Building to expand their reach out to the wider sidewalk. The building's flank will support a host of ground floor retail, catering to the re-created 'entertainment and commercial district.' Its Hill Street side will have a more residential feel, being occupied by a number of new restaurants, all with outdoor seating.

13.4 The Sears Building

While the Broadway Building traces its roots to upscale retail, the Sears Building has its beginnings as an industrial edifice. One of six Sears distribution centers in the United States, the building took its form over a period of 40 years, being constructed in nine distinct phases between 1927 and 1970. Aesthetically, it ranges from art deco to brutal industrial. Structurally, it is essentially ten separate buildings under a single roof.

Consisting of over 1,800,000 square feet of floor area and 13 stories in height, it has become an icon for the area surrounding downtown Los Angeles.

Unlike the Broadway Building that is situated along a redeveloping pedestrian corridor, the Sears Building sits amongst a district made up of tilt-up warehouses to the north and is flanked by housing and apartment buildings to the south. Through the proposed re-development/reuse it will become a neighborhood unto itself.

The ground floor of the Sears Building will consist of over 90,000 square feet of new retail, complemented by a food hall. Existing, abandoned freight loading railroad tracks will

FIGURE 13.6 Proposed rendering of exterior façade on Broadway and 8th Streets.
Source: Shimahara Illustration.

FIGURE 13.7 Proposed rendering of exterior façade on Hill and 8th Streets.
Source: Shimahara Illustration.

FIGURE 13.8 Photo of existing exterior of Sears Building.
Source: Hunter Kerhart.

FIGURE 13.9 Proposed rendering of central hub.
Source: Kilograph.

FIGURE 13.10 Photo of existing interior of typical floor of the Sears Building.
Source: Hunter Kerhart.

FIGURE 13.11 Photo of existing interior of tower at the Sears Building.
Source: Hunter Kerhart.

be used by 'pop up' operators in restored box cars, expanding the variety of dining experiences in this new neighborhood. The second and third floors will be occupied by over 200,000 square feet of office space, and 250,000 square feet will remain of the original Sears Store. This is in addition to the 1000+ residential units that will occupy the upper floors. In similar fashion to the Broadway Building, the roof top will be fully developed. Amenities will include two pools, a gym, theater, sports courts, and spa. The iconic tower element will house a restaurant/event space and one residential penthouse.

Two other examples of adaptive reuse include the Montgomery Park Center in Baltimore and the Ponce City Market in Atlanta. Both are completed and successful conversions that have preserved elements of their "shell" and created new "cores" of human activity. In the case of the Montgomery Park project, the old Montgomery Ward Center was converted to new office space. Likewise, the former Sears Building in Atlanta received new life as it now houses mixed uses apart from its original design.

13.5 Flexible design

The design approach to the renovation of the Broadway Building and the Sears Building is similar, in that the first design element taken into consideration is the notion of flexible spaces. Without knowledge of the future operators, the development of spaces had to consider a number of different possible functions and programs when laying out the interior space. In both projects, the ground floor is being programmed with restaurants, retail, and a large food hall made up of a number of vendors at one time, but the natural course will require a large host of revisions as the operators of each of these smaller spaces come into play. The third floors are to be set aside for office space, but again, this space may be carved into a number of small, medium, and large offices, or it may be occupied by one tenant. The upper floors are being laid out schematically as a hotel, however, due to lender restrictions, it is also being laid out and initially permitted as office space. This requires a heavily programmed use, like a hotel, to be conceptually worked out including mechanical, plumbing systems, kitchens, storage, etc., without guidance from an operator. The Broadway Building roof will house two pools, eight restaurant bars, an olive grove, event space, an urban farm, and a grassy knoll. These two roof spaces are designed and built as a "plug and play." This means all of the landscaping, railings, waterproofing, structural reinforcement, seismic upgrades, façade access cleaning systems, detailing, lighting, etc., are being designed, permitted, and constructed as a part of this first main building permit.

Whereas the city has processes in place for permitting shell and core spaces, they review the roof use as a new usable area in the building. As such, a 100% completed design at the roof level is required in order to evaluate all aspects of code compliance. The difficulty lies in the fact that the historic nature of the building requires that all penetrations and runs for mechanical or plumbing, etc., be directed up through the roof and they cannot traverse its façade. Therefore every square inch of the roof, while providing a large flexibility factor to the floors below, requires extensive detailing and lateral problem solving.

13.6 Ego-less design

As building systems are becoming increasingly complex and specialized, a non-specific design approach is more necessary. Likewise, as older buildings are transformed to perform new

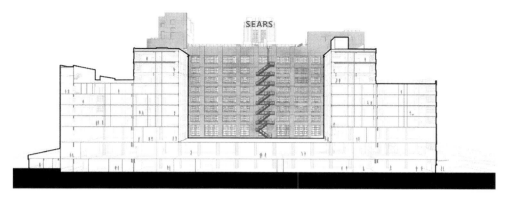

FIGURE 13.12 Proposed rendering of new lightcourt at the Sears Building.
Source: Author.

functions, the creation of the built object takes a back seat to the experiential quality of interior spaces. These two elements make up what is considered to be an "ego-less" design approach.

The Broadway Building and the Sears Building have over 20 design consultants each, ranging from the structural engineers to security consultants. The architect, now shifted from master designer to master manager, organizes and conducts meetings with the client and consultants, and ensures that the different consultants' drawings are permitted and coordinated for the 600+ large-format drawings.

The other aspect of "ego-less" architecture can be seen in the quality of the spaces that are created through the design process. The fascination with form is not present here as the form already exists as a framework for new design interventions. Examples of this notion can be found in both projects. New carvings into the building or "lightcourts," make dramatic cuts through the building shell, bringing natural daylight to the building's interior. They also break up the enormous mass of these buildings by connecting spaces horizontally and vertically. Through the restoration process of the building as a whole, the local, state, and national historic review agencies dictated certain conditions for the allowance of these lightcourts. The building was first built in nine phases, so the lightcourts were designed to tie into the hidden, original façades in order to restore them and bring them back into view.

In the Broadway Building, there are the three primary "lightcourts." While bringing daylight to the building's inner core, they also create visual connections throughout the building. They visually connect retail to office, restaurant to rooftop. In one lightcourt, a seven story concrete shear wall becomes the backdrop for large art installations and a point of reference in the building.

13.7 Culture hubs

In addition to the focus on flexible spaces and a turning away from form-based architecture, the design approach must emphasize the notion of a building as a "culture hub." That is to say, each building, through its approach to program and branding, will attract a certain and

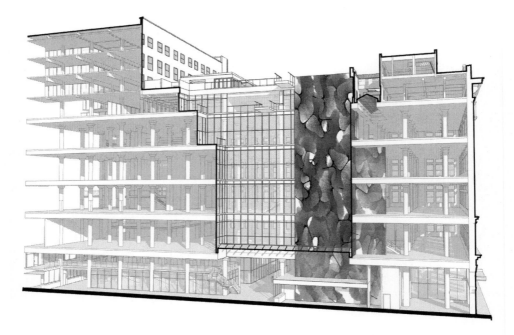

FIGURE 13.13 Proposed rendering of new lightcourt at Broadway Building.
Source: Authors.

desired sort of business and types of people to occupy its spaces. The specific culture of the building is initially conceived by the client/design team in conjunction with the building's form, its history, and the neighborhood context.

The Sears Building's new culture nods to the past and will become part of a new design district. The name of this new district will be "MOD" or Mail Order District, taken from the past days of Sears and Roebuck distributing their products through direct mail. The graphics and branding will tie visually to the postage stamps and brown packaging of this earlier era and its associated retro vibe of hard work, authenticity, and simplicity. It is to promote Sears today as a place where people meet face to face and interact in real time as opposed to doing so virtually through technology.

The Broadway Building's culture will guide one to a transcendental future. The cultural ideal here is to bring high-minded progressive people together to share and engage with each other to create new and better experiences, products, and most of all, ideas. This building aims to draw the crowd that wants to do more, do better, and do the next thing for our neighbors, for animals, and for our earth.

In these two cases, it is a culture that is decidedly urban, progressive, and sustainable. It is expressed by the programming and use within the building, the design elements, and of course the historic fabric and bones of the existing building.

With a desire to attract a certain kind of business, operator, and user of the building, the client puts the notion of the culture hub into play. It is then the focus of the architect to shape spaces of a certain variety and to likewise detail specific design elements of the building to attract this specific user group. This can be seen specifically in the use of the lightcourts, their

Omgivning **147**

FIGURE 13.14 Proposed rendering of partial roof amenities at the Broadway Building. *Source*: Shimahara Illustration.

detailing, and the manner in which they transform the building's inner spaces. It can likewise be seen in the way the roof amenities are organized to serve a particular variety of end user. The roofscapes are often the pinnacle of the project, complemented with amazing views and possible because of Los Angeles' temperate climate.

The Broadway Building's rooftops are alive with the humming energy of gathering, socializing, playing, and commerce. Each space is linked through a path of exploration to invite the users, most likely a visitor, to explore, connect, and engage with each other. Similarly, the Sears Building's rooftops mix private and public spaces, creating a physical social network amongst the building's inhabitants.

In addition to these elements already mentioned, the aspect of transforming each building's initial single use to that of multi-use is perhaps the most important. The buildings originally had single functions: one a large retail store, and the other a retail distribution center. Within this framework and while preserving the original historic fabric of the building, the structure is infused with a myriad of new functions. The existing elevations and details are to be restored. The floor plates, circulation systems, and cast-in-place-concrete structural system will remain largely intact and reused, only modified as required for the new functions of the building or as required to meet current code requirements.

13.8 Conclusion

Omgivning's approach to adaptive reuse projects in downtown LA comprises several aspects. As exhibited in the design and transformations of the Broadway Building and the Sears Building, these two projects embody the changing nature of the practice of architecture itself. The nature of the projects and the associated design approach thrust aside the creation of object and form and instead they focus on the end user's experience of a space; having to accommodate a series of functions into a building shell for which these uses were never intended. The architect's role as master designer has been transformed to that of master manager, being tasked with managing and coordinating an ever growing number of design consultants and technological systems. These new roles are coupled with a skill of navigating and a working knowledge of the myriad of local and federal codes and regulations that have to be accounted for in projects of this scale and type. As existing buildings continue to be reinvented to suit new needs it seems that the role of the architect as defined by Omgivning will become more and more the norm for the practice of architecture.

14

STRATEGIES FOR PLANNING, DESIGNING, AND OPERATING ADAPTABLE FACILITIES

John P. Petronis, Faye Whittemore, and Andy L. Aguilar

14.1 Introduction

As a private planning firm in Albuquerque, New Mexico with more than 40 years of experience, Architectural Research Consultants (ARC) has had many opportunities to observe and assist public-sector institutional clients to optimize facility use over a building lifecycle. This chapter explores strategies to promote adaptable facilities during each step in the facility delivery process (see Figure 14.1). Adaptable facilities in institutional settings accommodate the inevitable change in users and functions that occur during their long (50-plus year) lifespan. Facilities that are fit for purpose and fully utilized are also easier to justify and successfully compete for scarce capital and operating resources.

14.2 Use of planning standards to promote flexible collaborative work environments in the early facility planning phase

One strategy available to building owners to foster functional flexibility and adaptability in the early facility planning phase is to adopt broad standards that encourage space use flexibility throughout the life of the building. Owners and planners use these standards as a basis for allocating and assigning space during facility programming and design studies, as well as to benchmark existing space use. Space standards generally encourage more flexible, open work environments, and fewer private offices. The application of consistent space standards often results in an overall reduction of facility area required.

A powerful driver for adopting space standards is the effort by facility managers to more efficiently use existing space and reduce the need for new or leased space. In the past, many institutional space standards were based on a rigid hierarchical system of assigning space by personnel title, so that the higher an employee was in the organization, the more space and hard-walled privacy he or she was entitled to. More recently, space standards began shifting to a concept of assigning space according to "what you do" as opposed to "who you are." Many clients find that they can accommodate more staff in flexible, open workstation areas, rather than private offices.

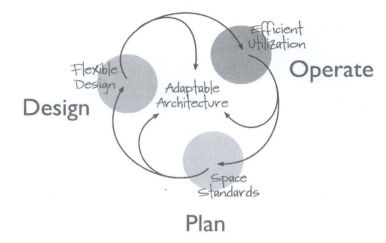

FIGURE 14.1 Strategies for planning, designing, and operating adaptable facilities.
Source: Authors.

The application of space standards also facilitates greater uniformity among workstations. Standardization of workstation types and infrastructure support, i.e., power, data, and mechanical, provides additional potential cost savings during initial installation, as well as future reconfigurations. As one client noted, with standardized workstations, employees only need to move "boxes and bottoms."

ARC recently worked with the State of New Mexico to update the State's space standards. The updated standards increase space flexibility and encourage innovation in work environments, including opportunities to work off-site. The revised standards include a simpler, more flexible way for state agencies to request and plan for leased or owned space. For example, agencies can use an expedited space request process if they stay within a maximum space target, e.g., 215 rentable square feet or 20 square meters per person. Alternatively, if agencies have specialized needs, they can use a more detailed process to justify them. The state landlord, i.e., General Services Department-Facilities Management Division, assists agencies in space planning using ARC's space standard guidance. Figure 14.2 graphically summarizes the State of New Mexico's space request process.

The State of New Mexico's and the State of Washington's space standards encourage open office workstations for most employees, with private hard-walled offices limited to a certain target percentage (30% in New Mexico and 10% in Washington) of total space and generally reserved for staff who regularly and consistently perform confidential work (see Figure 14.3).

New Mexico's space standards encourage meeting and collaborating in flexible common-use spaces outside of regular workstation areas. In addition to separate conference and collaboration rooms, other smaller areas—sometimes termed "huddle rooms"—provide opportunities for small meetings or respite from the hustle and bustle of the open office (see Figure 14.4). Huddle rooms may include technology to accommodate video conferencing and private conversations, and can function as transitional space for other uses as an organization's program requirements evolve.

Advances in technology have enabled employees to work from locations other than their desks. New Mexico Space Standards encourage agencies to consider alternative means

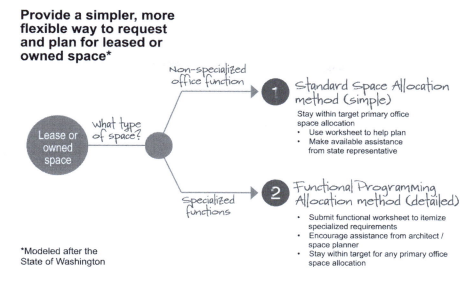

FIGURE 14.2 State of New Mexico's space request process. *Source*: Authors.

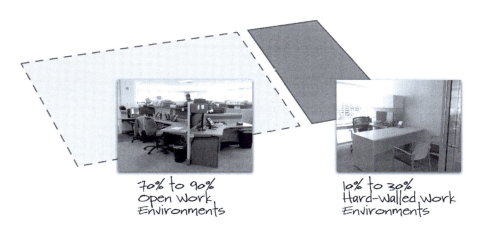

FIGURE 14.3 Open versus closed work environments. *Source*: Authors.

of working by providing more open, "hoteling" suites and fewer dedicated workstations. "Hoteling" workstations are flexible, unassigned stations that employees can occupy as needed. They make sense for employees who spend significant time working outside of the office and need only occasionally check in at the office, working at a hoteling space when they do so. Providing hoteling station options, rather than dedicated workstations, reduces facility operation and maintenance costs, and building mortgages or lease payments for only partially used space.

FIGURE 14.4 Huddle room.
Source: Authors.

While users often malign open work environments as a means to squeeze more people into less space for little money, this perception is, in ARC's experience, due to lack of proper planning and design. Adoption of space standard policies can promote good, creative solutions for providing healthy, collaborative, and flexible working arrangements. New Mexico State Space Standards provide good examples and web links to educate state agency users, and function as a source book for designers.

14.3 Incorporate building systems and configurations that support flexibility during the design phase

During the design phase of a project, the team can contribute to facility flexibility by incorporating layout configurations and building systems that support future modification. Starting with the building footprint, the floor-plate can be proportioned to allow natural light to penetrate most regularly occupied spaces. By placing hard-walled offices towards the interior, perimeter areas are available for open workstations. This gives open workstations access to natural light, views, and a generally more pleasant, healthy environment (see Figure 14.5). Where appropriate, interior windows and transparent walls can be incorporated to bring daylight and views to the interior spaces.

Architectural Research Consultants was part of the project team for a new office complex for a federal government client, which incorporated the strategies described above. The user groups include administrative functions and support teams including management, human resources, benefits, and medical/health services that are distributed across a large campus. Each building in the complex has a footprint that allows natural light to penetrate most areas

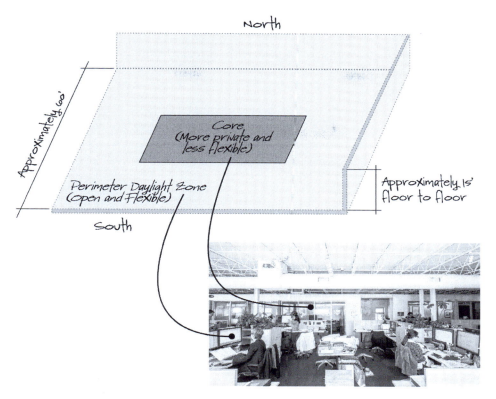

FIGURE 14.5 Conceptual diagram of a flexible floor-plate.
Source: Authors.

of the building, and locates hard-walled offices on the interior, and flexible, open offices on the perimeter. Applying efficient space standards and colocating common space, e.g., conference and training rooms, resulted in a 26% overall reduction in required space. Additionally, the design integrated sustainable design components reduce energy costs. As a result, the new office complex was projected to achieve operational cost savings for the client of over $7.3 million annually. Moreover, the new facilities will be flexible enough to accommodate a broad variety of users in the future.

Also during the design phase, the project team can select building structural systems to support flexibility. For example, long-span joist and beam systems that minimize columns and bearing walls are well suited for flexible, open office environments, and make future partition wall reconfigurations and utility pathway modifications more feasible and economical than bearing wall configurations. More generous floor to bottom-of-structure clearances allow for variations in ceiling heights and for future modifications to mechanical, electrical, and other building infrastructure to support different functions.

The Hartman + Majewski Design Group architects' renovation of their office headquarters in Albuquerque incorporates many planning and design strategies for adaptable buildings. Completed in 2010, the renovation renewed a 13,000 square foot building that was originally constructed in 1957 and housed a variety of functions, including professional offices, medical clinics, and, most recently, University of New Mexico graduate student architecture studios. The building's structural system includes steel beams and joists, exterior bearing walls, and interior columns. When the architects acquired the building, the interior had been partitioned into a maze-like configuration of small, dimly lit spaces with low ceilings.

The firm removed most of the existing interior partitions back to the columnar structural grid to open up space. The renovation removed the drop ceilings, which revealed the building's steel joists, metal decking, and generous floor-to-bottom of structure clearances. The architects left the building structure exposed to enable daylight to penetrate farther into the interior space.

Seeking to promote a flexible, collaborative environment for its employees, the firm created a centrally located open office area on the ground floor—arranged in four pods of four workstations—with central work tables. The open workstations are located to receive daylight from large, operable, south-facing windows with overhangs and translucent shades to control glare. Seven private offices and one huddle room line the west and north perimeter building walls. Because the architects limited new penetrations into the existing exterior masonry walls, the private offices have few exterior windows, but interior storefront walls "borrow" daylight from the open work environment (see Figures 14.6a and 14.6b).

Similar to the ground floor, the second floor also includes a daylit open area for six to eight workstations and three adjacent private offices with storefront interior walls. As the firm grows, it can expand into the upstairs leased office space.

The firm's headquarters also includes a large conference room that is used throughout the workweek for staff and large project team meetings, and available for after-hours use by community and neighborhood organizations.

14.4 Actively manage to achieve most efficient use during building operation

Even facilities that incorporate the most successful flexibility and adaptability strategies must have active management to achieve the most efficient use. Currently, planning of many sites and facilities focuses on accommodating peak user demands. For example, at colleges and universities, peak use of facilities ranges from 10 a.m. to 2 p.m. from Monday through Thursday, the most popular times for professors to teach and/or for students to take classes. At other times, facilities have significant unused capacity in many vacant instructional spaces. If use could be better distributed over the day and week, then fewer and smaller facilities would be necessary, with savings passed on to taxpayers and/or students.

In large, multisite institutions, understanding the details of current facilities use can be challenging. Architectural Research Consultants develops web-based tools to assist educational institutional clients to better understand the existing utilization and capacity of their facilities, and thereby optimize their use and plan for future needs.

Central New Mexico Community College (CNM) is the largest community college in New Mexico. The college enrolls about 24,900 students, as of fall 2015, and is comprised of seven campuses. Architectural Research Consultants used data from the college's 2012 fall and spring master class schedule—including course name, scheduled time, number of seats available and number filled—to analyze the utilization of every instructional space. ARC presented the results of the analysis graphically, using web-based software developed in-house. As Figure 14.7a shows, CNM's instructional spaces are almost 75% occupied on

FIGURES 14.6A AND 14.6B Photo/diagrams of a local architectural firm office.
Source: Authors.

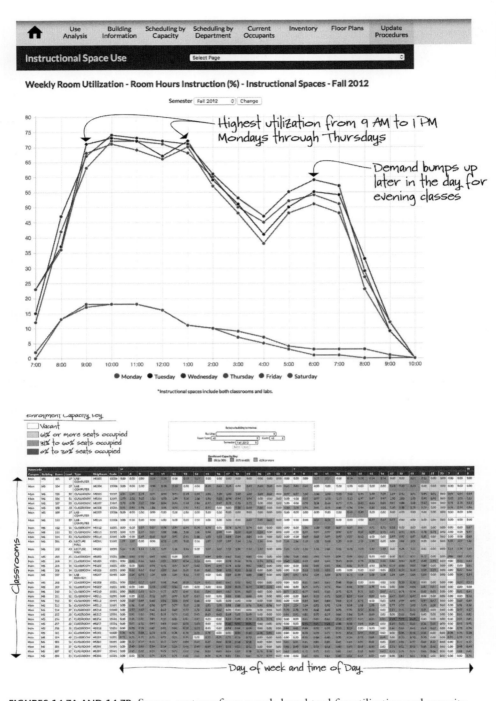

FIGURES 14.7A AND 14.7B Screen captures from a web-based tool for utilization and capacity analysis.
Source: Authors.

Mondays through Thursdays, from about 9 a.m. to 1 p.m. Instructional space utilization drops off quickly after 1 p.m., reaching a low of less than 50% occupancy by 4 p.m., and then picks back up for evening classes at 6 and 7 p.m. Figure 14.7b is a sample of a spreadsheet showing station occupancy, i.e., number of seats filled, by building and room. The analysis helps CNM understand occupancy and scheduling patterns, in order to optimize instructional space use and plan for future facilities improvements.

Joint-use facilities provide another strategy to improve utilization and decrease the amount of time that spaces are vacant. Primary schools provide a significant opportunity for joint use. These facilities are typically occupied from morning to late afternoon, and unoccupied during evenings and weekends. Through joint-use agreements, schools can increase their utilization and value to the community by providing public access to libraries, computer rooms, and recreational spaces after hours and on weekends. Joint use can be challenging for building owners and managers, as they require formal agreements, coordination of schedules, attention to safety and security of different types of uses, and other logistical details. As costs of building construction and ownership increase, however, we have seen increased application of joint-use facilities.

For example, San Juan College, a two-year community college located in Farmington, New Mexico provides joint-use facilities to offer college-level courses to high school students in partnership with the local school district, and upper division higher education with a number of other New Mexico universities.

Tierra Adentro of New Mexico (TANM) is another example of a high school that benefits from a joint-use agreement. Tierra Adentro of New Mexico is a charter public high school located in Albuquerque that emphasizes arts education, including Flamenco dance. The school leases dance studios during the day from its partner organization, the National Institute of Flamenco (NIF). In the evenings and on weekends, NIF conducts community dance lessons in the studios.

14.5 Conclusion

The economic context of the past several years has put pressure on public-sector building owners and managers to make better use of existing space and limit the amount of new area constructed. As a result, the public sector is adopting strategies in planning, design, and operation to increase building flexibility and adaptability—in effect to get better use out of less space. Successful strategies include the adoption of space standards during the design phase, incorporation of building configurations and systems to support flexibility in the design phase, and active management of space to increase utilization during building operation.

15

NATIVE MEETS HIGH-TECH: THE SOBOLEFF CENTER, SEALASKA HERITAGE CORPORATION

Zane M. Jones

15.1 Introduction

This chapter explores the effects of pairing Southeast Alaska Native art and architecture with contemporary design and construction practices in order to create a building that will fit within its current urban context and functions, serve future generations of Alaska Natives, and embody a rich Southeast Alaska Native historic past and present. It will discuss current cultural influences, location, and economy all within the realm of a multi-tasking space. The chapter will also outline how current construction technologies and digital design interface with Alaska Native art and architectural techniques and cultural spaces. It will analyze how Native materials and techniques create shapes and spaces that must merge with the site condition and local cultural challenges.

The case study will begin with cultural influences at the building scale and form, down to material detailing and fabrication. The chapter will argue that implications of multi-tasking design combined with Native design will reveal a symbiotic relationship that spans across time and culture. This relationship reveals how building materials used by Alaska Natives inform current and future art and architecture. Flexible multi-tasking design allows these Old World techniques to be continually re-thought within contemporary construction and design cultures. Noted architectural scholar of the North, Julie Decker, lays out these two forces driving design in the region, especially of the Soboleff Center.

> Long before the curious visitors and settlers migrated to inhabit the North, the indigenous people had learned to live in it. They understood survival in the North. More than that, native northerners knew how to thrive and develop rich cultures based on the place, maintaining a strong spiritual and physical connection to the landscape. (Decker, 2010a).

> But the North is growing and growing up and with it so is the architecture. Today, with either resident or invited architects creating more and more designs for buildings

at latitudes climbing above 60 degrees, an opportunity has arisen for a new definition of a northern building—one that is responsive to place and one that is, at the same time, aesthetically provocative. (Decker, 2010b).

Exploring the shapes and forms will reveal that not only do they meet the realities of the climate and culture they spawned from, they will set a precedent for design to adapt to the future culture and climate of Southeast Alaska. As MRV Architects were not the creators of the Native art, motifs and archetypes were borrowed with the guidance of Native design reviewers with a long history of design facilitation and understanding dating back to the founder of MRV Architects. Linn Forrest, who came to Alaska in 1938 to document Native villages for the U.S. Forest Service observed, "To many other Tlingit men and women who cooperated in the preparation of this account of their carvings, thanks are due, for it is their art and only they can explain it" (Garfield and Forrest, 1948).

15.2 Culturally adaptive architecture: reflecting the past and ushering the future

Completing the Sobeloff Center in the heart of downtown Juneau was a milestone accomplishment for the shifting social and cultural status of Native populations in Juneau and Alaska in general. The area's local Native people, the Tlingit, have a rich history of incorporating their distinct artwork into their dwellings and architecture. It is worth noting that similar regional tribes, the Haida and Tsmishain, share many common threads with the Tlingit, though they are distinct and different peoples; when referring to Southeast Alaska Natives in this chapter, the reference is to the Tlingit people.

FIGURE 15.1 Example of the Tlingit Naanyaa.aayí clan house known as the Chief Shakes House in Wrangell, Alaska.
Source: Linn Forrest image collection at Sealaska Heritage Institute.

One of the primary goals of building the Soboleff Center was to create a space to celebrate Alaskan Native heritage, to build from the past to create future heritage. Integrating an ancient art form into today's fast-paced construction practices and technologies proved to be a highly detailed task. Organizing the leading artists of the Tlingit community to have their and other Northwest Coast designs incorporated into the architectural detailing of a three dimensional building information model (BIM) challenged the notions of typical detailing and construction practices. The project looked to ancient Native construction techniques, specifically Northwest Coast longhouses built by Tlingit architects for thousands of years, and worked with a leading contractor and construction firm to translate those techniques into buildable details that fit within contemporary steel framing and high efficiency mechanical design. This combination of ancient and evolving ideas carried through to the construction practices and the cultural shifts happening in Juneau. The completed building stands today in the heart of downtown Juneau, representing a place in a new society that is shaped by an urban fabric and the natural world that still flourishes around Juneau. Not only is it a place where the Tlingit, Haida, and Tsimshian people can gather and have pride in their artistic and architectural heritage, it must also be supportive of a thriving business, the Sealaska Heritage Institute.

15.2.1 Contemporary construction in Alaska

When discussing the culturally adaptive aspects of the new design, the climate and technologies are a primary influencing factor. Likewise, the climate and environment of Southeast Alaska is arguably one of the strongest influences on local Native culture. Southeast Alaska is considered a temperate rainforest. This very specific climate dictates building design. With freezing temperatures and very few dry weather cycles, Southeast Alaska is a harsh climate for building materials and building occupants. For this reason, typically, well-insulated permanent dwellings have been an archetypal design form in the region. Recent research released by the Cold Climate Housing Research Center based out of Fairbanks, Alaska has strongly influenced current construction detailing. For example, controlling the location of the dew point on the exterior of the building is critical in the Southeast's environment. High humidity and precipitation combined with freezing temperatures require high insulation, breathability, waterproofing/rain-screening, and rot-resistant material. The Native longhouse in its simplest form addresses these issues. The current detailing in the Soboleff Center takes that logic a step further with today's technology.

15.2.2 Adapting contemporary construction technology to Alaska Native and architecture

Approaching the design from a space that seeks to incorporate historic ethno-technologies in longhouse construction, yet is able to be adaptive for the future, took the design out of the realm of typical contemporary construction practices. Disconnecting with typical industry standards was in a way connecting with what it meant to create a Native building. A statement by the Tlingit anthropological scholar, Thomas Thornton, highlights the influence that land and material have on the Native culture:

> A simple statement by Gabriel George, a middle-aged fisherman, particularly struck
> me. He said, "These lands are vital not only to our subsistence, but also to our sense of

being as Tlingit people." He did not elaborate on what he meant by that statement or by the phrase "sense of being," for it seemed self-evident to the mostly Tlingit audience (and painfully irrelevant to the professional planners assembled on behalf of the U.S. Forest Service). (Thornton, 2008).

The task, then, was both a sense of material, or, "being," that the building material and environment impose on the design. Instead of looking to leading products and the latest and greatest technology, the design team at MRV Architects looked to how the ancient practice of thick-cut yellow cedar could be added to a sealed envelope housing a contemporary high-efficiency mechanical system. Thick-cut yellow cedar planks, two inches or more, have incredible natural weathering properties. Yellow cedar is naturally anti-fungal, and is one of the slowest weathering local wood species. Existing Tlingit yellow cedar buildings had hundred-plus year lifespans. With this in mind, the design began to create a skin that would outlast the best metal panels on the market. The details aimed for a hundred-plus year lifespan. With this in mind, MRV treated yellow cedar like pre-fabricated metal panels, the best local technology. Metal panel construction, especially pre-fabricated insulated metal panel construction, is a common high-efficiency building technique in Alaska. Pre-made panels can be erected swiftly to enclose the building from the harsh Alaskan climate. In addition, extremely high construction costs make these pre-made panels cost effective from a labor perspective. The design team worked with the contractor to construct a variety of pre-fabricated panels up to three stories tall to be swung into place rapidly in order to enclose the building. Custom steel brackets received the panels, and the skin of the building was erected quickly.

15.2.3 Exterior skin

The exterior skin methods sought to use bands of glazing to accent the look of a Northwest Coast longhouse, and provided a contemporary feel while attempting to maintain the proportions of the Juneau historic district guidelines imposed on the design. Use of Northwest Coast formline designs within a "historic" district proved to be another daunting hurdle of the project. Like many cities, there is a history of racism in Juneau, which makes the location and architecture of the Soboleff Center a major triumph. Current local district historic guidelines required that the building keep the form of gold-rush and turn-of-the-century architecture up to the Second World War, which is mostly late Victorian to a few Art Deco buildings. After overcoming feelings of some conservatives in Juneau, compromises were made to "allow" Native formline and design elements in Juneau's historic district. In addition, city guidelines required a canopy around the perimeter to shelter pedestrians from the nearly constant rain—however, this was not an aspect of historic longhouses. Glass was chosen for this canopy requirement, as it has become an increasingly popular medium for Tlingit artists. Artists' designs were added to glass panels with etched Tlingit formline art. Light and shadow transfer the design to the walls and walk surrounding the building. The canopies and repetitive glazing are an echo of the urban fabric of Juneau, yet also have a unique Native feel with the added artwork.

Tlingit clan houses and individual houses were built of timber and adorned with large works of art externally.

FIGURE 15.2 Soboleff Center context view.
Source: Ken Graham Photography.

> Houses were raised from cedar posts capped by beams that weighed in excess of two or three tons each … The unpainted cedar siding weathered quickly to a silver grey and was never painted. An exception arose among the leading families of some villages who painted family crest designs in bold earth colors on their house fronts. (Malin, 1986).

This art typically consisted of totem poles, house screens, and painted formline. With the hundred-plus year lifespan on the building exterior, MRV aimed for weather-resistant art to be applied to the panels. Large cut metal panels were applied to the exterior of the building very much like the historic artwork that was carved or etched into the Tlingit buildings of the past.

Most notable on the design are the very large art panels applied on either side of the entry, typical of many Tlingit houses. These panels are the icons of the building, representing and describing its character and meaning to the owners.

> Visitors will first see huge, 40-foot panels on the exterior designed by the internationally celebrated Haida artist Robert Davidson. The design represents a supernatural being called the "Greatest Echo"—a theme chosen by Davidson because Dr. Walter Soboleff, the building's namesake, echoed the past to bring it to the present. (Sealaska Heritage Institute website, 2016)

The smaller detailing on the exterior took the form of weathering copper accents, another common material used by Tlingit artists. "Depicting coppers on carved columns was a

FIGURE 15.3 Soboleff Center entrance view.
Source: Ken Graham Photography.

widespread practice and reveals how old and entrenched the concept of wealth was within the culture" (Malin, 1986). Entries became a layering of materials and forms, which creates a dynamic welcome, much like the adorned entries of traditional longhouses.

15.2.4 Interior design

The interior design incorporated Native art and its place in a modern office setting. The building design was a complex mix of a museum and library area, visitor center and lecture hall, office, and admin space, along with lease space that could be used for any future expansion. The first floor is open to the public, with an emphasis on Native culture and education. The form of almost literally a clan house was added to the interior of the main floor. This required the structure to adapt to the form of a clan house, and acoustics were taken into consideration since the clan house is used as a performance space. Native materials like adzed cedar were specified and ordered much like long lead-time items because of their hand-crafted nature. Hand adzed cedar beams and panels were added throughout the clan house portion of the design, which added detail, texture, and the feeling of art created by hand. This technique of hand-swung adzing originally applied a resistant finish to add durability to the products. Some scholars are researching this ethno-technology and preliminary findings indicate that that adzing crushed and folded the wood fibers at a micro-level, making the wood more water resistant—a method that was both functional and aesthetic. Adzed planking has been left untreated, and is rated to last well into the future. The design of the center required that each piece of lumber had to be hand adzed after custom lumber mill cuts from regional forests. This is apparent from the Sealaska Heritage Institute's description of the interior adzing:

> The interior of the building is planked in cedar, which was hand-adzed by the Tlingit master artist Wayne Price. Adzing produces a texture that is commonly seen in Northwest Coast art, canoes, clan houses, and ceremonial objects. Price adzed almost every day for five months … At the end of the project he had made nearly one million adze marks on more than 3,200 square feet of wood! (Sealaska Heritage Institute website, 2016).

This process and design added a unique "hand-made" heritage to the building. In addition to this material and natural treatment, the cedar gives off a noticeable fragrance. Immediately it smells different than a typical building. Likewise, sound has been incorporated into the interior, with subtle audio of local birds and sounds from the forest playing over the audio system, deepening the sensory connection to the outdoors.

Many other materials also echoed the past while using contemporary techniques. Another example is the hand-selected marble tiles from Prince of Whales Island near Juneau, which were made for a portion of the flooring. These are filled with ancient fossils, which represent a connection to the outside, natural world that is so important to the Native culture. Native ethno-technologies and art forms are meaningful and vibrant. Expressions of glass and copper helped to give them a industrial/corporate feel. "A traditional clan house would have included a wooden house screen with posts on one side, but—in a nod to the modern world—we have rendered them in glass" (Sealaska Heritage Institute website, 2016). The clan house was fitted with projection screens, lighting, and sound systems for dance and ceremonies. The clan house thankfully provided excellent acoustics, as well as heavy timber

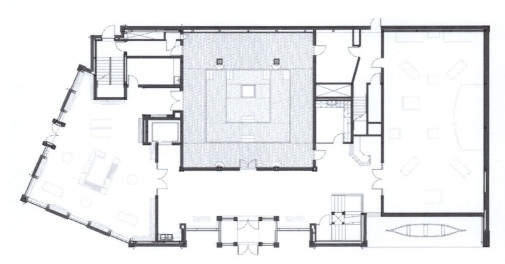

FIGURE 15.4 Soboleff Center floor plan 1.
Source: Author.

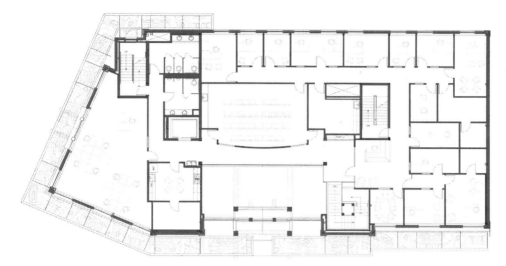

FIGURE 15.5 Soboleff Center floor plan 2.
Source: Author.

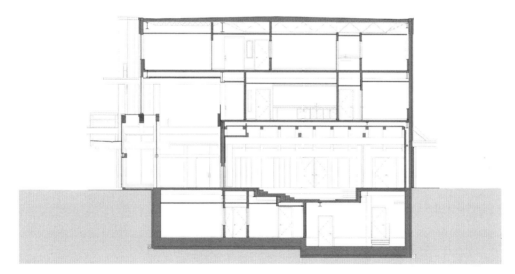

FIGURE 15.6 Soboleff Center section 1.
Source: Author.

fire ratings to code. Using the old-style construction proved to be compatible with, if not enhancing of, some of the best contemporary technologies.

15.3 Multi-tasking spaces: ancient culture in current business

While the building is mostly static, the activities inside that the design and users promote are not. The building is a snapshot of where NWC architecture has been and where it is

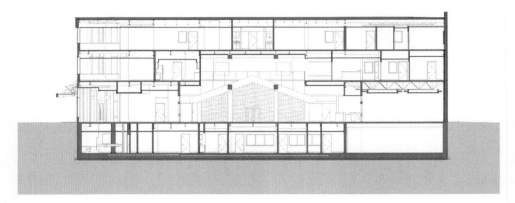

FIGURE 15.7 Soboleff Center section 2.
Source: Author.

going. The initial design planning, eventual detailing, and architectural design successfully paired NWC architecture and design with current urban business in downtown Juneau. The upper floors of the building serve as flexible lease spaces for business use, though the entry and circulation to those spaces moves through a clearly Native Alaskan work of architecture.

15.4 Conclusion

With a mission to make buildings "nurturing places for social and cultural designers," the Soboleff Center attempts to pave the way for socially concerned designers. The building itself nurtures budding Native designers, and those looking to create more pieces of NWC architecture. Carvers and artists work on site, showing not only their art to the public, but the actual process and craft of carving and creating the art that for so long shaped their communities. Ethno-technologies were sought out and applied through skilled craftsmen. Many of these craftsmen were influential on the building itself, and now they continue to inform future Native design, thus building on the movement. During the summer months, and tourist season, an outdoor caving area inset into the building just off the sidewalk shelters one or two carvers. The fresh smell of yellow and red cedar permeates the air around these carvers as they continue to practice their art.

> Socially concerned, environmentally savvy design is now a full-fledged movement. It has been codified and documented in such books as *Design Like You Give A Damn* (Stohr and Sinclair, 2006), *Expanding Architecture: Design as Activism* (Bell and Wakeford, 2008), and *Design Revolution* (Pilloton, 2009). (Szenasy, 2011)

The Soboleff Center is an example of what a piece of architecture can represent, while simultaneously nurturing places for social and cultural designers.

15.5 Bibliography

Bell, B. and K. Wakeford (2008). *Expanding Architecture: Design as Activism*. New York: Metropolis Books.

Decker, J. (2010a). *Modern North: Architecture On The Frozen Edge*. New York: Princeton Architectural Press.

Decker, J. (2010b). *True North: New Alaskan Architecture*. New York: Princeton Architectural Press.

Garfield, V. and L. Forrest (1948) *The Wolf and the Raven*. Seattle: University of Washington Press.

Malin, E. (1986). *Totem Poles of the Pacific Northwest Coast*. Portland: Timber Press.

Pilloton, E. (2009). *Design Revolution: 100 Products That Empower People*. New York: Metropolis Books.

Sealaska Heritage Institute website: August 2016. www.sealaskaheritage.org/true-southeast. Accessed March 23, 2017.

Stohr, K. and C. Sinclair (2006). *Design Like You Give a Damn: Architectural Responses to Humanitarian Crises*. New York: Metropolis Books.

Szenasy, S. (2011). "Toward Social, Economic, and Environmental Sustainability." *Universal Design Handbook*. Eds. W. F. E. Preiser and K. H. Smith. New York: McGraw-Hill.

Thornton, T. F. (2008). *Being and Place among the Tlingit*. Seattle: University of Washington Press.

16

BUILDING WITH BOXES: THE NEW JERUSALEM CHILDREN'S HOME

Mia L. C. Anfield

16.1 Introduction

This chapter will explore the design and construction process of the new "green" house for the New Jerusalem Children's Home, a non-profit organization situated in Johannesburg, South Africa. It will explain how New Jerusalem's vision affected the project: "To be one of the best children's homes in sustainable living, and in the provision of holistic and integrated quality care to orphaned, abused, traumatized, HIV positive, and vulnerable children in Africa" (New Jerusalem Children's Home, 2016). From the initial decision, the intent was to construct the house using recycled shipping containers and, where possible, recycled and repurposed materials. This chapter outlines the difficult task that 4d and a architects had in persuading the client to accommodate vulnerable children in the shipping containers, as they largely resemble the many shacks made of steel sheeting which still house the very poor in so-called "townships," i.e., the informal settlements, a legacy of the apartheid era. This chapter will also explore the design process of the project, including the building's sustainability features and the various materials used to complete the building. Lastly, it will touch on the affect that the building has on the perceptions and lives of the many children living in it.

16.2 The South African context

The client, non-profit organization "New Jerusalem Children's Home," always had a vision to become a leader in the provision of holistic and integrated quality care for orphaned, abused, traumatized, and vulnerable children. All of the children come from broken homes, with either a history of alcohol or drug abuse, deceased parents, or previous families that are homeless. They come from both the informal settlements and communities in the area (see Figure 16.1). New Jerusalem Children's Home owns the roughly 25 hectare site, housing and caring for up to 80 children at any one time. The children are placed in the home by social workers from birth up to the age of 18.

FIGURE 16.1 Typical informal housing.
Source: Caitlin Blaser Mapitsa

16.3 The brief, concept, and design process

The brief given was for the design of a low-budget, self-contained building to house 24 of the 80 children living at the New Jerusalem Children's Home, with the aim of building a further two houses in the future to house the remainder of the children once sufficient funds had been raised. At the commencement of the project, the children lived in dilapidated and cramped traditional brick buildings, which were the main buildings on the site. The original buildings, with various ad-hoc structures added on, were no longer sufficient or suitable to provide the space and services needed for these children.

Both intimate and public spaces were required for sleeping, eating, washing, relaxing, and studying. An important aspect of the project is that the New Jerusalem Children's Home is committed to achieving an environmentally sustainable framework in everything they do. Another focus of the home was that the client wanted to reduce their carbon footprint, making it vital that 4d and a architects re-used and recycled wherever possible.

4d and a architects wanted the house to be as "green" as possible, and the main driving force for this was the use of recycled shipping containers, giving them a second lease on life. The inspiration for this originated from 4d and a architects' long-time interest in the various designs of residential container units by the American architect Adam Kalkin. Contact was made with Adam and after the aim of the project was explained to him, he very kindly flew to Johannesburg during the initial design phase to give advice and valuable input. With that, the design for the children's home commenced, and the coordination and collaboration with the client began (see Figure 16.2).

FIGURE 16.2 Container House by Adam Kalkin.
Source: www.inzombie.com (accessed March 23, 2017).

16.4 Persuading the client

The proposal of putting vulnerable children in recycled shipping containers typically used on construction sites as site offices or storage for building materials was initially rejected.

Considering this, the design team employed the aid of a company to produce 3D images of the proposed building to present to the board, as the client struggled to understand what the design was trying to achieve solely based on the plans and other drawings. It was only after the presentation of these 3D images to the board that 4d and a architects received approval for the design (see Figure 16.3).

16.5 The design

The design uses 28 recycled shipping containers, of 6 m (20 ft) and 12 m (40 ft). The building has an area of 550 m^2 (5920 sq ft) and adjoins a refurbished brick structure. It includes a large open communal living room, made up of three high cube containers, providing the dining area, kitchen, homework/computer area, male and female ablution facilities, four to eight private bedrooms, two private living units for the housemothers, first floor balconies, and access to an outside patio and a large garden. The neutral cream-colored interior allows for the use of brightly colored bedding and furniture. The whole space is therefore light and airy, in contrast with the original enclosed shipping containers. It is not a hidden fact that the structure is made of shipping containers, which is an important aspect of the project to the design team. Due to the repetitive building-block nature of the containers, they are positioned adjacent to and on top of each other in such a way that the building is well modulated, i.e., alternating between solid and transparent, utilizing a variety of materials, for a universally playful appeal.

FIGURE 16.3 3D image generated for a client presentation.
Source: 3D ImageWorks.

In regards to the overall site, the new container building's position allows for the incorporation of an existing brick structure. This renovated structure is used as a kitchen and dining area for the house. The re-use of this existing space and the incorporation of it into the new structure reemphasize the idea of reusing materials and spaces. The containers are orientated to provide visual and physical connections to the surrounding garden (see Figures 16.4 and 16.5).

16.6 The construction

Stemming from the goal of keeping this project environmentally sustainable, there is minimal disturbance of the original site. The only wet-work required on the site prior to the delivery of the containers was the construction of numerous 600 mm × 600 mm × 800 mm (1.96 ft × 1.96 ft × 2.62 ft) deep steel reinforced concrete plinths to support each corner of the containers, thereby minimizing site disruption. At a later stage, these concrete plinths were covered in brightly colored mosaics, using donated ceramic tiles. These were broken up and put together into various fun designs by volunteers, including many schoolchildren (see Figure 16.6).

The containers were pre-painted, the openings for the various doors and windows were pre-framed, and the first fix plumbing happened at the container depot. They were then delivered to site on large trucks, over a period of a few days, and then positioned onto the already cast concrete plinths using a crane, reminiscent of a large game of Tetris.

The containers were stacked next to and on top of one another. They were welded together and then the entire top of the containers were waterproofed to prevent water penetration. The remainder of the construction process took place on site – i.e., installation of the doors and windows, insulated ceiling and wall cladding, floor finishes, plumbing, light

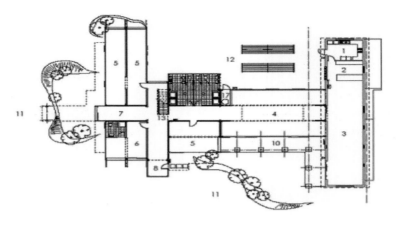

GROUND FLOOR PLAN

1. Scullery
2. Kitchen
3. Communal Dining Room
4. Communal Lounge/TV Room
5. Children's Bedroom
6. Housemother's Living Unit
7. Communal Homework/Computer Area
8. Main Entrance Lobby/Tower
9. Communal Ablution Facilities
10. Covered Patio
11. Garden
12. Washing Yard

FIGURE 16.4 Architectural ground floor plan.
Source: Author.

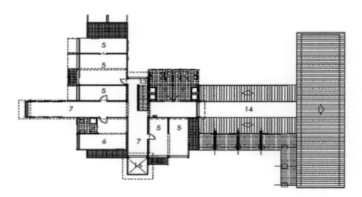

FIRST FLOOR PLAN

1. Scullery
2. Kitchen
3. Communal Dining Room
4. Communal Lounge/TV Room
5. Children's Bedroom
6. Housemother's Living Unit
7. Communal Homework/Computer Area
8. Main Entrance Lobby/Tower
9. Communal Ablution Facilities
10. Covered Patio
11. Garden
12. Washing Yard

FIGURE 16.5 Architectural first floor plan.
Source: Author.

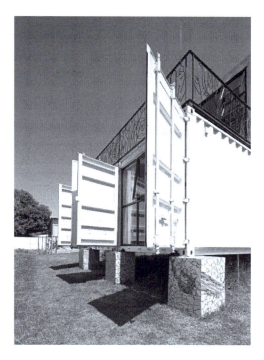

FIGURE 16.6 Mosaics were used to decorate the concrete plinths supporting the containers
Source: Dennis Guichard on behalf of Safintra SA.

fittings, and electrical. This process occurred in the same way as would happen on a standard brick and mortar building.

The whole construction process took six months. Typically, this period would have been quicker, but in this case, construction was delayed slightly due to the nature of the project depending on the donation of funds and materials and/or certain installations being done at cost. It was amazing to see how many companies and individuals contributed to the project.

16.7 Sustainability and recycling

Throughout the design process, emphasis was placed on the project being environmentally friendly. It was vital that the use of environmentally responsible products and the reuse of materials was adhered to. A major priority was given to the reuse of materials in a creative way to be sustainable and to keep the project's budget within the means of the NGO. An example of this was the repurposing of the vinyl material used on large signage boards into individual, fun, colored shower curtains in the communal bathrooms.

Special consideration was given to the building's thermal performance to ensure comfort in the hot summers and cold winters of Gauteng (a province in South Africa), and to reduce the building's energy usage. Both the walls and ceilings of the containers were clad internally where required with skimmed gypsum boards on a galvanized steel sub-frame, with the cavity filled with an environmentally friendly, non-allergenic polyester insulating product made from recycled PET bottles. The original timber floors were sanded and sealed. They were left exposed in the main circulation areas, with repurposed carpet tiles from office refurbishments and donated vinyl sheeting used elsewhere. Large powder coated aluminum doors and windows were installed between the steel framed openings, with opening sections for natural ventilation. These were positioned in such a way to maximize natural light without excessive heat gain. Horizontal and vertical sunscreens, made from eco-friendly composite decking planks on a steel sub-frame, were utilized to help reduce direct sun penetration.

The design features both passive and natural environmental controls. Lifting the containers on concrete plinths and floating the insulated roof above the tops of the containers, natural airflow surrounds the volume, helping to keep the interiors cool. Heating, where required in winter, has been introduced by the use of energy-efficient infrared heaters. A 3 kW single-phase photovoltaic system with back-up batteries, donated by the Dutch division of Lidl, was also installed, to supply electricity for the energy-efficient LED lighting.

The design did not stop with its concerns for energy usage as water use was also a design factor. The reduction of water usage was achieved by the installation of water-saving taps and showerheads. A domestic effluence system was used to convert all suitable effluent into environmentally safe water for irrigation of the large permaculture gardens, where the children grow their own vegetables. A 500 liter (132 gallon) solar tank system was installed to provide the hot water, donated by "Sonnenkraft SA", with a heat-pump back-up system.

16.8 The children

The unique approach to environmentally friendly construction is also an opportunity to educate the children within the building about waste, energy, and creative design. The children are more conscious of the need to reduce, reuse, and recycle, and are making increasing

FIGURE 16.7 Two of the children of the New Jerusalem Children's Home.
Source: Author.

FIGURE 16.8 The completed house.
Source: Dennis Guichard on behalf of Safintra SA.

efforts in this regard. To increase their understanding of environmental issues and to inspire them to initiate and implement environmental projects at the home, four of the children even attended the TUNZA International Children's Conference on the Environment which was held in Rio De Janeiro, 2012. The children, as part of their effort to commit to recycling, separate all inorganic waste on site for collection.

How does one measure the success of an architectural project of this nature? Feedback from the children, the housemothers, and even their schoolteachers is very positive. Before the construction of this building the children shared everything, had no personal possessions, and no personal space. Now they have their own beds, wall space on which to hang pictures, and a cupboard where they can securely keep their own clothes and possessions.

Orphanage co-founder Anna Mojapelo agrees:

> Since the children moved into this house, their self-esteem has increased. Now they have their own personal space, they are free to dream their dreams. They are friendlier, they participate more in daily tasks, and they are starting to take care of the environment. They see the world in a different light. (Taylor, 2012)

16.9 Conclusion

This project revolutionized how South Africans see shipping containers: the old ones are most often recycled individually into local spaza shops or used as site offices/stores on construction sites. What this building achieved is not only provision of a unique, fun, and spacious building for the children but it also raised the profile of the home, which is critical to ensure a continuation of monetary donations to keep it running. It has also raised awareness of the use of "green" technology and the use and adaptation of different materials. By adapting and reusing something as "modular" or "box-like" as a shipping container, a culturally appropriate solution can be derived from a low acquisition cost and a bit of persuasion, resulting in a piece of architecture that has both timeless simplicity and beauty. When a local newspaper published an article about the new facility, one of the young children living in the house cut it out, stuck it up on her cupboard, and in her own hand wrote: "My lovely home, 5 star hotel."

"Building with Boxes" is the epitome of how adaptability influences architecture today.

16.10 Acknowledgements

"4d and a architects" were runners up in the residential category at the 2013 "eta energy efficiency awards" sponsored by Eskom (the South African electricity public utility) for their New Jerusalem Children's Home Container House. This was due to the success of the design, the use of sustainable materials, and technologies to reduce the building's energy consumption requirements.

16.11 References

New Jerusalem Children's Home (2016). Accessed March 23, 2017, from http://newjerusalemchildrenshome.org/about/.
Taylor, S. (2012). "A place called home." *Earthworks,* issue 8, June/July.

REFLECTIONS ON PART IV

Michael J. Crosbie, Ph.D., FAIA

"Tradition and connection promoting adaptability"

Adaptable architecture at the scale of the building allows architects, designers, and environmental scientists to work on a multitude of levels: interiors, the building envelope, the exterior, the way the building impacts the site, and (particularly in urban contexts) how the project connects with its immediate neighborhood. Part IV provides a well-rounded range of building case studies: purpose-built new construction, adapting existing buildings to new functions, sustainable projects with an accent on recycling, design and construction with an emphasis on responding to indigenous existing cultures, and the application of broad planning principles for adaptability.

The role of POE is particularly strong in the case study of the Keren Or Jerusalem Center for Blind Children with Multiple Disabilities. Authors Preiser and Wilhelm explain the process of working closely with the design architect and the client to develop design and planning guidelines and performance criteria for the variety of spaces. Examining precedents was a priority in formulating the criteria, as were interviews with staff and reviewing POEs of similar kinds of facilities for the blind. After construction was completed, POEs of the facility were carried out on a regular basis (the first one took place on the building's opening day!). This represents a closed loop of research, application, and feedback. Subsequent POEs occurred one and three years after opening, resulting in further post-construction design recommendations. This casts the design process in a new light: rather than coming to a stop at construction, design can continue to evolve during the building's life, informing its future performance. New findings can also have an impact on the design of other facilities around the world. The key is to translate the building's embodied knowledge into research for application.

Echoing Preiser's and Wilhelm's emphasis on formulating performance criteria, ARC argues that achieving adaptability in the design of new facilities requires one to think of spaces as multi-use from the day the building is completed. They urge designing spaces from the start for multiple, flexible uses, based on broad guidelines. In offices, for instance, open space planning provides this kind of flexibility, but it requires the right corporate culture to support it. The trend in today's office design is to assign space calibrated to the task to be performed rather than the person's rank in the organization. Certain work activities can take place off site, which can have a huge impact on office design, with a combination of collaborative team rooms along with open offices. "Hoteling" allows employees to temporarily work in spaces not assigned to them. Such flexibility is supported by generous amounts of natural light and views throughout the office. Building structure also has an impact: long spans obviously contribute to plan flexibility by avoiding repetitive columns. Such beefy structure is what makes old mill buildings in places like New England so valuable today as flexible "maker" spaces. Tracking space use is a design strategy that can help a client get the most flexibility out of existing space that might not be utilized at the same intensity throughout the day, permitting spaces to "multi-task" just as people do. Joint use is also helpful, and a growing trend in inner-city religious congregations is to share their space with potential neighborhood users during the week.

An ambitious revival of two downtown Los Angeles buildings from the early 20th century shows how adaptability can be extended through restoration, preservation, and reuse. Liljegren and Kish make a strong argument that the greenest project is one that takes a building that already exists and adapts it for new life. In the case of both the 1908 Broadway Trade Building and the 1927–1965 Sears Roebuck Distribution Center, the architects describe their "ego-less" design approach as focused on creating interiors that are to be experienced and used, rather than form-making for its own sake. Both these buildings were originally built for single uses—Broadway was a department store and Sears a vast distribution warehouse of nearly 2 million square feet. They are being transformed into mixed-use projects of intense variety: parking, retail, food, hotel, offices, gyms, housing, entertainment, green space, and recreation. These projects are essentially vertical neighborhoods. Particularly interesting for Broadway is how the adjacent sidewalk was widened to encourage street life along the building's edge (certainly a new direction for LA, not known as a pedestrian-friendly city). These projects tap into a trend of urban revivals in neighborhoods that have "good bones," such as these two buildings, and also the reuse of abandoned infrastructure (think of the High Line in New York City). Both Broadway and Sears have fully populated green roofs, enlivening the building's "fifth façade" and getting more value out of these multi-use projects by creating "culture hubs" that give their neighborhoods identity.

Another way to "re-use" history is to mine cultural identity and building tradition in creating new flexible buildings. Jones' case study of the Sobeloff Center in Alaska tells the story of how Native American multi-tasking space and art traditions were incorporated into a new cultural center and museum. The choice of thick-cut yellow cedar planks for cladding not only connected with traditional Native American building practices but increased the building's potential longevity because of the material's superior performance in this harsh climate. The designers developed a prefabricated metal panel clad with cedar planks, which simplified construction. The cultural center's ground floor contains program spaces while the second floor was designed to be leased, flexible office space. The architecture's use of tradition, rendered in a contemporary way, gives this building a close connection to indigenous people and their lives.

A very similar tie between local people and architecture was achieved in a new home for destitute children in South Africa, built with recycled shipping containers. Anfield reports that sustainability was valued by the client and was a key factor in the design. Recycling shipping containers to create the new building was a sustainable solution (the project also re-used an existing brick building on the site). In this project, sustainability extends beyond the building itself, to educating the young residents about sustainability as a way of living. The architectural quality of the building and its sustainable features contribute to the self-esteem of the children, and have raised local awareness to the potential of shipping containers as a sustainable choice.

All of these case studies in one way or another tie into the local context, making each of the solutions carefully calibrated to the needs to the users, the role of the building in the neighborhood, and the potential for the building to ' teach" about adaptability and reuse. The lessons here are that buildings can be adapted in different ways, such as understanding their multi-use possibilities during design; exploring how material choices can make buildings adaptable by users responding to those materials in different ways; and how large elements of a building can be adapted from some other use, such as the shipping container example. The POE is one tool that permits us to test this adaptability at a range of scales and functions, and validates the design decisions of space programming, material choice, and building identity.

PART V
Urban scale

Preamble

Andrea E. Hardy

Addressing adaptive architecture at a larger scale, Part V demonstrates the reuse of large infrastructure and multi-building campuses. These five chapters cover the potential of public urban infrastructure such as alleyways, the repurposing of campus environments such as airports and army barracks, the collaboration of multiple government departments to create an interdisciplinary campus, and lastly, the use of building information modeling (BIM) to connect people, professionals, and buildings on an equal, if not larger, scale.

In Chapter 17, the focus is on an existing, underutilized infrastructure and its possibilities for reuse and revitalization. Through the exploration of existing research on public spaces, it is discovered that alleyways hold the scale, connectivity, and resources needed to generate an activated public space. Several case studies are provided at the end of the chapter demonstrating existing uses of the theories discussed throughout the chapter.

Rath and Hodulak, in Chapter 18, discuss the use and process of integrative planning. The chapter uses the example of the Otto-Lilienthal TXL Airport in Germany, specifically that of Terminal A, by outlining how it is planned to be reused as a higher education research facility, to exhibit how dated infrastructure can have a second life for new users. While reviewing the building life cycle of the TXL Airport, the authors explain a holistic approach to adaptive architecture, which is an integrative planning process implemented in the early stages of building delivery.

Similarly, in Chapter 19, Schramm showcases adaptive reuse of a Prussian Artillery Barrack complex as it evolved from its original conception to its current use. Through outlining the building's original use, transformation into an educational center, and its growth from there, Schramm discusses the goals, successes, and failures of the complex's evolution as a result of the programming and planning process. This chapter not only identifies the adaptability of a historical complex but also the importance of involving all building users in the design process, including students.

Murray's chapter, Chapter 20, provides the unique example of an urban municipality project in Gartcosh, Scotland. His project, at Ryder Architects, shows the development of a multi-department complex through the collaboration of multiple government agencies. Each stage in the design, construction, and occupancy process focused on interdisciplinary interaction to help government agencies adapt to the idea of collaboration in a more technology based age.

Focusing further on the impact of technology on the built environment, in Chapter 21, Kato, Mori, and Taniguchi talk about the use of building information modeling (BIM) within the field of design and construction. By implementing BIM at the beginning of the project, they discuss its influences on planning, programming, design, and construction. The chapter concludes with an example of BIM used for a Pediatric Intensive Care Unit with specific examples on how it influenced the authors' design, construction, and building commissioning phases of their project.

17

REAPPROPRIATION OF CITY INFRASTRUCTURE: ALLEYWAYS

Andrea E. Hardy

17.1 Introduction

The dark, dirty, and unsafe characterization that many associate with American alleyways today is a stark contrast from historical understandings of these in-between spaces. The term alleyway has multiple meanings and definitions worldwide. Some common translations include small streets, lines of trees or shrubs within the landscape, and less traveled "back-roads" typically planned for utilities, such as trash pick-up. This chapter focuses on the latter of these uses: the reuse of alleys planned for utilities and narrow passageways, and how to embrace them as new sites for design and culture.

After briefly outlining the historical development and uses of alleyways from around the world and in the US, adaptability will be evaluated through public space theories and three examples of repurposed alleys. Case-study examples are given to promote the education of environmental issues, highlight local culture, and demonstrate opportunities for micro-housing. The City of Chicago, Illinois, is redeveloping alleys with sustainable materials to assist in the reduction of Urban Heat Island effects, i.e., the collection of heat within the built environment during the day that increases the average temperature of the surrounding area even at night, a problem that affects many cities around the US and worldwide. In contrast to the technical revisions of Chicago's alleys, the city of Phoenix, Arizona, is becoming known for its display of cultural murals in the urban infrastructure. The last example of this chapter considers the development of micro-housing within narrow alleys, citing the Sliver House by Boyarsky Murphy Architects in London. With the current movement of tiny houses, alleys provide the perfect space for small structures, if permitted by local zoning and planning departments.

17.2 Past approaches: historical uses of alleyways

The term itself comes from the French word "allee," which refers to lined landscaped pathways with trees to shield views into private gardens. Trees were needed because walkable pathways were frequently traveled by people, as cars were not yet in the picture. Alleys have existed for the past 2000 years – as their existence predates this terminology. The concept of an alley, more recently defined as a narrow passageway, can be referenced back to the layout of medieval towns. Structures were built close to one another and housed both business and living spaces. Folks who lived in these work/live structures would also set up shop just outside their homes to sell goods. The fact that both business and living were off of the same passageway meant that it was constantly being traveled, and, as such, was an interactive space (Zeidler, 1983). Structures were built and organized by the citizens of the towns and cities, not planners, so they directly related to the needs of the people: what outdoor spaces were needed and where they were needed (Gehl, 2011).

In London during the Industrial Revolution, this model of work/life shifted. Industries were centered in the city, with workers typically living close by. Alleys and boulevards were the frequented pathways for individuals to move throughout the city (Zeidler, 1983). Due to major industries taking over the land and polluting the city, many sought refuge from the smog out in the countryside. The foundation of the movements of Utopianism and Functionalism originated from this need for clean air, and led to questions of how to balance the necessity for both conflicting environments.

How does one create a balance between the city's industrial pollution and the open clean air of the country? "Le Corbusier wanted to bring nature into the city, in the form of parks, [Frank Lloyd] Wright suggests the exact opposite; take the city into the countryside" (see Figure 17.1) (Rybczynski, 2010). Wright, with his theory of large lots and individual homes, greatly influenced city planning in the Southwest of the United States. For example, both Phoenix, Arizona and Houston, Texas have a rolling suburbia with looped highways and shopping centers spaced within a certain distance of driving. These extensive suburbs create a network of interconnected infrastructures including utility alleys. Service roads and other in-between building spaces are not thought about from a social point of view

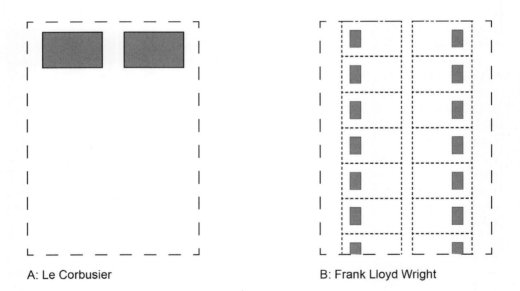

FIGURE 17.1 Le Corbusier's versus Frank Lloyd Wright's illustrated spatial utopian theories.
Source: Author.

and are not designed for specific outdoor activities (Gehl, 2011). Such alleys are typically only used for trash collection and electrical services, and thus developed "public ways in private locations," typically located at the rear of the private residence (Clay, 1978). Alleys, with their evolving needs and use, developed from a landscape terminology, to a walkable urban pathway, to a utility and trash-collection corridor, typically seen as dark and unsafe. How do we get alleys back to a usable, interactive, and beneficial element within the public realm?

17.3 Theories behind reuse and habitability of public infrastructures

Since alleys originally existed as energized and walkable environments from the Medieval era through the Industrial Revolution, theories behind the activation of public space are crucial to restoring value to these forgotten spaces. Theories by Jan Gehl and Nan Ellin on the activation of public spaces, and the spatial activation through the use of multipurpose spaces, as studied and developed by Gillian Tett with her findings in *The Silo Effect,* are outlined to demonstrate the potential of alleys from the immediate scale of the alley, to neighborhoods, up to the urban scale. These theories interpret qualitative understandings of alleys and people to target urban issues concerning the larger metropolitan area.

In cities with alleys, there is the challenge of scale and dimension. San Francisco, Boston, New York, and Philadelphia contain narrow alleys, mainly due to their antiquity. Similar to the implications of historical precedent and the Industrial Revolution in London, these older cities were built prior to the introduction of the automobile industry. Newer cities, such as Phoenix and Houston, developed the opposite issue. In these two cities, urban planning revolves around the car, and therefore buildings are pushed apart to accommodate vehicles and utility services.

Regardless of geographic location, all alleys are characteristically closed off. A majority of these spaces have 6–8 ft (1.82–2.44 meter) high walls that separate them from adjacent residential neighbors, or are directly adjacent to tall buildings. So, what makes alleys a good opportunity for social interaction?

Possible access to contact at other levels, maintenance of existing contacts, social environments, sources of inspiration, stimulating experiences, activities as attraction, play habits, seating preferences, car travel volume, hierarchy of public spaces, and intimacy of spaces are the main topics when discussing "life between buildings." Jan Gehl, in his book *Life Between Buildings: Using Public Space*, identifies these aforementioned traits as necessary to creating a well-balanced, interactive social environment. The proximity of surrounding buildings and their use dictate whether people are around to use the outdoor space, while appropriate seating, activities, car speeds, and the like are all specific attributes required to bring people together. An isolated space typically contains walls, long distances, high speeds, multiple levels, and orientation away from others. To create contact, Gehl states that a space must contain no walls, have short distances, low speeds, one level, and orientation toward others. Although alleys contain three of the five listed isolation characteristics identified, there is opportunity with the contact traits that they do have. Low speeds: they are not wide roads with multiple lanes of fast moving cars. The absence of the automobile can lead to a pedestrian friendly environment. Single level alleys, even though they typically have a great distance spanning a whole neighborhood, provide an opportunity to connect neighbors locally. The length of alleys is an opportunity to explore the scale of space required for different

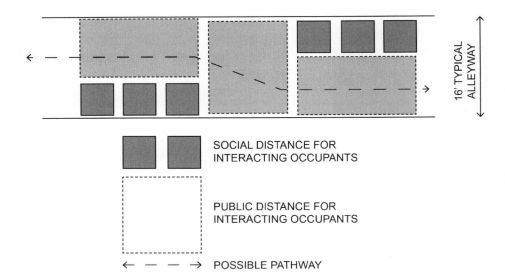

FIGURE 17.2 Graphic illustration of possible arrangements of Gehl's comfort levels/sizes within the size limitations of an alley.
Source: Author.

interactions. Gehl also outlines what distances are required for personal comfort within a public place: social distance being 1.3–3.75 meters (4½–12 ft), and public distance being greater than 3.75 meters (12 ft) (Gehl, 2011). The width of a typical Phoenix alley is 16 ft (4.88 meters). These "narrow" spaces therefore provide an opportunity for friendly, social, and public interactions in both length and width. Walls and distances of alleys are the main hindrances for activating the space.

In demonstrating Gehl's theories as to how alleys obtain the fundamental properties of what it takes to create usable space, one can ask: how can they be further engaged to provide enlivened spaces and a new social realm?

Porosity and connectivity are solutions to the activation of space. As previously mentioned, many residences have a wall at the rear of their property that limits visibility to the adjacent alley (see Figure 17.3 for an image of a typical Phoenix alley). Common tasks such as disposing of trash into the dumpster are quick and hurried, as it is natural to be timid of what could be further down the alley or hiding behind a neighbor's wall. There needs to be hybridity, connectivity, porosity, authenticity, and vulnerability (Ellin, 2006) amongst neighbors to openly access the space, connect with one another, and appropriate it as their own. In her book *Integral Urbanism*, Nan Ellin suggests that by creating integral spaces we will "heal wounds inflicted upon the landscape" and develop a more sustainable urban environment through the creation of thresholds. Ensuring alleys flourish includes development of new, layered boundaries between residences and this public space through open, porous walls that provide visibility. "The porosity of threshold boundaries permits acts of sharing to expand the circles of communing through comparison and translation" (Stavrides, 2015). Neighbors can share, but so can communities. Through the sharing of artwork, as will be discussed later in the example of Phoenix, communities can be educated and cultures put on display.

Alleyways **189**

FIGURE 17.3 Photograph of a typical Phoenix alley adjacent to residential properties.
Source: Author.

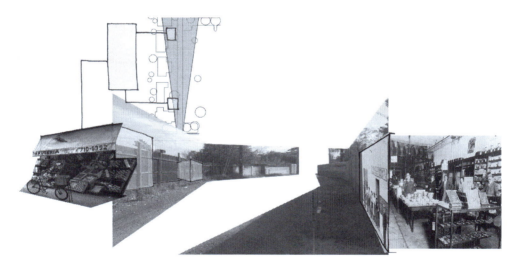

FIGURE 17.4 Collage by author outlining possible uses of alleyways by displaying historic and potential future uses in or off of alleyways.
Source: Author.

Alleys are a space between a usable public network of roads, private residences, private businesses, and at times even public parks. In this sense, alleys are a transition space between public and private (Stavrides, 2015). How can municipalities use and benefit from miles of underused alleyways?

Design teams are composed of architects, engineers, specialized consultants, owner representatives, and contractors. It is natural to designers that there is a collaborative process and that cross-professional coordination is required. Urban planning facilitated through municipalities is typically restricted within certain departments. Cities are constantly dealing with new issues that should be approached by multiple departments, each with their own focus, data and analysis, networks, etc. When brought together, creative solutions are possible that have the potential to solve more than one issue. This can be referred to as "silo-busting" (Hayes, 2015), a theory developed by Gillian Tett, as explained in her book *The Silo Effect* (Tett, 2015). The process of using a multi-faceted, multiple department approach to solving problems proves critical in this era of multitasking devices and upper-level education, typically pushing for collaborative design. The following section on Chicago exemplifies how multiple departments can come together and provide a whole array of solutions by looking into the details of standard maintenance of the city's alleyways. By looking at alleys from an urban perspective, larger scale issues can be resolved, but they must be complemented by the neighborhood and local scale solutions.

It is through multiple-angle urban analysis, cultural neighborhood representation, and creative designs for small spaces that alleys begin to take on the life inherent in old cities. The next three sections of this chapter will describe the characteristics of successful examples of repurposed alleys: The Green Alley initiative in Chicago, a ground-up movement of murals in Phoenix, and a tiny house in London. Each example will be related back to the aforementioned theories and scales of alleys.

17.4 Examples of re-appropriated alleyways

17.4.1 Grid of sustainability

What if cities were to combine Tett's theories of a multi-point approach and the reuse of alleyways? The City of Chicago is that example with their Green Alley program. Looking at their approximately 1900 miles of alleyways, the City of Chicago asked the important question of "can you make it do more for you?" (Saulny, 2007). They decided to tackle many of their other city wide concerns, such as water drainage, light pollution, material recycling, and urban heat-island effects.

In 2010, Chicago's Department of Transportation released *The Chicago Green Alley Handbook: An Action Guide to Create a Greener, Environmentally Sustainable Chicago*. The handbook utilized a landscape architect (Hitchcock Design Group), a civil engineer (Knight E/A, Inc.), an environmental engineer (Hey and Associates, Inc.), and materials testing (STATE Testing, LLC). In addition, the booklet provides links and contract information for the Chicago Department of Transportation, Chicago Department of Environment, Chicago Center for Green Technology, and Chicago Department of Water Management. In addition to renovation, conservation, and development of alleys in the city, the booklet provides information for adjacent properties on sustainable practices: recycling, composting, the benefits of trees, native landscaping, rain gardens, rain water collection, bio swales, and more. What could have been a standard repaving of alleyways and standard maintenance turned into a silo-breaking, multi-department, and multi-field solution to the city's stormwater management, heat reduction, material recycling, energy conservation, and glare reduction.

As the "alley capital of America" (Saulny, 2007), Chicago is working on developing solutions for sustainability within urban planning. Although, Chicago is not the only city starting an initiative to revitalize their alley infrastructure. San Francisco pushed, in 2008, to develop restaurants in alleys with the goal of creating lively areas that become a destination instead of an avoided back alley (McKinley, 2008). Following that, Austin, Texas, released a report on their approach for activating their downtown alleys (City of Austin Downtown Commission Alley Activation Workgroup 2013). There is a focus to not only make alleys a more central part of the solution for downtown issues, such as with Chicago, but to also make them cultural destinations, as is currently happening in Phoenix, Arizona.

17.4.2 Art and culture in alleyways

Grassroots organizations in Phoenix, Arizona started growing before, during, and after the 2007 recession, which hit the Phoenix housing market in a particularly severe manner. In this developer-driven city, organizations such as Roosevelt Row, Local First, Paint PHX, and others spearhead events that generate public attention while also highlighting the needs of the community regarding sustainability, culture, and local economics.

Paint PHX is an annual event held in March that connects artists with building owners. Many of the works produced reflect the Mexican and Native American heritage of the participants, exemplified in distinct districts such as the Calle 16 along 16th street, Grand Avenue, and Roosevelt Row. This heritage comes through in Figures 17.4 and 17.5.

Looking at the theories, outlined earlier in this chapter, by Jan Gehl and Nan Ellin, and given Phoenix's location and history, this artwork is an integral part of the urban fabric of the city. There is an inherent need for neighborhoods to reflect their culture. As the historic Mexican and Native American cultures adjust to modern times, heritage, tradition, and belief are displayed throughout Phoenix in the form of murals. This further stimulates education

FIGURE 17.5 Mural by Lalo Cota and El Mac, south-facing wall at Barrio Café on Calle 16. *Source*: Author.

FIGURE 17.6 Mural by Douglas Miles: Native American Women with historical and present images in their hair.
Source: Author.

through exposure, putting culture on display for better understanding. "Public space is not only instrumental in the social (diversity) education of citizens, it is potentially the place of political expression" (Bodnar, 2015). Not only do they create the feeling of an energized space, they also provide thresholds between different areas of Phoenix; they "encourage differences to meet, to mutually expose themselves, and to create grounds of mutual awareness" (Stavrides, 2015).

17.4.3 Small creative design

In many older US and European cities, alleys are much narrower and typically are barely the width of a car. These wedge voids throughout the cities challenge land owners, designers, and architects to generate creative small spaces. Part of this solution is the current trend of small/tiny housing that further pushes architects to design livable, flexible, and multi-use small spaces. Tiny homes are also a challenge for municipalities with zoning setbacks, land uses, and densities designated throughout the city or town. Boyarsky Murphy Architects accomplished this with their Sliver House in Vale, London.

The modern Sliver House is an unapologetic example of how to create a livable environment within a tight space in the fabric of the city. Measuring only 11 metres (36.09 ft) deep and 7.5 metres (24.61 ft) wide and with a street frontage of 3 metres (9.84 ft), the site is fixed between two Victorian-style structures (http://boyarskymurphy.com, accessed April 2, 2017).

This building provides an example of how to infill the "unusable" wedges throughout a city. Programming for these spaces does not need to be a park or a solution to a drainage issue; the solution can be to generate higher density.

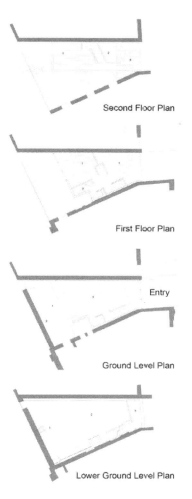

FIGURE 17.7 Plans of Sliver House designed by Boyarsky Murphy Architects.
Source: Plans by Boyarsky Murphy Architects, with overlaying text by author.

17.5 Conclusion/recommendations

To solve many of the urban issues that plague modern cities, the author encourages interaction in the public realm, porosity and connectivity, and using alleys to solve multiple city planning issues, including increasing density. All of these lead to the conclusion that alleys can be used for multiple purposes by numerous people and can support their community in various ways. Not only do alleys have the opportunity to be repurposed but, by applying the theories discussed throughout this chapter, public spaces can be more interactive, neighborhoods can be safer (Newman, 1973), and the social realm within our built environment can be reinvigorated with another layer of social interaction. Additional added benefits by silo-busting include reducing the heat-island effect, putting culture on display as thresholds throughout the city, and demonstrating that these small alleys can be transformed into living spaces.

17.6 References

Bodnar, J. (2015). "Reclaiming Public Space." *Urban Studies Journal,* February 18, 2016, http://journals.sagepub.com/doi/pdf/10.1177/0042098015583626. Accessed April 2, 2017.

City of Austin Downtown Commission Alley Activation Workgroup. (2013). *Activating Austin's Downtown Alleys as Public Spaces.* Austin: City of Austin Downtown Commission Alley Activation Workgroup.

Clay, G. (1978). *Alleys: A Hidden Resource.* Louisville: Grady Clay.

Ellin, N. (2006). *Integral Urbanism.* New York: Routledge.

Gehl, J. (2011). *Life Between Buildings: Using Public Space.* Washington: Island Press.

Hayes, C. (2015). "'The Silo Effect' by Gillian Tett." *The New York Times,* September 2, 2015.

McKinley, J. (2008). "Alleys for Cool Cats." *The New York Times,* March 30, 2008.

Newman, O. (1973). *Defensible Space: Crime Prevention Through Urban Design.* New York: Macmillan Publishing.

Rybczynski, W. (2010). *Makeshift Metropolis: Ideas About Cities.* New York: Scribner.

Saulny, S. (2007). "In Miles of Alleys, Chicago Finds Its Next Environmental Frontier." *The New York Times,* November 26, 2007.

Stavrides, S. (2015). "Common Space as Threshold Space: Urban Commoning in Struggles to Re-appropriate Public Space." *Commoning as Differentiated Publicness,* Spring.

Tett, G. (2015). *The Silo Effect: The Pearl of Expertise and the Promise of Breaking Down Barriers.* New York: Simon & Schuster.

Zeidler, E. H. (1983). *Multi-Use Architecture in the Urban Context.* New York: Van Nostrand Reinhold.

18

CONCOURSE TO CAMPUS: TRANSFORMING BERLIN TXL AIRPORT INTO A HIGHER EDUCATION SPACE

Una Rath and Martin Hodulak

18.1 Introduction

In recent years, the increasing mechanization of buildings has posed additional tasks for engineers and architects, requiring greater involvement with new technologies. Meanwhile, the functionality of buildings is substantially determined by their technical services. The resulting complexity of building projects necessitates a rethink among all those involved in planning and construction. A holistic, building life-cycle-oriented, and interdisciplinary approach has evolved against this background: the integrative planning process.

Integrative planning is not new, and this term has generally been applied for some years now to projects with high complexity and challenging tasks for architects and engineers. However, to date, there isn't any definition as to what integrative planning implies, what its distinguishing processes are, and what type of project organization it necessitates. In the understanding of the authors, integrative planning is first and foremost about collaboration on equal footing among all those participating in the project, implying a common start, consistent communication, and the continuous support by an integration planner.

This chapter describes the process of integrative planning based on the case study of the transformation of the Berlin TXL airport. It focuses on the conversion of the Terminal A building, which will move from aviation use to that of a higher education facility.

18.2 Background

The existing "Otto-Lilienthal" Airport TXL will be shut down once operations start at Berlin's single airport BER. The airport closure is a unique chance to design a new sustainable urban development. It will include a university, industrial and production facilities, service industries, cultural institutions and housing, as well as gardens and open spaces.

In 2009, the Berlin Senate Administration initiated an open discussion on future options for a new use of the current airport site. In the course of the workshops conducted at the time, the participating multidisciplinary teams developed a range of different future scenarios.

Following an evaluation of the risks and opportunities for the city, the State of Berlin voted for the development of a research and industrial park, the "Urban Tech Republic" (UTR). The future UTR will link research-focused university departments with start-ups and enterprises and enhance synergies between research and production.

Prior to planning, a key question arose: how can a former airport site, with its building stock and vast open spaces, be transformed and developed into an innovative and multi-functional area whilst not losing sight of the history of this extraordinary place. Thanks to its combination of functional logistics and aesthetical clarity, Tegel Airport can be regarded as an icon of Berlin's post-war modernity. Its characteristic architecture, featuring forms typical of the period, the clear delineation of the functional units and easy orientation, combined with short distances between arrival and departure, still delight both travelers and experts.

The distinctive airport elements are to be retained; however, they will have to be transformed by altering their current functions for a new future use. At the same time, new elements will also be introduced, and the combination of new and re-used old components will represent UTR's one-of-a-kind characteristics. It is intended that the Terminal A building and its site will remain a unique feature. The change from ramps, driveways, and car parking to open public spaces will generate a new perception characterized by experimentation and adaptability. The prominent hexagonal terminal building, today's face of the airport, will remain and be kept as a relict in the new urban context. The spatial concept of today's mono-functional terminal building can easily accommodate a completely different future use. It will be converted into a multi-functional structure in accordance with sustainable building requirements and responding to future changes.

This scope of work requires a mutually supportive and integrative approach in the thinking of architects, engineers, and landscape designers. As project experience shows, intense communication and interdisciplinary collaboration are the key assets for successful planning. An integrative planning team working on an equal footing is able to define and agree on viable goals at an early stage, and to communicate these at the project start.

18.3 Concept

Almost all of today's terminal buildings, i.e., Terminals A, B, and D, as well as a number of maintenance buildings and hangars, were identified and selected for future functions. These are all clustered and in close vicinity to the central Terminal A hexagonal building. They will accommodate incubator businesses or start-ups, small and medium-sized enterprises, and shared functions, such as site maintenance, infrastructure, conference facilities, and exhibition spaces. The site layout will follow the central theme: from idea to experiment to market production.

The same holistic approach of converting the area by means of integrative planning is being applied to the transformation of the Terminal A building. It relies on overlapping architectural aspects and technical issues, as well as linking the building and its surrounding urban fabric.

18.3.1 Program development for Terminal A

Terminal A, as the future site of Beuth University's urban technologies departments, will be transformed into a research facility and the starting point for new products and developments. Beuth University, one of Germany's ten largest universities of applied sciences,

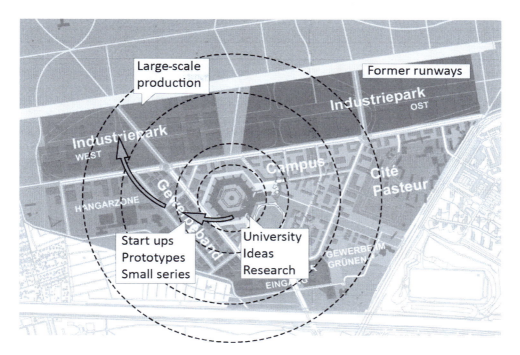

FIGURE 18.1 TXL concept – from idea to market production.
Source: Authors.

has decided on splitting its departments across two sites – the existing campus in Berlin-Wedding and the new site in Berlin-Tegel. Research and teaching at their Berlin-Tegel site will be located in one place. Adjacent outdoor experimentation fields, start-ups, and production facilities will complement the research laboratories. The site will support a close-knit network of students, scientists, founders, and entrepreneurs. The terminal building itself will accommodate teaching and research facilities, a library, retail areas, conference and convention facilities, child care and general services, as well as a start-up center. The former terminal will become a multitasking space and the focal point of the industry and science park.

The university's core function will be arranged lineally along the existing hexagon-ring. Nearly half of the ground floor area will be converted into research laboratories and related workshop areas for the various departments. Regarding the immediately adjacent tarmac, the area on the outer perimeter and parking decks within the inner perimeter will serve as field laboratory, outdoor experimental area, and delivery access. The indoor–outdoor relationship of the existing structure will be preserved, albeit serving a new and different use. Lecture halls, seminar rooms, and workshops, as well as offices for the academic staff, will be located above the laboratories on the upper floor – the former passenger level. They will be functionally clustered and spatially linked to ground-level laboratories.

The basement level will accommodate technical services and infrastructure, including electrical services, water, heat, and telecommunications. They will be linked and distributed via existing vertical shafts to the laboratories above. The library, refectory, additional seminar rooms, and student studios will be located on the second level. The roof terrace above will accommodate further experimental assemblies, e.g. solar arrays and rooftop greening.

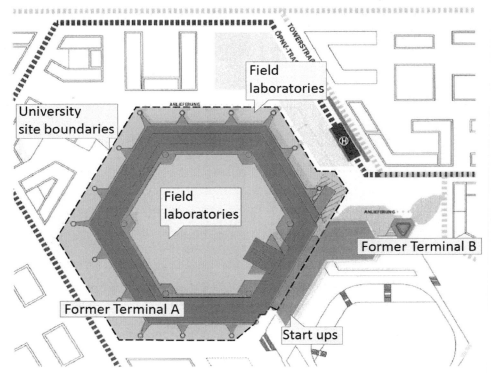

FIGURE 18.2 Extent of university site with field laboratories.
Source: Authors.

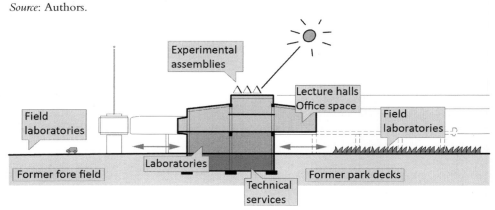

FIGURE 18.3 Schematic section of terminal building converted to university use.
Source: Authors.

The conception and design of the hexagonal ring seemed to be a challenge at the start of project but turned out to be a stroke of luck as it proved to be an almost ideal structure for a research-focused university. It provides outstanding prerequisites for the highly diverse space schedule of the departments with their specific curricula, research activities, and their need for flexibility and future adaptability.

18.4 Process – from idea to feasibility

18.4.1 Basic understanding

The goal of integrative planning is to generate functional, efficient, and ecologically sustainable buildings, hereafter referred to as sustainable buildings. As organizations and work environments are in a constant flux, and in need of frequent reorganization, flexibility in built environments is of major significance. To achieve maximum flexibility, the amount of remodeling and retrofitting measures needs to be kept low. Reassembling flexible wall elements and reprogramming the building automation software, for example, are easy, quick, and economic ways of adapting a building when changing its use. Sustainable buildings are also energy efficient. Moreover, they are characterized by availability, utility, and low overall operating costs.

As a holistic approach, integrative planning consists of a large and rising number of individual processes, as well as the growing interrelation of processes throughout the project. The quality of integrative planning increases with the synchronization and optimization of the interrelations of processes. In order to fully comprehend the significance of integrative planning, it is necessary to understand the processes involved. Probably the most significant features are a fully established team at a very early stage, the focus on the users' needs, and a consideration of the building life cycle from the outset. Contrary to common practice, where architects make the first move and then gradually involve further planners, specialists, and consultants, integrative planning involves all parties from the start. This requires a clear project description and well-communicated objectives, thus it is important to focus on the user and client needs prior to the start of planning.

Consideration of, and alignment with, the building life cycle is characteristic of a holistic approach. The building life cycle generally starts with an idea, combined with the need for space at a specific location. The initial idea in the planning phase is followed by the programming, design, construction, and occupancy phases as depicted below (Preiser & Schramm, 2005, reissued 2015 by Routledge). In the sixth phase, the building life feeds into the next building cycle, namely adaptive reuse or recycling. The phases described in this chapter, i.e., programming, concept, and feasibility, are all part of the programming phase within the depicted building life cycle.

18.4.2 The concept

Prerequisites and goals: the statement of a client's goals and the documentation of his needs and requirements are two essential prerequisites for integrative planning. The concept phase therefore starts with the building program and project initiation. The aim of the project initiation is to establish a project structure and organization which will support the integral approach and ensure that the program can be completed.

At this stage of the project, the range of possible options is broad. Decisions can still be made on the appearance and perception of the future building, its properties and qualities, as well as the investments and future operating costs. Prior to the start of creating a concept and planning, these parameters can be influenced by up to almost 100%. Once project work has commenced, the range of possible options diminishes with the growing number of decisions made and the interrelations and interdependencies among them.

FIGURE 18.4 Building life cycle.
Source: Authors, based on Preiser & Schramm (2005).

Building quality: the overall quality of sustainable buildings is determined by numerous factors, including usability and ecological sustainability. Usability can be further differentiated in terms of architecture and design, convenience and flexibility, comfort, and wellbeing. Ecological sustainability refers to such aspects as the use of regenerative energy, space requirements, energy efficiency, and the type of building materials that are envisioned to be used.

Quality criteria: the emphasis and priority, as specified by the client, allow one to state and document an overall quality definition of the building on an abstract level, and at a very early stage. The definition of quality is a prerequisite for holistic solutions. It needs to be adequate and measurable in order to enable quality control to be implemented in later project phases.

18.4.3 Integrative planning process

Programming: data about the users' and client's needs and requirements are collected during the concept phase and documented in a building program. Establishing a building program is labor intensive, but, in the authors' experience, it contributes substantially to a project's success, and is a prerequisite for later quality management. A building program is a means for establishing measurable targets and requirements for planners and firms, and facilitating continuous quality and control of project progress.

The building program includes general project data, such as aim and purpose, scope, participating parties, and responsibilities. Moreover, it includes general parameters, goals, needs, requirements and their priorities, functional proximities, risks, and financing. The general approach and the methodology involved correspond in large parts to facility-programming guidelines as described in *Facility Programming* (Preiser, 2015), *Architectural Programming* (Hershberger, 1999), *Problem Seeking* (Pena & Parhsall, 2001), or *Nutzerorientierte Bedarfsplanung* (Hodulak & Schramm, 2011).

Project organization: a project organization defines the project, team, and process structures. We distinguish between a traditional project organization and a project organization with integrated partners. In a traditional project organization, the architect is commissioned by the client, which includes assuming the overall responsibility for his work, as well as that of his experts. Each of these experts conducts tasks or develops and designs solutions within his/her area of expertise. The architect's task is to integrate the experts' solutions into his/her design. This integration is not to be mistaken for integrative planning. Integration by the architect is rather about adapting the experts' designs into the leading architect's design.

As is common knowledge, complex and challenging projects depend in large part on the planners' know-how, but, above all, on their ability to collaborate. The overall solution is always a result of individual contributions, however these might be coordinated, discussed, optimized, and brought together. Integrative planning is about bringing together individual know-how in order to achieve overall concepts by linking architecture, building structure, energy concepts, building operation, and environmental services. Integrative planning is an interdisciplinary planning approach with the goal of achieving a higher overall quality, better investment and operational efficiency, and at reduced lower cost and expenditure of time.

The rising complexity of building, automation, and technology increases the number of experts involved and the level of communication that is necessary. The coordination effort of building services engineering, structural design, structural physics, fire protection, etc., is high, even in medium-sized projects. Successful planning requires an integration planner who must be a generalist with a technical and engineering background, and a thorough understanding of information technologies and building automation.

Figure 18.5 depicts the position of an integration planner within a reformed project organization structure. In the initial phase, it is the integration planner's task to coordinate the planning of the various technical and building services. The resulting cross-disciplinary organization is then reviewed and integrated with the architect's own planning.

The integration planner can be regarded as the architect's generalist counterpart for all technology-related aspects of the building. He is the link between the architect and the involved building technology experts. As a result, the architect now has access to a competent response and is relieved of a number of coordination tasks. The technical experts obtain a highly qualified coordinator, who is sensitive to their specific topics. Last but not least, the client will achieve better quality in planning and design. The overall concept of building technologies and architecture leads to a systemic solution for building and technology.

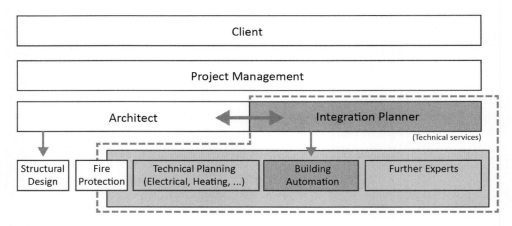

FIGURE 18.5 Organization structure of an integral planning.
Source: Authors.

18.5 Project status – Terminal A conversion

The transformation of the Terminal A building from airport use into a higher education facility started with a building program. Beuth University had established a space program in 2011, which was used as a basis for checking, updating, and providing details in terms of required building qualities and spatial proximities. A series of 20 interviews with various departments and service sections was conducted. They included general needs, as well as specific requirements of the indoor and outdoor research laboratories. The interviews included questions concerning the current as well as new and evolving processes and work styles in order to validate the stated needs and ensure a future-oriented concept outcome.

The next step saw the project team being initiated. According to the aforementioned integrative planning principle, all of the participating professionals already mentioned were involved. This included the architect, the landscape designer, environmental design engineers, structural engineers, experts on façades, fire protection and contaminants, as well as a project developer. Most of the planning processes started at the same time and were conducted in parallel. Project team meetings were held every two weeks with additional bilateral meetings in the intervening period. The planners neither revised the university tasks, processes and work styles, nor the respective requirements. However, the resulting spatial layouts and technical concepts were frequently reviewed, discussed, and optimized. The project team was involved, along with university representatives as future users of the building. Traditional lecture halls and office concepts were examined and new spatial concepts for teaching and academic work were developed. These discussions ensured an overall functionality in terms of organization, process, and communication structures.

Since the entire team of planners and experts were involved from a very early stage, it needs to be stressed that the whole range of interdisciplinary competences was available and could be used. In addition to spatial feasibility studies by the architects, the engineers developed energy and infrastructure concepts, a fire protection concept, as well as a superstructure of environmental services. The results form a reliable basis for further cost planning and project schedule development.

The team summarized the users' expectations as well as the experts' estimates, perspectives, considerations, concepts, and feasibility studies in a single document. This document is the basis for a political decision on the project's budget and start. It is also a credible basis for all of the following planning and construction decisions

18.6 Conclusion

We are experiencing increased correlation and interdependency among technical systems and technologies, as well as a rising complexity of requirements that are the outcome of what are at times even contradictory goals – such as operational safety, energy efficiency, and preventive fire control. Projects of this scope can no longer be mastered with traditional processes that rely on the division of work, disciplines, and responsibilities. Technically challenging building projects require a large amount of interdisciplinary communication and collaboration, and constitute a paradigm change to integrative planning.

It would be short sighted to restrict the practice of interdisciplinary planning to large projects. We all know of small catastrophes from real life – this can even happen when planning a family home. A planning process characterized by sequential processing of tasks within individual disciplines will lead to frequent changes in design, delays, and unplanned resulting costs. This is the result of neglected involvement of participating trades and disciplines.

A decisive factor for achieving success is to anticipate a new understanding of the planner's role. Technical experts need to be involved from the outset, assume more responsibility from the start, and, most importantly, work on an equal footing with the architects. In theory, this has been acknowledged for some time. With the Tegel conversion, it is currently being put into practice.

18.7 References

Hershberger, R. G. (1999). *Architectural Programming and Predesign Manager*. London: McGraw-Hill. Republished in 2015 by Routledge.

Hodulak, M., & Schramm, U. (2011). *Nutzerorientierte Bedarfsplanung*. Berlin: Springer Verlag.

Pena, W. M., & Parshall, S. A. (2001). *Problem Seeking: An Architectural Programming Primer*. New York: John Wiley & Sons, Inc.

Preiser, W. F. E. (2015). *Facility Programming*. London: Routledge.

Preiser, W. F. E., & Schramm, U. (2005). A conceptual framework for building performance evaluation. In W. F. E. Preiser, & J. C. Vischer (eds.), *Assessing Building Performance*. London: Routledge.

19

AN ADAPTIVE EVOLUTION FROM PRUSSIAN ARTILLERY BARRACKS TO INTELLIGENT CAMPUS BUILDINGS

Ulrich Schramm

19.1 Introduction

This chapter will trace the adaptive evolution of a group of military buildings in Minden, Germany, which were built in 1897. The buildings were converted from singular-purpose structures serving the Prussian artillery, the German Wehrmacht, and British occupying forces to today's highly specialized spaces currently used by the Bielefeld University of Applied Sciences, Minden Campus. Although this chapter focuses on a campus as the predominant scale of the environment, a range of buildings will be considered as well, with their re-used spaces where activities take place and behavior occurs. Thus, on the one hand, this chapter will deal with the interrelationships among environmental influences and people. On the other hand, it will focus on the process of creating built environments in general and adaptive architecture in particular.

19.2 Utilitarian buildings serving for defense in Minden

19.2.1 Design of the barracks

According to contractual agreements in 1894, the City of Minden had to provide the construction site with the technical infrastructure and to build the barracks, whereas the military administration was responsible for the furnishings. The barracks were to house 36 officers and other ranks, six married administration officials, one gunsmith, and 273 enlisted men. The idea was to place the buildings on the site in such a way that a big training ground for artillery could be arranged as well. Accordingly, the new buildings were grouped on the rectangular plot that is 340 m/1,115 ft in length and some 120 m/400 ft wide. Viewed from the main entrance in the north-east corner of the site, the family house, the kitchen and wash house, and the latrine were on the left hand. The dominant dwelling house with the men's quarters was on the right hand with its back to the spacious training and riding grounds, located in the center of the plot. On the long sides, the other buildings were to be found (see Figure 19.1). The idea to

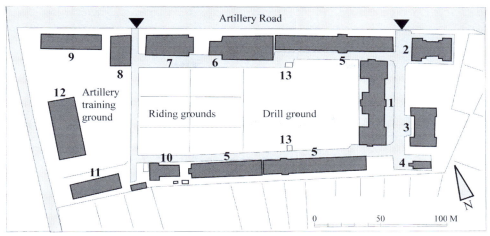

FIGURE 19.1 Map of the artillery barracks.
Source: Author, based on Korn (2005).

build the houses in a light half-timbered manner was dismissed in favor of a monolithic brick construction method.

- Men's quarters: The three-story building was 65 m/215 ft long, had a basement, and was mainly used to accommodate the enlisted men.
- Family house: In order to accommodate the families of officers and administration officials, six apartments were fitted in the two-story family house.
- Kitchen and wash house: A one-story building was designed to house the kitchen and two dining halls, one for lower ranks and the other for all enlisted men. Moreover, the building accommodated an apartment for the sutler as well. The attic was used as storeroom for his goods and as a drying area for the men; the basement had a wash room and showers.
- Latrine: A small building was built with 13 toilet stalls for the men and three stalls for sergeants and other ranks.
- Stables: Along the north and south sides of the site, stables were built in brickwork, mainly one story high.
- Riding-stable: An indoor riding area was constructed, a long and deep building with nine windows, each of them 2 m/6 ft high.
- Vehicle shed: A shed was built to accommodate vehicles and harnesses.
- Artillery shed: Another shed was erected as a one-story hall to house the artillery, with three broad doors opening towards the grounds.
- Stable for the sick: A stable for sick horses was built, one story high.
- Blacksmith's/armorer's workshop: In the south-west corner of the training grounds, this one-story building was constructed next to the stables, with two high chimneys.

206 Schramm

- "Remonten" stable: A stable for three- to four-year-old horses was built. These horses were still in training in order to later replace other horses determined to be unfit for service.

In 1897, the construction work was done. The tenements were initially used by the IVth Section of the Imperial Field Artillery Regiment 22 (Tippach, 2005).

19.2.2 Next tenants

With the end of the German empire in 1918 and the dissolution of the imperial armed forces, the 5th Battery of the 6th Prussian Artillery Regiment that was conscripted in 1921 moved into the barracks. Later, the German Wehrmacht, which emerged from the German army after 1935, used the barracks until the end of World War II. At that point in time, the new training hall was built along the west edge of the site, in 1936.

Since 1945, the British occupying forces used the barracks under the name of "Springbok Barracks." Some business enterprises were established on the site after 1949; for example, a business for metal finishing occupied the former "Remonten" stable. The fire department, too, used parts of the barracks: the former vehicle shed was converted and complemented with a seven-story tower in order to dry the fire hoses. In 1957, the British army left the site, and in 1971, the fire department moved out as well (Tippach, 2005).

19.3 Adapting the buildings for education

19.3.1 From barracks to university buildings

In 1964, with the establishment of the State School for Construction Engineering on the eastern part of the site, the barracks started to change significantly: the users were no longer soldiers, but students; instead of drilling, studying became the main activity; thus, the buildings were no longer used for defense, but for teaching and academic purposes. Subject areas of the school were at first structural engineering (1964), then construction management (1965), followed by transport and hydraulic engineering (1966). Starting in 1965, the first laboratories were installed in the former military buildings.

In 1971, the Bielefeld University of Applied Sciences emerged out of six regional facilities for education – the State School for Construction Engineering was one of them. Consequently, the Minden site – with 300 students and 25 instructors – established itself as a separate location to study some 45 km/27 miles from Bielefeld, where five other departments were located. Beside the subjects in the field of civil engineering, architecture became a new field of study at this time in Minden, constituting the department of "architecture and civil engineering" (Fachhochschule Bielefeld, 1996).

19.3.2 Revitalization of old structures

Although the structures of the former barracks were classified as a historical monument in 1993, more and more buildings were converted for the needs of a university, like the main building, housing offices, seminar rooms, and lecture halls (see Figure 19.2). From 1996 to

FIGURE 19.2 The former men's quarters turned into the main building on the Minden Campus. *Source*: Author.

2002, the stables along the south edge of the site were re-used as an auditorium building with three lecture halls and a hydraulic engineering laboratory with related research facilities. The stables on the north side, along Artillery Road, were turned into a laboratory for building materials and a workshop for making architectural models.

Parallel to this development, in 2000, "construction project management" was introduced as a new bachelor's program in addition to the two established courses in "civil engineering" and "architecture." These programs were augmented in 2007 by the introduction of a consecutive master's program called "integrative construction," a new program for graduates of the three bachelor's programs. At this time, the Minden Campus had about 650 students, i.e., roughly 10% of the student body at the Bielefeld University of Applied Sciences.

19.3.3 Increasing enrollment by 500 students

In 2008, the state government of North-Rhine Westphalia mandated that the Bielefeld University of Applied Sciences increase enrollment by 500 students at the Minden location within five years. The university administration decided to introduce the following six bachelor's programs: "business engineering" (2009); "electrical engineering," "computer science," and "nursing" (2010), "mechanical engineering" and "infrastructure management" (2011). In order to meet the spatial requirements, the former blacksmith's workshop was quickly converted into a computer lab (see Figure 19.3). In the former family house, too,

FIGURE 19.3 The former blacksmith's workshop now used as a computer lab.
Source: Author.

offices for staff and a skills lab for nursing were accommodated. Instead of the former training hall, seminar and practice rooms were placed. Some buildings, like the "Remonten" stable or the vehicle shed, are still occupied by third parties and unavailable for university use. Although the adapted facilities like the lecture halls or seminar rooms are used by the different programs from morning until night, an analysis of space in 2010 showed the need of additional 3,768 m^2/40,500 sq. ft. of net usable space – to be created as an entirely new building on the campus (HIS, 2010).

19.4 A new campus building to meet the university's needs

19.4.1 Beyond assembly-line education

With the increase of enrollment by 500 new students, specific educational policy objectives were pursued: on one hand, the introduction of so-called "MINT" subjects (mathematics, information technology, natural sciences, and technical disciplines) aimed at educating the specialists the local economy was looking for. On the other hand, existing academic structures were to be broken up – similar to the idea mentioned at the beginning of this book (see the Introduction by Preiser, Fisher, and Hardy): instead of disciplinary monocultures with standardized curricula, interdisciplinary, collaborative education, and research was the aim of the new concept. This was already realized on a small scale with the introduction of the master's program "integrative construction," where graduates from "architecture," "civil

Evolution from barracks to campus **209**

engineering," "construction project management," and, recently, from "infrastructure management" are trained together on integrative construction projects. On the larger scale of a university campus, the range of curricula and research offerings were to be broadened from the topic area of "architecture and civil engineering" to the new subjects of "technology" and "health." This provided for more synergistic education and interdisciplinary collaboration. And lastly, in terms of reorganizing the campus, it was planned to unify the three departments, combining all programs within one common unit.

19.4.2 "Democratize production" as a prerequisite for adaptive architecture

In view of the plan to use the increase of enrollment for an organizational and structural realignment of the Minden Campus, one would expect a sophisticated strategy for operational implementation in the form of a new campus building – a new approach that is intended "to democratize production" (see the Introduction by Preiser, Fisher, and Hardy). With regard to the "production" of the new and shared building, such an innovative approach could include: first, the goals of three departments and 11 programs need to be identified, with different histories, cultures, structures, and expectations; and, second, the requirements of all direct user groups like professors, research assistants, or students need to be clarified, as well as of those other stakeholders like businesses in the area, Minden marketing, or the interested public. These goals and requirements need to be considered at an early stage and translated into a facility program. Such a program will later be used by the designer to develop an appropriate design solution, an adaptive architecture that can accommodate required multiple functions at the same time, both sequentially and in periodically recurring fashion.

What sounds great in theory may be difficult in practice at a university with its traditional hierarchical structures. The organizational integration of all programs within one unified department was imposed from the top – the new name "Department Campus Minden" as a minimal consensus emphasizes the location, but not the disciplines that are represented. The facility program for the new building was also not developed jointly with the future building users, but it was basically defined top down in 2010. A programming workshop offered a year later surprisingly was scheduled between terms. Only three students were therefore involved, who eventually called the workshop a placebo, as their input seemed to have no impact on the facility program at all (Lögering & Szymura, 2013). In the final program, almost no space was designated for the existing architecture and civil engineering disciplines; most of the space, i.e., two thirds, was for the new MINT subjects and at least one third for common or shared facilities like the library and cafeteria to be used by all.

During the following phases of design, design development, and building construction, ten professors started to participate in the process as an interdisciplinary research group "InteG-F." As they are focusing on "Well-Being and Acceptance in the Intelligent Building," they use the new campus building as a major case study. While those professors followed the building progress with interest, students remained broadly excluded from the building delivery process: they were neither invited to the ceremonial laying of the corner stone for the new building, nor to the joint topping-off ceremony. Finally, they were not part of the opening ceremony. Without user participation, the opportunity to "democratize production" as a prerequisite for adaptive architecture was wasted.

19.4.3 Rough landing: early feedback from building users

In August 2015, the new campus building (see Figure 19.4), located amidst the former riding area, was officially opened. Now, the offices are occupied, the library is in use, and teaching has started. The cafeteria opened six months later, and, finally, the social areas were furnished. Commissioning of building technology and automation is currently delayed, and building defects need to be remedied little by little. Accordingly, it is still too early to assess the building performance objectively by carrying out post-occupancy evaluations. However, first comments and casual feedback from building users – professors, research assistants, and students – show the following: the landing of the occupants in the new building has been rough! As users were barely involved in the building delivery process, many of them feel like strangers, unable to understand basic functional, technical, or aesthetic decisions.

19.5 Conclusions

An adaptive evolution from Prussian artillery barracks to intelligent campus buildings has taken place. The barracks were adapted to the needs of the university, commensurate with spatial flexibility and structural capacity of the old buildings (see Figure 19.5). Many of them are networked with one another and the main campus in Bielefeld. The Minden Campus as

FIGURE 19.4 The new campus building (middle) with the auditorium (left) and the former tower of the fire department (right).
Source: Author.

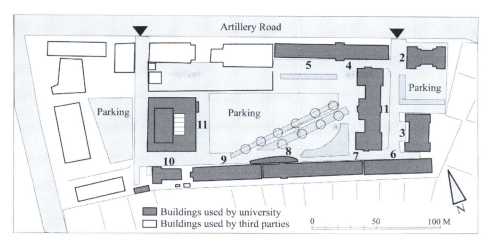

FIGURE 19.5 Map of Minden Campus, Bielefeld University of Applied Sciences, 2016.
Source: Author.

a place to study is well accepted as the programs are attractive and the concept of interdisciplinary, collaborative education is future-oriented. Thus, the number of students increased not only from 650 to 1,150, but to 1,600 as of this date, and it appears that the new building is already too small to meet the current need for functional space in a satisfactory manner. Apart from that, an energy-efficient building was planned, using intelligent technology like geothermal energy, photovoltaics, and building automation systems. Moreover, seminar rooms have floor ducts offering flexibility for cable connections. Finally, light-weight construction walls allow for adapting the existing cellular offices to team or group offices, if required later.

But for many people, the process to meet the space requirements, to deliver the new building, and even the building itself seem to mirror the past: significant decisions were made from the top down, and old "us versus them" thinking of the former departments became cast in concrete, at least to some extent. User involvement was close to zero and many occupants are unable to identify with the resulting building. Yet there are other examples in the surrounding area like the Detmold School of Architecture and Interior Design that show how to do it differently: the new building on Campus Emilie was designed by the architectural students themselves, with flexible and adaptable interior spaces. A post-occupancy evaluation, carried out just recently, indicates a high degree of user satisfaction – of both professors and students – with "their" building (Rüterkamp & Janzen, 2014).

From today's perspective several opportunities were not taken advantage of in Minden to see the campus building project as part of a change management process, to unify the different disciplines, to overcome cultural differences, and to create a common identity. Now it remains to be seen whether, and to what extent, common or shared facilities like the library and cafeteria will attract people from all programs in the new building (see Figure 19.6).

FIGURE 19.6 Atrium of the new library, located on the second floor of the new campus building. *Source*: Author.

The cafeteria on the first floor with its adaptive architecture in particular has the potential to encourage interdisciplinary exchange among those who are studying, teaching, or doing research: this space accommodates multiple functions simultaneously, such as meeting, eating, talking, working, or relaxing, as well as periodically recurring events like receptions, exhibitions, ceremonies, and summer or Christmas parties.

19.6 References

Fachhochschule Bielefeld (ed.). (1996). *Hochschule der Praxis: Fachhochschule Bielefeld 25 Jahre*. Bielefeld: Presse- und Informationsstelle.

HIS Hochschul-Informations-System GmbH (ed.). (2010). *Einpassungsplanung neuer Studiengänge der FH Bielefeld am Standort Minden*. Unpublished project report. Hanover, Germany

Korn, U.-D. (2005). Minden – Stadt und Festung. In Landschaftsverband Westfalen-Lippe, Westfälisches Amt für Denkmalpflege (ed.). *Bau- und Kunstdenkmäler von Westfalen/Bd. 50. Stadt Minden Teil 1. Einführungen und Darstellung der prägenden Strukturen Teilbd. 2. Festung und Denkmäler* (pp. I & 801). Essen: Klartext-Verlag.

Lögering, M. & Szymura, M. (2013). *Berücksichtigung der Interessen und Bedürfnisse der Nutzer an der Fachhochschule hinsichtlich der Ausführungsplanung für die Campuserweiterung Minden*. Unpublished student specialization project, Fachhochschule Bielefeld, Germany

Rüterkamp, Y. & Janzen, M. (2014). *Detmolder Schule für Architektur und Innenarchitektur: Evaluierung offener Seminarräume*. Unpublished student research project, Fachhochschule Bielefeld, Germany

Tippach, T. (2005). Städtische Artilleriekaserne. In Landschaftsverband Westfalen-Lippe, Westfälisches Amt für Denkmalpflege (Ed.), *Bau- und Kunstdenkmäler von Westfalen/Bd. 50. Stadt Minden Teil 1. Einführungen und Darstellung der prägenden Strukturen Teilbd. 2. Festung und Denkmäler* (pp. 801–812). Essen: Klartext-Verlag.

20

A CASE STUDY ON THE DESIGN OF THE SCOTTISH CRIME CAMPUS

Gordon Murray

20.1 Introduction

The Scottish Crime Campus is a Scottish Government-funded facility providing 23,600 sq. m (254,000 sq. ft.) net of high-quality office and support accommodation for up to 1,200 people; total development value £73M (US$102M).

The complex comprises four block structures, each of which is four storeys in height, arranged around a central atrium with a diagonal cross route providing controlled access. The brief for this project called for a facility to bring together key law enforcement agencies within one building to promote collaboration and innovation across multi-agency services. For the first time, law enforcement agencies are working for both devolved and UK legislation whilst operating under the same roof. All agencies share an atrium space. It is the social core of the building, the place where employees meet, interact, and circulate. The intention of this interaction is to encourage the dissemination of ideas and help create a sense of community. It is a significant component in a wider exploration of architectural quality on government buildings working to parameters set out in the Scottish Government's architecture policy. This chapter will outline how present research was consistently maintained through the design of the project and through all elements of the construction phase.

20.2 Client and stakeholders

A Project Board made up mostly of Scottish Government civil servants, following the Scottish Public Finance Manual/Office of Government Commerce model, was established. The Project Board was ultimately responsible for ensuring the building was delivered on time, within budget, etc., and helped to ensure that design outcomes were locked in. A Programme Board, made up of senior civil servants but also senior representatives from all the occupying agencies, was also established to ensure the agencies were closely involved in the detailed design and progress on site. The primary aim of the Programme Board was to oversee the delivery of a benefits realisation and change programme to enhance collaboration between various anti-crime agencies. To accomplish all of this it also assisted in

FIGURE 20.1 View of campus.
Source: Keith Hunter Photography.

coordination of the user input to the design. This board morphed into a management board, which oversaw occupation and continues to manage the building on behalf of all users.

A client advisor was in place from the very start of the Crime Campus project alongside a dedicated procurement specialist allocated to the project. The client advisor played a crucial role in keeping track of design, development, technical design, and construction stages of the process, including providing market and investment views at the heart of the construction procurement. Given the complexity of the project and the high quality expectations, special consideration was given to the selection of the contractor with emphasis on their design capability. The four-way split of contracts and the use of different types of contract (ICE, JCT, Design & Build) at different stages also ensured design expertise among contractors was optimised because of the early focus on maintaining design quality.

20.3 Objectives

Stakeholder visits to successful projects like the BBC/Pacific Quay in 2008, to the Gartcosh site, and to building precedents and comparable institutions in the UK and Europe also helped to ensure that 'stakeholders were on board', as well as build relationships between stakeholders. Client education, focus on design outcomes, and coordination between stakeholders were all important factors in ensuring that intended outcomes were achieved. 'Process maps' developed by BMJ as a part of their briefing role by engaging with the users were used very effectively by the composite design team to confirm adjacencies and the rhythm of the building. The Programme Board and occupying agencies referred to the 'Process Map' to illustrate and explore different organisational relationships, potential spatial organisations, functions between the different groups, and just how the building would operate day to day. The campus aims were to:

- improve the efficiency and effectiveness of the multiple agencies involved;
- foster proactive cooperation and collaboration between these agencies;
- provide world-leading expert forensic scientific support to local and national partners.

The function of the building defines its architecture; the design creates a practical yet iconic building that will encourage disparate groups to work together collaboratively and creatively. Adopting a geometry informed by the immediate context, programme, and chromosome form, the design of the building references genetic structures and imagery associated with identity; it emphasises uniqueness and, at the same time, common bonds.

The original design competition project brief in 2007 emphasised the following building and design outcomes:

- bring together various detection agencies under one roof to develop ideas of collaboration, exchange, participation to accelerate information dissemination, and co-operation;
- deliver a sustainable building with useable, functional space for each of the agencies to maximise the potential of the building;
- deliver a resilient building to ensure continuity of power/services supply and sophisticated IT infrastructure to the agencies;

FIGURE 20.2 Chromosome and DNA patterns.
Source: Author.

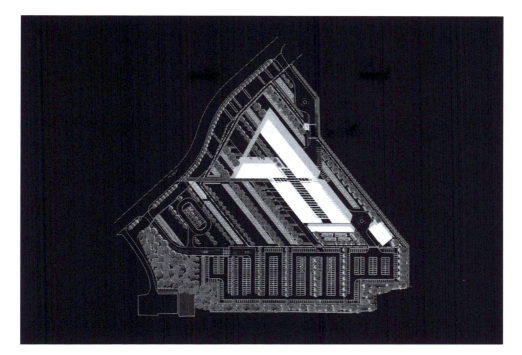

FIGURE 20.3 Site plan of Campus.
Source: Author.

- deliver a building that met the unique set of design conditions imposed by the multiple occupants and address the varying and potentially conflicting requirements for collaboration and segregation;
- deliver a high environmental performance and a range of relevant community benefits.

20.4 Context

The brief and accommodation schedule for the building were extremely complex in terms of adjacencies, the hierarchy of levels of security, and non-contamination of evidence. By locating the forensics in a separate leg of the building, we avoided any risk to the integrity of the scientific evidence and acknowledged the importance of managing any risk of contamination. This created a complex network of relationships. Collectively it was a principal objective of the client to simplify the strands of this network by encouraging collaboration through exchange, i.e., the agora or marketplace of information defined as the atrium space.

20.5 Multi-purpose spaces and building systems

20.5.1 Campus atrium

All elements of the offices that can be are open to this atrium, further reinforcing the shared nature of the building and the contact across the space. Building wings are also physically

FIGURE 20.4 View south in atrium showing level changes.
Source: Keith Hunter Photography.

connected to each other with the bridge elements through this space. The atrium can be used for large gatherings, multiple breakout and informal meeting areas as well as allowing the canteen to spill into the space if desired. Architectural elements like bridges and visible informal meeting areas were also made explicit to enhance the chance meeting and visual connectivity. The floor is stepped up over accommodation on the lower floors creating a greater degree of privacy and quietness through the shared space. While the main purpose of the atrium was for the social interaction and flexibility of building occupants, it is also key to the ventilation strategy in the building. Warm air rises to the top through a natural stack effect. Heat is then mechanically removed through a heat exchanger and recirculated back into the office spaces. This allows clean air to be preheated for the office spaces and dirty air

FIGURE 20.5 View of atrium.
Source: Keith Hunter Photography.

220 Murray

to vent naturally through the atrium space. It is aligned to offer the best open views of the Campsie Hills to the north.

20.5.2 Building form

Many of the functions carried out within the building are concerned with identity and identification. The façade and building concept take some of the visual references associated with the process of identification and abstracts them into the building itself. Vertical orientation of the façade breaks up the horizontality of the massing, providing rhythm and variety, and is inspired by various visual references, including DNA sequences, barcode banding, and fingerprint dermal ridges as formal devices. Three significant ideas generate the form of the building. The discrete functions in each wing of the building are set against one another as blocks in the personification of the chromosome form. The distinct role of each wing is in contrast to the collective shared space of the atrium. The building is also rooted in the specific geology of the site in North Lanarkshire. This geological form rises from the earth into the atrium as the base of the building, i.e., a series of stepped plinths, in turn enclosing support accommodation.

A limited palette of standardised bands of deep solid masonry are repeated in sequences around the façade in arrangements that reference the male and female chromosome sequences. These waves are denser at closed elements of the façade and provide contrast at large glazing areas. Deep window reveals generate a columnar or pillastered effect on the façades, providing considerably more shading than a flat façade. The patterned form both minimises solar gain and provides relief to the otherwise regular and long façades. This verticality and the deeply modelled façades also strongly ground the building with a gravitas suited to its functions.

Numerous visits to the site and to comparable institutions in the UK and Europe provided a basic tool kit and reference points for the development of a design strategy for the building. Extensive discussions were held with the various client bodies to unlock the solution, a synthesis of objectives for the six disparate organisations. Context, precedent, and metaphor were combined with these analyses to develop a physical manifestation of the essence of the development in a semiology which would be capable of being read at various levels and provide building users with a way to understand the nature of the building.

20.5.3 Design approach

Rootedness, security, stability, confidence, and intelligence were all essential characteristics of the brief, which were required to be embodied in the design solution. The dynamic nature of the plan evolved from the geometry of the site boundaries, such that the principal entrance would be on a diagonal route, parallel to the railway, as is the secondary entrance to the east. It is intended that this would allow connection through to future expansion wings. These geometries generate a language and dynamism entirely appropriate to the nature of the agencies operating inside the campus facility. These form the starting point for the building shape, along with the systematic analysis of the building's programme as evolving in multifaceted aspects of performance.

It was important that a strong design ethos be established for this building. As previously described, DNA and chromosome biology were selected as important new technical

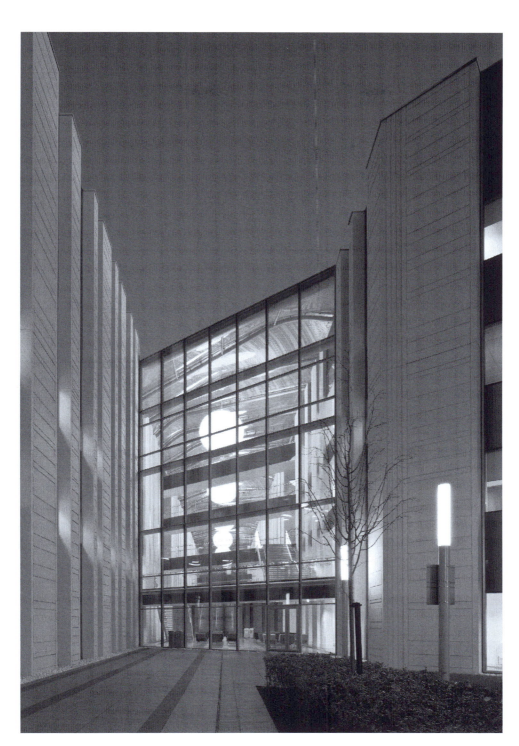

FIGURE 20.6 Glazed wall on north end of atrium.
Source: Keith Hunter Photography.

FIGURE 20.7 Evening view of campus.
Source: Keith Hunter Photography.

detection tools with their corollary in determining the rigour of the process of identifying guilt and innocence: the basic principles in human rights and the rule of law. The primary circulation is at the centre of the building at the point where the two chromatids would touch. Connecting bridge elements through the atrium were also initially inspired by diagrams of DNA chain connections. These concepts were the starting point for iterative processes whereby design options were tested in terms of accessibility, legibility, internal ambiance, environmental performance, and structural expression, which ultimately permitted a solution with some depth and purpose. The early concept studies of chromosome shapes and other genetic forms remain detectable in the overall design. These technologies were selected for their subtle yet explicit exposition of the detection process as themes to influence the design of the structural support devices, shading, solar control, and ventilation systems, and support a sustainable approach within an envelope design. Concurrently, a variety of programmatic solutions and spatial permutations developed alongside the detailed three-dimensional design, whose complexities were tested through model-making, animations, and other forms of visualisation. The essence was to translate the abstraction of the idea into a concrete form, options of which were tested to optimise the environmental performance of the façades and surfaces. The design of the façades and surfaces were required to embed the ethos of the design solution for the 'Institution' as a highly contextual approach in terms of site, accommodation, objectives, and character of the institutions as one organisation.

The design approach permeates and synthesises all aspects of design from spatial organisation to detailed fabrication. Façade engineering, as seen through the repetitive use of a small number of components or subsets of components, has encouraged manipulation of the façades through the use of pattern making.

In his essay, 'Symbolic and Literal Aspects of Technology' (Colquhoun and Frampton, 2008), Alan Colquhoun defines the essence of the argument and the basis of our approach:

The science of building, the rationalisation of construction and assembly, however vital in themselves, remain in the world of literal action. It is only when the architect seizing this world organises it according to the logic of symbolic forms that architecture results. (Colquhoun and Frampton, 2008)

The principle of a concrete or steel frame sheathed in some form of curtain wall is often such a meagre translation of the ideals of the Modern Movement, masking an apparently logical and functional system enough that the essential features of good architecture are being overlooked. It is still possible to achieve the effect of mass, which is not a necessarily a product of programme and its structural interpretation. "Massiveness" in such construction can be exaggerated to embody enclosure, protection and civic authority reminiscent of a walled town. We have sought to exemplify this approach.

Colquhoun poses a further problem:

if buildings are to retain their quality of uniqueness as symbols, how can they also be the end products of an industrial system whose purpose is to find general solutions. We have a confusion between technology as a means to construction and technology as the content of the building form itself. (Colquhoun and Frampton, 2008)

20.6 Culture and communication

The distinction is false, Colquhoun suggests, as it ignores the fact that architecture belongs to a world of symbolic forms in which every aspect of building is presented metaphorically not literally. Semiotics is seen as having anthropological dimensions, and is a means of determining visual communication. In *Umberto Eco: Philosophy, Semiotics and the Work of Fiction*, Caesar suggests all cultural phenomena can be studied as communication. These signs have psychological and biological roots. This pattern language can be simplistic or complex visual mathematics to enrich the meaning or understanding of the complexities of the building codified in a manner that both aids understanding and enriches experience (Caesar, 1999).

Design outcomes were clearly identified and articulated in the business case from 2006/7. This early clear reference to intended organisational objectives such as the focus on collaboration between various anti-crime agencies, functionality, and sustainability ensured that there was clarity and consistency in approach. This helped inform the procurement strategy. The author was also appointed Client Design Champion for the project to ensure design outcomes were locked in and regularly occurring design workshops were convened with the composite design team. The emerging design was seen to meet the intended outcomes within the agreed budgets and could be flexed to take account of the vagaries of annual budgeting at a time of budget cuts. The Scottish Government also built in flexibility to accommodate scope changes through the adoption of the four-contract strategy. Whilst a Post Occupancy Evaluation Research exercise is underway and the building is to be featured as a case study in the, as yet unpublished, Scottish Government Review on Design-Led Construction Procurement (one of five case studies, the others being projects in health, housing, learning and infrastructure), several aspects of the original objectives are now bearing fruit.

As planned, incidental meetings, viewed as being important, allow informal conversations to happen that might not otherwise occur. The building encourages people's paths to cross

FIGURE 20.8 Detail of façade.
Source: Keith Hunter Photography.

The Scottish Crime Campus **225**

to facilitate these unplanned conversations and introductions. Being located adjacent to one another means meetings happen more regularly, happen faster and can involve people who might not otherwise be involved. Equally, just being co-located is not enough and management needs to change to ensure more effective collaboration happens in some cases.

Most agencies have changed the way they work as a result of moving into the building. Some emergent findings are:

- Moving into open plan was a concern for some staff, and agencies have worked with their employees to minimise negative perceptions.
- More space for some agencies has allowed them to work in different ways and the space has facilitated the inclusion of higher tech equipment and allowed people to form new multi-agency teams who can sit together in a space.
- Offering spaces to mitigate the loss of private offices such as the inclusion of quiet rooms has been important.
- Most agencies are at or near capacity in terms of numbers and some may have to consider how the Scottish Crime Campus can support flexible working, e.g. desk sharing, in the future.
- Informal working, e.g. use of the atrium, is not something that all building users are comfortable with and some are still working towards knowing how to use this space effectively.

20.7 Conclusion

The concept developed for the research project was to find an architectural form and pattern language that would provide a semiological basis for the essence of the building's operational techniques and also give outstanding environmental performance. This was achieved in the choices of both external and internal enclosing surfaces and the forms generated from them. The outcome of the research into these shapes and materials led to the design decisions for four blocks in a formal arrangement around a common gathering space, i.e., the series of horizontal and vertical planes. The organisation of the internal façades enclosing this space reflected the semiology contained in the external façades that enclose the buildings as well as on the roof surface of the atrium.

The questions originally set out to be answered in this research programme have been successful visually, programmatically, and as a built structure. Defining a new semiology for buildings that reflect the ethos behind the brief, satisfy the technological requirements in terms of built environmental performance, and offer constructional advantages in terms of cost and quality has made an early and lasting impact on this mixed-agency facility.

20.8 Acknowledgements

From the bid-stage, design quality, design research and control were the responsibility of the author. For specific fiscal reasons the Government procured the project in three stages. The first was designed by Ryder and implemented by Sir Robert McAlpine as a standard works contract. The second was designed by Ryder who were then novated to Graham Construction as construction architect under a design and build contract with bmj as lead consultant – client representative. On the third, the fit-out was a management contract with

226 Murray

Balfour Beatty Construction Ltd; bmj were architects and lead consultant and the author was client design advisor.

The other main consultants were Arup Civil, Structural and Transport Engineer; Wallace Whittle, Environmental Engineers; Ian White Landscape Architects and Thomas and Adamson Cost Consultants with Sweett Group as project managers. Jeremy Smart Associates undertook client liaison between the Government bodies and design and construction teams.

20.9 References

Caesar, M. (1999). *Umberto Eco: Philosophy, Semiotics and the Work of Fiction*. Malden, MA: Polity Press.
Colquhoun, A. and Frampton, K. (2008). *Collected Essays in Architectural Criticism: Alan Colquhoun*. London: Black Dog Publishing.

21

MULTI-TASKING ARCHITECTURAL COMPUTER PROGRAMS: BIM

Akikazu Kato, Shiho Mori, and Gen Taniguchi

21.1 Introduction

The challenge of using Building Information Modeling (BIM) systems is becoming an important issue in the building industries of the USA and Japan, as well as in other countries. Building Information Modeling enables front-loading decision-making in the planning, programming, and design phases, meaning more is discussed and decided in the basic design stage, rather than in the succeeding detailed design stage. This shift of workload increases liability issues for the architects and engineers; however, the process enhances the quality of each phase in the project's development. The use of BIM provides a holistic picture for the general contractors, where in the conventional construction process the information is scattered throughout architectural, structural, mechanical, and electrical drawings. Thus, the system will increase productivity in the construction phase. When the information needed in the management and operation of the building is suitably extracted before the actual completion of the building, as in the virtual handover stage, the use of BIM can support efficiency in the facility management stage. Lastly, BIM enables simulations by use of evidence uncovered through research, benefitting the building performance assessment stage. By using the case study of a children's hospital redevelopment project in Japan, this chapter explains these advantages and discusses the development of meta-BIM as a major player in the current innovations to the building delivery cycle.

21.2 Background

Building Information Modeling is one of the most promising developments in the architecture, engineering, and construction (AEC) industries (Eastman *et al.*, 2011). Fundamentally transforming modes of design practice and standards of building design, delivery, and operation (Kensek and Noble, 2014), it is promising that BIM will benefit the process of building performance evaluation.

The introductory stage of BIM is now evolving, with more participants than previously involved. Clients/users, planners/designers, contractors, and facility managers seek the innovative process during design and construction in order to re-examine workflow, increase productivity, and solidify industry leadership among competitors. This chapter aims to clarify the current status of BIM usage mainly in the USA and Japan, and to compare the differences and similarities in the cross-cultural context so that the most useful methodology is found. This methodology can then be applied to guide students in higher education who will be the next leaders and practitioners in the coming years.

21.3 Current literature on BIM

In American academia, *The BIM Handbook* (Eastman *et al.*, 2008) was published as an informative seminal book describing the state-of-the-art technology of BIM systems in 2008, updated in 2011. The book provided powerful examples of BIM use for owners, managers, designers, engineers, and contractors. *Building Information Modeling: BIM in Current and Future Practice* by Kensek and Noble stretches the boundaries of BIM, and challenges the profession to examine its full potential. It considers, for example, how BIM could support design thinking and reasoning, support simulation, and provide insights into the profession and the direction it is heading (Kensek and Noble, 2014).

In professional practice, a similar publication on integrating BIM and sustainability appeared in 2008, i.e., *Green BIM: Successful Sustainable Design with Building Information Modeling* (Krygiel and Nies, 2008). The American Institute of Architects (AIA) upholds that these two revolutionary movements are intended to create environmentally friendly design through a streamlined process. Industry leader Kimon Onuma claims to have used BIM as early as 1993, leading *BIMstorm* from 2006. *BIMstorm* is a cloud-based charrette on architectural design projects, joining multiple owners, users, and consulting members. In Japan, an introductory publication *Innovating Industry: BIM Construction Revolution* (Yamanashi, 2009) noted that the IT revolution lead by BIM will impact business and the economy to a greater degree than the Industrial Revolution.

A number of publications on operating manuals for BIM have been published in the USA and Japan, including those by Kensek (2014) and Ieiri (2014). Additionally, guidebooks were published for facility managers, including those by Teicholz (2013) and the JFMA BIM-FM Research Council (2015).

21.4 Important features of BIM

When BIM is used in a project's planning, programming, and design, all of the information regarding the building is linked automatically. When a designer changes the geometric shape of the building plan, like those in elevations, sections, detailed working drawings, information in finishing schedule charts, and structural, mechanical and electrical drawings, related pieces of building information are changed automatically. It could be said that the geometric shape is only one portion of information regarding the building.

Building Information Modeling systems also give accurate figures of used building materials, like volume of concrete, total area of wall paper, number of door knobs, and others. They detect potential incidents – for example, an air-conditioning duct colliding with a structural beam – and warn designers and supervisors to make necessary adjustments.

21.5 BIM for hospital projects

In the case study of Maryland General Hospital (MGH) in Baltimore, Maryland, an expansion project of approximately 9,600 square meters (103,000 square feet) was carried out, reaching completion in March 2010. It was connected to an existing structure built in the 1950s, and included eight new operating suites, four specialty rooms, an 18-bed intensive-care unit (ICU), a pharmacy, and a laboratory (Eastman et al., 2011). Maryland General Hospital, founded in 1881, is part of the University of Maryland Medical System. On June 6, 2013, Maryland General Hospital was renamed "University of Maryland, Midtown Campus."

Throughout the development of this project, information from different sources was integrated using BIM to form a system consisting of a centralized database and integrated facilities management software. The system also uses bar coding for equipment and tablet PCs for on-site data handling. This made data available at all times, helping to eliminate waste from facilities management, optimize and increase the lifecycle of equipment, increase efficiency in preventive maintenance, and provide accurate and electronic as-built documents.

21.6 Aichi Children's Health and Medical Center

The authors are involved in a redevelopment project of a 200-bed children's hospital in Ohbu, Aichi Prefecture, Japan. Designed by Yasui Architects & Engineers and completed in September 2015, the additional 7,200 square meters (77,500 square feet) consists of a tertiary emergency department, a new operating department, a pediatric intensive care unit (PICU), and support facilities, and is gradually showing its performance capabilities. Because there is

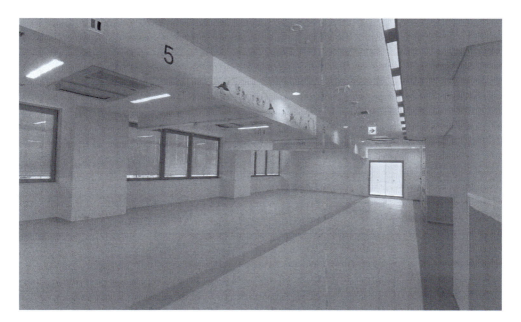

FIGURE 21.1 PICU of Aichi Children's Hospital, photographed immediately after building completion.
Source: Authors.

FIGURE 21.2 BIM view of PICU with expected medical equipment and furnishings.
Source: Yasui Architects & Engineers, Inc. and Kato Laboratory, Mie University.

the existing main building, a full-scale BIM was not used. Autodesk Revit Architecture software was used to develop 3D drawings of major functional areas of the new addition, with renovations to be made to portions of the existing structure. During the construction period, 3D drawings of rooms, including medical equipment and furnishings, were developed to facilitate final working drawings presented to hospital staff. This practice was to ensure the staff had a better understanding of the room by room utilization contents. Presently, a FM system development project is being carried out using similar BIM data, and the case of MGH outlined above has been quite informative because of the similarities between the two projects (Seki *et al.*, 2016).

21.7 Towards meta-BIM

In the course of the evolution of mankind and architecture, the initial breakthrough might have been the use of triangulation drawings, or triangular surveying, to verify one's land holdings in the fertile flood plain along the Nile River of Ancient Egypt. The second might have been in the Renaissance, namely the use of perspective drawings first described in 1435 by Leon Battista Alberti in his *Della Pittura* (Bertol, 1996). The third epoch was the use of computers starting in the 1960s (Kalay *et al.*, 2014). It should be noted that in the same era the Environmental Design Research Association (EDRA) was founded, and post-occupancy evaluation (POE) became a mainstream field of specialization, which later produced the Building Performance Evaluation (BPE) (Preiser and Hardy, 2015). Thus, the current use of BIM is staged as the fourth major innovation.

Early BPE projects of hospital facilities started with the behavioral tracking of pathways of building occupants, including one carried out in a hospital ward (Nuffield Provincial

Hospitals Trust, 1955) and another in the simulation of the Yale Traffic Index (Thompson and Goldin, 1975). Inspired by these studies, the authors carried out a time-motion study of nurses' activities in hospital wards and conducted simulations of nurses' walking distances to evaluate ward floor-plan types (Taniguchi *et al.*, 1984). These BPE studies are now accumulated to create a knowledge base on the planning, design, and management of hospital and healthcare facilities.

Starting from the latter half of the 1990s, with more efficient personal computers and Internet access, studies on computer usage in architectural planning and design became easier. Fuzzy inference and genetic algorithms in workplace studies were carried out using the open environment of AutoCAD software by evaluating the performance of floor plan types and creating a suitable floor layout (Kato, 1994; Kato *et al.*, 2001). Application Programming Interface (API) is provided in current BIM software like Autodesk Revit, which has a similar interface to AutoCAD, where an external program can be loaded and performed on the geometric shape of BIM.

By combining the knowledge base of BPE studies with simulations using API in BIM systems, a complete design interface can establish a BPE feedback loop in the early stages of planning, programming, and design. As the automated development of geometric forms continues, the next phase of evolution will lead to the development of meta-BIMs.

21.8 References

Bertol, D. (1996). *Designing Digital Space: An Architect's Guide to Virtual Reality*, John Wiley & Sons.

Eastman, C. *et al.* (2008). *BIM Handbook: A Guide to Building Information Modeling for Owners, Managers, Designers, Engineers, and Contractors*, John Wiley & Sons, first edition.

Eastman, C. *et al.* (2011). *BIM Handbook: A Guide to Building Information Modeling for Owners, Managers, Designers, Engineers, and Contractors*, John Wiley & Sons, second edition.

Ieiri, R. (2014). *BIM in This Much* (This Much Series), Shuwa System Publishing, in Japanese.

JFMA BIM-FM Research Council (2015). *BIM Utilization Guidebook for Facility Manager*, JFMA, in Japanese.

Kalay, Y. E., Schaumann, D., Seung, W. H., and Simeone, D. (2014). Beyond BIM: Next-Generation Building Information Modeling to Support Form, Function, and Use of Buildings, Chapter 24 of Kensek, K. M., and Noble, D. E. (2014).

Kato, A. (1994). A Study on Development of Floor Zoning Support System, Facility Management Tools Using Fuzzy Inference, *Strategies and Technologies for Maintenance and Modernization of Building*, CIB W70 Tokyo Symposium, Vol. 1, pp.231–236.

Kato, A., Le Roux, P. C., and Kitakami, Y. (2001). Application of Genetic Algorithms in Office Building Configurations, Reproduction Model Simulation in a Japanese Local Government Office, *Proceedings of EDRA32* and paper handout, Environmental Design Research Association, Edinburgh, UK.

Kensek, K. M. (2014). *Building Information Modeling*, Pocket Architecture Technical Design Series, Routledge.

Kensek, K. M. and Noble, D. E. (2014). *Building Information Modeling: BIM in Current and Future Practice*, John Wiley & Sons.

Krygiel, E. and Nies, B. (2008). *Green BIM: Successful Sustainable Design with Building Information Modeling*, Sybex.

Nuffield Provincial Hospitals Trust (1955). *Studies in the Functions and Design of Hospitals*, Oxford University Press.

Seki, S. *et al.* (2016). Development Studies on Facility Management System Using BIM for Children's Hospital, Utilization of BIM in Renovation and Extension Project for Aichi Children's Health and

Medical Center, *Research Paper Report of Tokai Branch Conference*, Architectural Institute of Japan, Vol. 54, No. 402, pp.317–320, in Japanese.

Taniguchi, G. *et al.* (1984). A Study on Nursing Activities in Hospital Wards, *Transactions of the Architectural Institute of Japan*, No. 344, October 1984, pp.116–125, in Japanese.

Teicholz, P. (2013). *BIM for Facility Managers*, IFMA Foundation, John Wiley & Sons.

Thompson, J. D. and Goldin, G. (1975). *The Hospital: A Social and Architectural History*, Yale University Press.

Yamanashi, K. (2009). *Innovating the Industry: BIM Construction Revolution*, Nihon Jitsugyo Publishing, in Japanese.

REFLECTIONS ON PART V

Michael J. Crosbie, Ph.D., FAIA

"Managing ever-increasing complexity and scale"

Part V examines adaptability in the built environment at the scale of neighborhoods and urban precincts, as well as large chunks of infrastructure, developments, and groups of buildings such as military installations and campuses. Some of the case studies focus not only on what was done and why, but how it was accomplished: the tools available to professionals and ways of organizing projects at this scale.

Hardy provides an insightful look into a piece of urbanism that is rarely considered: alleyways. Alleyways are part of the spatial fabric in every city, but they are often invisible—behind or between buildings, inaccessible, and often not very pretty. These are transition spaces between the highly public realm and the private realm in cities. Sometimes alleyways run parallel to the main street, providing access for services, utilities, and trash removal, while at other times alleyways are perpendicular to the main thoroughfare and are "blind" or a dead end. They typically lack regular flows of traffic and pedestrians. How can we celebrate alleys as a part of the city, transform them, reinvent them? Older cities that grew before the advent of automobiles tend to have narrow alleys, while newer cities, such as those in the American Southwest, have wider alleys. To give them life, alleyways need pedestrian traffic and slow or no auto traffic. Walls and long distances can hamper pedestrian activity. But such transition spaces are perfect for overcoming the "silo effect" of single-use spaces in the city. Might restaurants commandeer alleyways on a temporary basis for serving patrons, in a similar way that some establishments now take over parking spaces in front of their shops to set up tables? Alleys can also become settings for vegetation, water management, composting sites, or landscaping. Hardy notes that they can have a cultural role, as they do in cities such as Phoenix, where alleyways become canvases for colorful murals that raise awareness of the city's diverse ethnic culture. Might an alleyway host a small work of architecture? One of the most amazing buildings I ever visited was architect Jakub Szczesny's Keret House in Warsaw, which at 5 feet at its widest point between two buildings is currently the narrowest house in the world.

Two chapters here are case studies of what to do and what not to do. Schramm's account of the transformation of a German military barracks dating from the late 19th century into a college campus today demonstrates the perils of ignoring the building's potential users in its design and construction. Not only was the recent design of a new building at Bielefeld University's Minden Campus carried out without the input and involvement of faculty and students—the completed structure has been coldly received by its users. Ironically, it is part of a university for applied sciences, some of which include the built environment! Some faculty and researchers at Minden saw this as a perfect opportunity for a POE, which concluded that professors, staff, and students feel alienated by the new educational facility because they were not consulted in its design and construction, and are mystified by the implied functions of the spaces, not understanding how the design is to accommodate their needs. They feel like strangers on their own campus, victims of a top-down decision-making culture.

Minden is in marked contrast to Murray's case study of the Scottish Crime Campus, the design of which was carefully carried out to involve professionals and staff from six different anti-crime agencies in Scotland who would work together in the building. The goal was to create a place that would not only accommodate each agency's needs but would enhance the opportunities for information sharing and collaboration. The designers used a Programme Board and Process Maps to articulate how the agencies operate and reveal how spatial organization and adjacencies might be most effective. The key element in the building is a central, light-filled atrium around which the six agencies are housed—a space that encourages casual and serendipitous exchanges, collaboration, and efficiency. Opportunities for social engagement in the atrium attract people to it. Visual connections between departments encourage chance meetings and exchanges. The atrium has also become a work site for some in the building. The atrium appears to be functioning like the central square of a small city, all thanks to a thoughtful design process that relied on the building's likely users.

Two chapters in Part V concentrate on the design/construction process as a way to build in flexibility and adaptability. Rath and Hodulak's account of the re-use of a former airport in Germany as a new research and industrial park focuses on the use of "integrative planning." The authors describe this method as scaled to complex, large projects with a lot of pieces—veritable cities in scale. There is intense communication and collaboration among scores of consultants. Conventional processes place the architect at the very center of the project, working with a cadre of consultants who join the project team sometimes at different intervals. The work of the consultants is blended with the architect's design (seamlessly, in the best of all possible worlds). Integrative planning places the architect and the integrative planner on the same level, although the authors' description of the process gives more latitude to the planner. Team members are involved from the very start, and flexibility of the facility over its projected life cycle is considered at the beginning of design—it becomes a functional/performance metric. The planner, who guides the team's collaboration, is more of a generalist with technical and engineering knowledge, ideally an expert in information technologies and building automation. The integrative planning process described is becoming more commonplace, and it gives some architects pause to find themselves not at the center of the process as has traditionally been the case.

Kato and his co-authors provide a view into what might be called "integrative BIM," in the way software tools are co-joined with BIM (building information modeling) to give the project team seamless coordination and the ability to test potential solutions. As the authors point out, with BIM design decisions are made early in the project, loaded into the BIM model, which then compels project team members to make coordinated design decisions. Up-front decisions make the project more reality-based early in the process. Building information modeling has the potential for clients to better understand the building as it is being designed because of its three-dimensional modeling. Building information modeling also allows for the study of functions in spaces (such as time-motion studies and building traffic analysis) and to model how they might be more efficiently accommodated. Taking data collected in POE and BPE and using it to analyze plan layouts, it can later feed into commissioning and performance evaluation, facility management, and maintenance. The authors make a persuasive argument that BIM supports greater performance and sustainability in the built environment, provides swift feedback to the project team as the design progresses, and signals in real-time conflicts in the design based on faulty decision making.

Part V ramps up the scale of flexibility and adaptability in the built environment on the urban level, but it also gives us a glimpse into the future of design as projects become more complex and the number of collaborators on project teams grow. It is difficult to determine whether the growing complexity and scale of projects is happening because of new computing power and ways to organize our work, or whether the tools are the products of greater design complexity and scale.

PART VI
Epilogue

22

THE INTERNATIONAL SPACE STATION: ADAPTIVE HUMAN ACCOMMODATIONS IN AN EXTREME, ISOLATED ENVIRONMENT

David J. Fitts, Jennifer L. Rochlis, Ph.D., Mihriban Whitmore, Ph.D., and Alexandra Whitmire, Ph.D.

22.1 Introduction

The International Space Station (ISS) is Earth's largest human-habitable orbiting research platform. Designed and built under agreements among the US, Russian, Canadian, Japanese, and European space agencies, ISS has been continually inhabited since November, 2000. The vehicle supports a complement of six crew members of both genders and different cultural backgrounds.

Several forces operate to make ISS unique among habitats presented in this book. The vehicle operates in an extremely hostile environment, and carries its own self-sufficient, atmospherically-pressurized volume to support the lives of its crew. Although it only operates at an altitude of approximately 400 kilometers (240 miles) above Earth's surface it is very difficult to access because only a small set of vehicles – each with their own transport limitations – can attain the orbital velocity of approximately 27,600 km/h (17,100 miles per hour) required to reach ISS. At a high cost per pound to deliver anything to Earth's orbit there is severe scrutiny on the size, weight, volume, and applicability of every resupply item. ISS's costs are shared across 26 nations, adding political complexity to every decision from the makeup of the crew to short- and long-term planning for ISS's utilization. All of these constraints have required the vehicle's design and operation to be adaptable to change in order to remain useful and relevant over ISS's 20- to 30-year life.

22.2 ISS composition, modularity and adaptability

ISS comprises a central structure, core systems, and human-habitable modules. The most visible exterior elements are a 109 meter (358 feet) truss that provides the backbone of the vehicle and four 73 meter (240 feet) solar arrays that provide electrical power. All other elements of ISS are attached to the central truss including mechanisms that keep the solar arrays pointed toward the sun, thermal control systems, docking ports for visiting vehicles, robotic manipulators, communication antennae, and, most importantly, the habitable modules that appear as canisters grouped near the mid-point of the truss (see Figure 22.1).

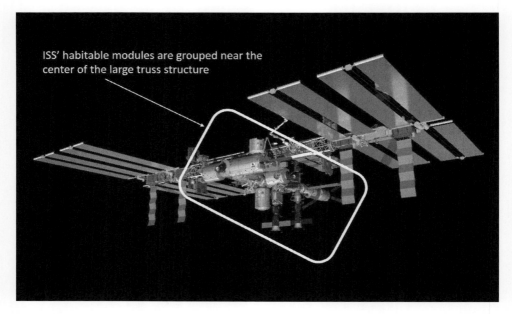

FIGURE 22.1 Exterior view of ISS.
Source: NASA, Public Access.

The pressurized human-habitable modules of ISS have hatches at each connection point that allow isolation of a module in the event of an emergency – i.e., depressurization, fire, or toxic spill. Except for modules provided by the Russian Roscosmos space agency, whose designs are derived from the earlier Mir space station, all modules are outfitted with interchangeable racks in the four quadrants of the circular cross-section. The faces of the racks leave a cross-sectional square of habitable volume along the central axis (see Figure 22.2). The number of racks a module can accommodate depends on the length of the module. Though some racks were pre-installed before modules were delivered to orbit, the racks are sized to be transportable to orbit by visiting vehicles and to be maneuvered through vehicle hatchways. Using two crewmembers, most racks were installed in the vehicle on-orbit in this manner.

There are four types of racks:

1. System racks. As in terrestrial buildings, these support basic engineering capabilities such as electrical power management, thermal control, air handling, data, and communications.
2. Habitability racks. These uniquely support human habitation of the ISS modules. Though some may also be deemed system racks, e.g., human life-support systems, others are unique to the daily living requirements of the crew, e.g., food preparation, communal dining, exercise, crew health care, and human waste capture/disposal. Even private quarters for individual crewmembers are provided within rack volumes.
3. Utilization racks. Sometimes called science or experiment racks, these provide dedicated locations for the scientific investigations that are the raison d'être for the ISS. If ISS racks were to be mapped to the "Live; Work; Play" paradigm mentioned in the introduction to this book, these utilization racks would be where the meaningful work of ISS is conducted.

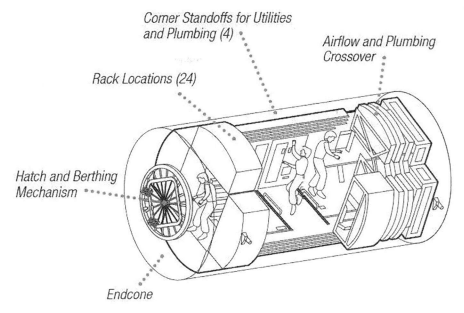

FIGURE 22.2 Rack system within ISS habitable volumes.
Source: NASA, Public Access.

4. Storage racks. All racks noted above interface with utility connections provided by each module's infrastructure, but there are also an extensive number of passive storage racks needed to keep the large amounts of loose equipment from filling up ISS's corridors. Loose equipment might be crew food and water, spare system parts, science equipment and supplies, maintenance tools, clean clothing, etc. The ISS contains 111 racks of which approximately 30% are for storage.

The ISS rack system's modularity allows change-out of racks on-orbit, but the designs of systems and subsystems within ISS racks are also modular so that they may be maintained, rearranged, or modified. In particular, eight of the utilization racks are designed for sub-rack-sized science experiments that can be changed to meet the changing needs of scientific research (see Figure 22.3).

The major components of ISS were assembled in orbit over a sequence that lasted from 1998 to 2011. During 85% of the construction, the ISS was permanently occupied by crewmembers who finalized the installation of elements and systems using robotic arms and extra- and intra-vehicular crew activity. The largest ISS elements were delivered to orbit by the US Space Shuttle before its retirement in 2011. Even after major assembly was declared complete in May 2011, additional pressurized volumes have been added, the interior has continued to be rearranged, and newer rack and sub-rack systems have been delivered to expand capability and better utilize available space. In short, the ISS can be modified and updated despite the extreme isolation of space. As new utilization demands and new technologies become available, ISS's design and operation allow for change and improvement. Several new habitable modules and large systems are scheduled to be added to the vehicle in upcoming years. This

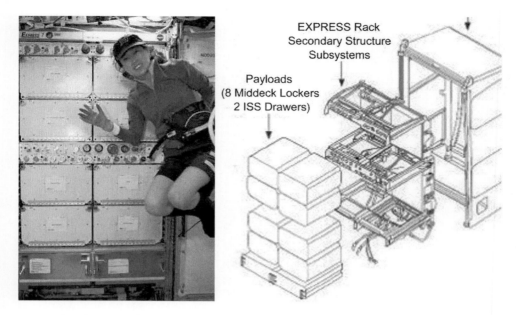

FIGURE 22.3 Crewmember Naoko Yamazaki prepares to transfer sub-rack experiments during transfer vehicle docking; ISS rack showing integration of smaller sub-rack experiment packages. *Source*: NASA, Public Access.

adaptability makes ISS a valuable laboratory for "post-occupancy evaluation" of a spaceflight habitat and habitation systems.

22.3 Life aboard ISS

The tasks that crewmembers perform during a "day in the life" of ISS are similar to those of terrestrial humans. Crewmembers live – i.e., eat, sleep, hydrate, perform hygiene, exercise; they work – i.e., conduct science, maintenance, habitation chores; and play – i.e., spend communal time, retreat to privacy, and communicate with family. The unique challenges of ISS, and of human spaceflight in general, include living and working every day in the same relatively small space, having little to no connection with nature, and living with zero gravity. Crewmembers' days are filled with planned activities, often pre-scheduled down to five-minute increments. Functions to be performed are typically sequential, i.e., individual members aren't typically required to multi-task at a given moment. When tasks are performed, crewmembers typically go to a unique location within ISS to perform them. Major ISS reconfigurations occur only when visiting vehicles bring and take away sizable components or large quantities of resupply materials.

22.4 Habitability and adaptive architecture: what is habitability?

As early occupation and operation of ISS began, it quickly became evident that users and resuppliers were making plans and assumptions with limited awareness of their impact on available ISS habitable volume, e.g., utilization and system designers were planning large

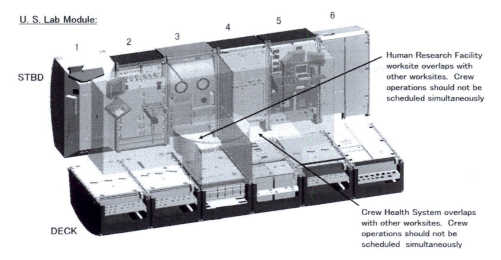

FIGURE 22.4 ISS interior volume configuration analysis for resolving conflicts.
Source: Authors & NASA, Public Access.

attachments on rack fronts that would negatively impact neighboring racks and a module's central corridor. Habitability planners created an internal volume configuration (IVC) forum that required hardware developers to share their designs early in their conception and to meet established, published habitability criteria designed to prevent conflicts and preserve the crew's habitable volume and ability to function, e.g., by establishing "off-limit" zones around emergency equipment (see Figure 22.4).

Establishing habitability criteria for early design concepts was revolutionary in that it allowed human factors engineers to have an early, continuous voice in shaping and controlling the integrated crew environment. Since conceptual design may begin ten years before flight, waiting until systems are delivered to assess their impact on habitability is too little, too late. Operations planning must start early, when designs are being formulated, so that operations don't become a patchwork of reactionary workarounds to make delivered systems useful and habitability tolerable. Providing habitation design criteria and performing human-centric evaluations during system development allows human factors engineers to recommend improvements when designs are still conceptual and able to be cost-effectively modified.

Habitability may be defined as "fitness for occupancy." However, it can be challenging to characterize objectively if a particular environment is "fit" for an individual or group of occupants. Due to zero gravity and full-time confinement, habitability can be even more challenging in space where crews interact with their environment differently than in terrestrial spaces. The spacecraft becomes both home and workspace, thus demanding challenges in terms of user needs. NASA and other countries' space agencies endeavor to consciously identify, quantify, and document key characteristics of habitability design. The generation and implementation of concept-ready ISS habitability requirements has served as a model for future human-habitable spacecraft design within the US National Aeronautics and Space

244 Fitts *et al.*

Administration (*NASA Space Flight Human-System Standards* and *NASA Human Integration Design Handbook*). For next-generation exploration-class vehicles, NASA human factors engineers are also developing advanced iterative user-in-the-loop evaluation processes for early assessment of the acceptability of human habitable volume concurrent with vehicle concept maturation.

22.5 Net habitable volume

Several terms are used to describe spacecraft volume as related to human habitability:

- Pressurized volume – the total volume within the pressure shell.
- Habitable volume – the volume remaining within the pressurized volume after accounting for all hardware and systems. Sometimes called "sand volume," this is equivalent to the volume of sand that would fill the spacecraft around hardware, including gaps, crevices, and other volumes inaccessible or unusable by crewmembers.
- Net habitable volume (NHV) – the functional volume left available to the crew after accounting for losses of volume due to deployed equipment, stowage and trash, and the exclusion of human-unusable volumes.

"Acceptable" minimum spacecraft NHV must support effective and efficient human functionality but must also serve to be behaviorally supportive. What is behaviorally acceptable varies from mission to mission, e.g., what is acceptable for a relatively short transition from the Earth to the Moon will likely not be tolerable for an extended-duration mission to Mars (see Figure 22.5). Acceptability is impacted not only by the volume available, but by the quality of the environment, i.e., factors such as lighting, temperature, humidity, acoustics, and

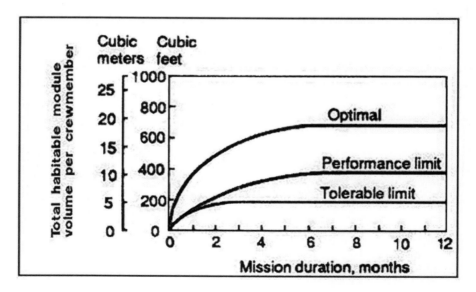

FIGURE 22.5 Graph showing NASA-recommended NHV as a function of mission duration. *Source*: NASA, Public Access.

odor. Such factors must be within their acceptable ranges, with some being user-adjustable to provide crewmembers control over their domain.

Since the dawn of human space exploration, the cost of putting mass into space has put tremendous engineering and management pressure on keeping habitable interiors of spacecraft as small as possible. On the US Gemini program (1961–66) the vehicle provided only about 1.25 m^3 (44.1 ft^3) of habitable volume per crewmember for missions that lasted up to two weeks. In contrast, the ISS must be considered spacious, with over 100 m^3 (3532 ft^3) of pressurized volume available for each of its six human occupants (see Figure 22.6).

Vehicle design engineers tend to focus on systems and hardware, often perceiving the volume needed to accommodate the human crew as an afterthought. In designing the vehicle, it falls upon human factors engineers, psychologists, and crewmembers themselves to emphasize the quantity and quality of NHV. In addition, human spaceflight programs have a history of underestimating the amount of loose equipment required for a mission, e.g., spare parts, experiment equipment, tools, and especially crew consumables. As a result, pre-planned storage volume is typically under-sized during vehicle design and loose equipment ends up being secured in what was originally conceived as unencumbered NHV.

Evaluating the minimum acceptable NHV per crewmember and designing the right qualities into provisions available to support healthy, fulfilling life is an ongoing endeavor for spaceflight agencies. Human spaceflight programs recognize that the volume needed to viably support human habitation increases with mission length and complexity. Durations for exploration class missions to Mars and beyond will extend into years. To evaluate and plan for living and working in the same enclosed volume for such durations, ISS is being utilized for research studies evaluating the behavioral health and performance of crews over extended durations. Such studies yield insight into habitability design criteria for future exploration vehicles. Additionally, space agencies are conducting extended-duration analog

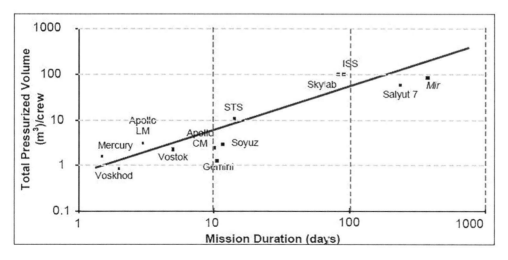

FIGURE 22.6 Graph showing NASA historical spacecraft NHV as a function of mission duration. *Source*: NASA, Public Access.

space missions in terrestrial habitats, e.g., the Mars 520-day chamber study conducted by the European Space Agency in 2011 helped to systematically characterize human behavior in prolonged isolation and confinement. One finding from Mars–520 was that crewmembers became increasingly sedentary over the duration of the mission, highlighting that optimizing future long-duration vehicle layout for maintenance of physical activity sufficient to support bone and muscle health in zero-gravity will be an essential consideration (Basner *et al.* 2012). Few completed analog studies to date, however, have lasted the duration anticipated for a Mars mission. Deriving a NHV and habitat layout that is acceptable for such an endeavor is dependent on developing evidence-driven criteria for judging adequate volume limits for extended-duration exploration missions.

In 2014, the NASA Human Research Program supported a two-day consensus session which brought together experts in the areas of architecture, environmental psychology, cognitive psychology, and industrial ergonomics, with representatives from NASA behavioral health, human factors, and habitability communities. The panel produced a document describing a process to be used to assess NHV and a set of volume-driving tasks to be critically evaluated for long-duration missions. The panel also defined minimum acceptable NHV as:

> The minimum volume of a habitat required to assure mission success during exploration-type space missions with prolonged periods of confinement and isolation in a harsh environment. This definition acknowledges that, in theory, smaller volumes are possible; however, these would be unacceptable from human factors and behavioral health perspectives with likely negative consequences for psychosocial well-being. Considerations in defining minimal acceptable volume include requirements to support tasks as well as requirements maintaining psychological and behavioral health for extended durations – e.g., 1 to 2.5-year missions – in an isolated, confined spacecraft. (Whitmire *et al.,* 2015)

An acceptable minimum NHV of 25 m^3 (883 ft^3) per person was recommended, with several caveats, e.g. based on a crew of six. Importantly, the panel recommended that individual private crew quarters be twice the size of current quarters on the ISS.

22.6 Psychological factors and future roles for ISS

The ISS was developed as an international laboratory where crews could perform critical tasks in microgravity, gathering knowledge to push mankind beyond low earth orbit. ISS is a technological *tour de force* and ISS designers, managers, and users continually investigate new technologies that could expand vehicle capabilities, e.g., original data busses are enhanced with much faster onboard wireless networks; new exploration-class oxygen generation and water reclamation systems have been installed for long-duration mission testing; and advancements in visiting vehicle capabilities may deliver greater mass to orbit at lower costs.

Engineers initially provided for functional human life support and subsequently implemented habitation features with psychological benefits, e.g., private crew quarters for sleep, personal tasks, and private communications with home. ISS communal activity has been supported; e.g., in the galley crewmembers eat most meals together. Additionally, large bay windows that allow crew to gaze at the Earth – a favored leisure pastime – were installed in 2010 near the end of ISS's assembly. The benefit of windows is evident in the thousands of pictures that crewmembers take of Earth and publish through social media. Recently, the ISS program approved an advanced, flexible lighting system that mimics Earth's 24-hour day/night cycle. Several new habitation and system elements are planned, including the first inflatable space habitat, a structural technology that could cost-effectively increase available NHV for future space vehicles. Each of these habitability-enhancing functions have yielded psychological benefits, as evidenced by crew comments in post- and in-flight debriefs.

It is important to remember that the ability to provide upgrades is facilitated by ISS's proximity to Earth, the vehicle's relatively large volume, and its modular construction. As exploration missions shift beyond Earth's orbit and as mission durations increase far beyond what has currently been experienced, many or most aspects of a spacecraft's configuration will be fixed at launch, making pre-flight vehicle design and habitability concerns more critical and salient. It will become increasingly critical to evaluate private crew quarters, communal spaces, meaningful work, and activities during spacecraft design to ensure the psychological health of exploration-class crews. Exploration missions will be quite different from current and past human spaceflight. Long-duration exploration crews will necessarily be more autonomous from Earth-based mission control since there will be long delays in communications due to the long distances and the maximum speed of light.

In the remainder of its useful life, the ISS is positioned to serve as a unique test bed for future beyond-Earth-orbit spacecraft and mission design. Mission simulations are being planned on ISS to model and emulate such missions. Currently, studies are being conducted to evaluate the effect of long-duration zero-gravity exposure on humans. Soon, simulated light-speed communication delays will be introduced to simulate great distances and to evaluate the impact on terrestrial-based mission support, the need for operational autonomy, and the psychological impacts of impaired communications. One of the biggest differences between an Earth-orbiting mission and Mars-or-beyond exploration missions is that the latter will have no option for resupply, so long-duration ISS missions with no resupply have been proposed as potential test cases.

Discussions occur regularly on how the vehicle might serve to support exploration missions directly, e.g., as a way-station or departure node for beyond-Earth orbit. ISS is currently approved for operations through 2024, but this timeframe has been extended in the past and may be extended again.

22.7 Conclusion

In its relatively short history, human space flight has been a process of incremental learning. ISS is a major contributor to our understanding of how to live and work in space for extended periods of time, including not only advances in the mechanics of keeping humans aloft and alive, but advanced understanding of the very real challenges of keeping humans healthy, productive, and reasonably happy in contained environments (see Figure 22.7). ISS is helping the international partners build a better definition and understanding of the totality of what "habitability" means in such environments and missions, and is increasing our awareness of how to ensure that knowledge continues evolving to inform the design of future human spaceflight systems and missions.

FIGURE 22.7 The Expedition Two and Space Shuttle crews convene for a group portrait aboard the ISS.
Source: NASA, Public Access.

22.8 References

Basner, M., *et al.* (2012). "Mars 520-day mission simulation reveals protracted crew hypokinesis and alterations of sleep duration and timing." *Proceedings of the National Academy of Sciences,* vol. 110, www.pnas.org/content/110/7/2635.full. Accessed March 23, 2017.

Whitmire, A., *et al.* (2015). "Minimum Acceptable Net Habitable Volume for Long-Duration Exploration Missions." *NASA, Johnson Space Center.* Houston, TX: NASA/TM-2015-218564. http://ston.jsc.nasa.gov/collections/TRS/_techrep/TM-2015-218564.pdf. Accessed March 29, 2017.

APPENDIX

The habitability paradigm – key elements and concepts for a humane architecture

Wolfgang F. E. Preiser, Andrea E. Hardy, and Jacob J. Wilhelm

A.1 The habitability paradigm

Habitability research was initially carried out by federal agencies including the US Navy, NASA, and the US Army Corps of Engineers in an effort to improve the quality of designed and built environments, for example, in shipboard habitability research. A working definition for the term 'habitability' is offered: 'Habitability refers to those qualitative and quantitative aspects of the built environment which support human activities in terms of individual and communal goals' (Preiser, 1983).

The term is derived from the original meaning of the word 'habitat', i.e., a given species' natural home, which is comfortable and fit for human use. In essence, then, habitability constitutes the quality of the environment.

A philosophical base and set of objectives for environmental design with adequate habitability includes the following considerations, according to the authors:

> Habitability defines the degree of fit between individuals or groups and their environments, both natural and man-made, in terms of ecologically sound and humane key elements and concepts. Habitability is not an absolute but a relativistic concept, subject to different interpretations in different cultures. A future-oriented, evolutionary approach to environmental design should consider worldwide equitable resource allocation, in the interest of long-term survival. Habitability further implies the objective of minimizing adverse effects of environments on their users, e.g. discomfort, stress, distraction, inefficiency, sickness, as well as injury and death through accidents, radiation, toxic substances, etc. (Preiser, 1983).

This habitability paradigm is a proposal that relates buildings and settings to occupants and their respective needs versus the environment. It represents a conceptual, process-oriented approach that accommodates social science concepts in applications such as facility programming, building performance evaluation (BPE), and database development for any type of building or setting. This paradigm does not claim to become a theory of person–environment relationships, although it does permit concepts concerning such relationships to be 'plugged in' where appropriate. Presented in hierarchies from smaller to larger scales, or numbers from lower to higher levels of abstraction, respectively, the paradigm can be transformed into a checklist format to permit systematic handling of information.

A.2 Habitability paradigm elements

Habitability paradigm elements include buildings/settings, occupants, and occupant needs, similar scales to those outlined in the different parts of this book. The physical environment is dealt with on a setting-by-setting basis, and is built up in scale from the proximate environment. Each higher order scale of the environment is comprised of aggregates of units at lower scales. Thus, the built environment is addressed using the following hierarchy of scales:

- region: an assembly of communities at the geographic scale;
- community: an assembly of city blocks or neighborhoods;
- facility: a complex of buildings such as a military base or a campus;
- building: an assembly of rooms or spaces;
- room: an assembly of workstations or activity/behavior settings;
- activity setting: the proximate environment in which behavior occurs, e.g. a workstation.

The workstation–proximate environment scale can be equated with behavior settings or archetypal places (Barker, 1968; Spivack, 1973). In general, it needs to be recognized that the scale of the environment, as described, directly influences interaction between the user and their surroundings (Emami *et al.*, 2015).

Archetypal places are accommodating needs and activities that are generic and applicable to most populations. Since environmental design relates behavior to space in time, Spivack's categories of basic places and people types appear to be appropriate for adaptation in the

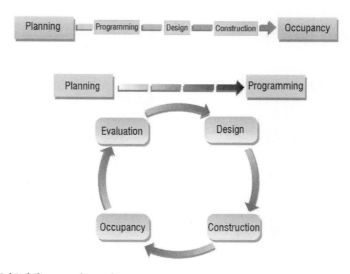

FIGURE A.1 Habitability paradigm elements.
Source: Author, Jacob J. Wilhelm.

proposed habitability paradigm. Archetypal places are designated to provide for activities common to virtually all human beings, i.e., shelter, sleep, mating, grooming, feeding, excretion, storage, territory, play, routing, meeting, competition, and work.

For each setting, each occupant group and its respective habitability level, a pertinent sensory environment and its quality performance criteria are devised, e.g., for the acoustic, luminous, gustatory, olfactory, visual, tactile, thermal, and gravitational environments. Although it cannot be sensed by humans, the effect of radiation on the health and well-being of people, from both short-term and long-term perspectives, is also included for completeness sake.

Occupants within the same setting are differentiated according to life-cycle phases and special requirements they may have in the use of the environment, based on physical or mental impairments, cultural heritage, or other differences. Life-cycle stages, as described by Spivack, include infancy, childhood, adolescence, courting-mating, reproduction/child care, middle life, and ageing (Spivack, 1973). For example, the need for personal space, and other psychological aspects, within a public or private environment, varies depending on age (Gifford, 2002). Limitations of the elderly and persons with disabilities may consist of impaired vision, as well as physical and mental disabilities. Fine differentiations are made within some of the life-cycle phases, where warranted, e.g., concerning developmental phases of children and their special environmental needs. Occupant needs in the built environment are conceived of as so-called habitability levels. Grossly analogous to the human needs hierarchy of self-actualization, love, esteem, safety, and physiological needs, a three-level breakdown of habitability levels reflecting occupant needs in the physical environment has been devised (Maslow, 1948). This breakdown also parallels the three basic requirements buildings should meet according to Vitruvius: firmness, commodity, and delight. The habitability levels refer to the following elements:

- health and safety level: preventing accidents and injury, disease, vandalism, etc., in the built environment;
- functional and task performance level: providing conditions conducive to the efficient performance of a job; for the proper functioning of living environments, adequate amount of space, etc.;
- social, psychological, and cultural comfort and satisfaction level: providing environmental conditions conducive to territorial integrity; speech and visual privacy; access to valued resources; expression of individuality; status; identity, etc.

Behavioral science research specializing in person–environment relationships provides data for potential use in guidance literature at all three levels of habitability, including research applications into human factors and concerns of environmental psychology. It is at the psychological comfort and satisfaction level of habitability that most concepts dealing with person–environment relationships can be identified, categorized, and applied. It is also true that at this level more qualitative than quantitative data exists, a fact that should not obviate its importance in analyzing effects of the physical environment on its occupants (Berlyne, 1960; Fayn and Silvia, 2015).

Spatial characteristics, such as those manipulated by environmental designers, include aspects of location, dimensions, proportions, distributions, and orientation. These serve to further such phenomena as communication, expression of status, socio-petality (layout spatially attracting people to a central focus point), and socio-fugality (layout dispersing people spatially).

Occupants' needs are not always easy to separate into neat levels and categories. Further, as the work of Dewey and Humber implies, there is a complex interaction of a variety of forces at work on occupants, their attributes, and those of the environment (Dewey and Humber, 1966; Preiser, 1983; Bechtel and Churchman, 2002). According to Dewey and Humber's framework, interacting processes and forces in the human organism are grouped into three categories:

- Biological heritage includes a person's given cognitive and emotional characteristics, motor and sensory potentials, biogenic impulses, health, race, sex, somatotype (basic emotional disposition), and stature.
- Environment constitutes the physical (geographic, geological, and meteorological), the biological (human and nonhuman), and cultural (material and nonmaterial) factors that impinge upon people.
- Acquired personal attributes refer to people's covert attitudes, beliefs, knowledge, concepts, and skills and overt motor habits, such as speaking, writing, walking, and idiosyncratic mannerisms.

Social-psychological processes considered essential in interactions with the human and nonhuman environment seek to facilitate accommodation, communication, compensation, learning projection, role playing, and rationalization (Pastalan, 1974; Gifford, 2012).

A.3 The habitability paradigm and the triad of programming/building performance evaluation/database development

The relatively young subfields of programming, BPE, and database development have made, and will continue to make, significant contributions to architecture in the quest for improving the quality of the built environment (see Figure A.2).

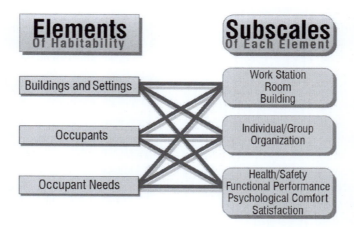

FIGURE A.2 The triad of facility programming/building performance evaluation/database development.
Source: Author, Jacob J. Wilhelm.

Value-based programming, as described by Hershberger (1999), and research-based programming both attempt to identify the value positions and their relative importance as determined by major stakeholders. As a feedback mechanism, post-occupancy evaluation (POE) has evolved into an integrative framework for building performance evaluation (Preiser, 2003), focusing not only on the built outcome at the time of occupancy and post-occupancy, but also on the entire building delivery and life cycle.

Taken together, the triad of programming, BPE, and database development holds great promise for improved quality of many varying environments of the future.

A.3.1 Programming

In facility programming, building-use information is identified and documented in the form of the functions, activities, and performance criteria a proposed building is to accommodate. For further information on the process of programming, see *Professional Practice in Facility Programming*, which presents methods and applications of programming from the perspective of user needs in buildings (Preiser, 1993).

To understand the habitability of spaces, we refer the reader to the basic seven steps in the programming process (Hershberger, 1999).

1. Organizational goals. The objectives of the client need to be obtained and documented, whether they are formal, informal, personal (e.g., those of the managing director), or hidden. Frequently, difficulties exist in reaching stated goals and objectives, and inferences will have to be made from existing operations. Further, pertinent constraints such as codes and regulations need to be analyzed.
2. Organizational objectives. Objectives are translated into functions that the organization needs to carry out, e.g., administration, instruction, etc. Usually, department names and breakdowns of organization reflect the major functions they are to carry out. Petronis attempted to describe the process of arriving at facility requirements in programming through strategic planning and systematic translation of sets and subsets of organizational goals and objectives (Petronis, 1993; Cherry and Petronis, 2009).
3. Functions of organizations. Functions are broken down further into activities of programs that need to be spatially accommodated. Activities refer to specific work processes, such as writing, assembling, etc., which take place in specific activity settings or workstations.
4. Performance requirements. Environmental criteria and performance requirements are formulated for each activity setting.
5. Time/space utilization. A schedule and adjacency requirements are devised in order to establish priorities and trade-offs concerning time/space utilization.
6. Designation of spaces. This occurs after all activity settings with appropriate space estimates have been compiled, thus providing the first gross area estimate.
7. Options. Options as to different program resolutions are presented, usually tied to time phases and cost considerations. Examples are no-cost solutions (based on exchange of existing furnishings, donated labor and goods), medium-cost solutions requiring some capital expenditure (e.g., painting and remodeling), and high-cost solutions requiring major investment (e.g., structural changes and additions to existing or entirely new buildings).

A couple of other programming step-by-step outlines provide a similar process, but include fewer steps. Edith Cherry and John Petronis (2009) outline six steps that are driven by more technique and quantitative considerations of a building's program. William M. Peña and Steven A. Parshall have outlined even fewer steps in their book *Problem Seeking: An Architectural Programming Primer* (2012). They outline a five-step process for evaluating and developing programming.

The program clarifies for the client, user, and the architect the facility requirements that may exist for an existing or potential project. The program may indicate organizational changes or functional realignment of the organization's existing space without necessarily resulting in a new design project or building. Different formats have been developed for presenting building use information and specification, usually on an activity-setting basis.

A.3.2 Building performance evaluation (BPE)

Data-gathering techniques in the evaluation of performance in buildings will only be mentioned in passing, and where appropriate. Post-occupancy evaluations (POEs), which can stand alone or be a part of the more involved building performance evaluations (BPEs), are distinct from post-construction evaluations in that they deal specifically with the use performance of a building. They are also distinct from merely descriptive studies of buildings in that they require criteria standards, objectives, or threshold values to evaluate the performance of a building against.

Information on the client organization, its structure and objectives, functions, activities, and required support facilities is gathered and transferred to performance requirement sheets. Measurements concerning the physical environment are made, as are inventories of existing equipment and furnishings. Means of eliciting open responses from the users of the facility are devised. Problems and conflicts in the existing offices are identified and documented. Three options at different cost levels, developed to resolve the problems, are then identified.

Comprehensive reviews of the evolution of POEs and BPEs over the past 50 years can be found in chronological order in the following key publications: *Learning from Our Buildings: A State-of-the Practice Summary of Post-Occupancy Evaluation* (Federal Facilities Council, 2002); *Improving Building Performance* (Preiser, 2003); *Assessing Building Performance* (Preiser and Vischer, 2005); *Enhancing Building Performance* (Mallory-Hill *et al.*, 2012); and *Architecture Beyond Criticism: Expert Judgment and Performance Evaluation* (Preiser *et al.*, 2015).

A.3.3 Database and design guideline development

Large organizations engaged in a considerable amount of construction, especially repetitive facility-type construction, greatly benefit from user feedback. Easily measured in hotel chains, these benefits are affecting shifting habitability requirements at the room scale. While already in the habit of regularly conducting guest surveys, applying the same thinking as described in the proposed habitability paradigm revealed misunderstandings of the performance requirements, time/space utilization, and designations of spaces in hotel rooms within the Marriot International chain (Petersen, 2015). The development of the Marriot International Innovation Lab reconsiders and tests design guidelines of new rooms, leading to a new prototype of what the 21st-century hotel room looks like. Additionally, new spaces that resist previous understandings of programming, such as 'innovation centers' for employee collaboration, are increasingly included in new design guidelines.

As other private-sector corporations shift to the internet, the greater need for a sense of place within a market that is literally placeless is being considered. Tech companies, as we know them today, are still very much in their first generation of architectural development; most tech-giants have humble beginnings, moving into existing models of office spaces as they grew.

In the same way that Einstein's theory of relativity changed how we think about space in a different dimension, changing parameters brought on by new technologies can be seen to drive the next generation of architectural response (Angier, 2015). The inherent logic that guides these projects is the general understanding and exploitation of habitability, whether it is explicitly stated in guidelines or exists under the approach of architectural movements like Parametricism. While rejecting repetition, Parametricism still understands the tightly-woven interconnection of each element of the habitability paradigm. Emerging social media and tech companies, online marketplaces, and other startups require designs that address the same habitability concerns that plagued 19th-century company towns (Green, 2010), with the added requirement of adaptable spaces that embody the long-term goals of their creator. Enlisting so-called 'starchitects', Google partnered with the Danish Firm B.I.G. and Heatherwick Studio, Apple commissioned London-based Foster+partners, and Amazon is tied to NBBJ to materialize the utopian office for a type of workplace that hasn't existed until the 21st century. Already built projects include Zaha Hadid Architects' Galaxy Soho in Beijing, China and Gehry Partners' Facebook campus in Palo Alto, California.

Google, as with many of the other mentioned tech conglomerates, currently requires design guidelines to uphold graphic standards, an idea that is slowly transferring into architecture. These guidelines, when they fit within the habitability framework, could ease the transition from headquarters to hub locations, meaning the expansive Mountain View, California campus maintains and improves in quality as it adapts to the London, Tel Aviv, Seoul, or São Paulo campuses. Looking at completed company towns as databases that can inform

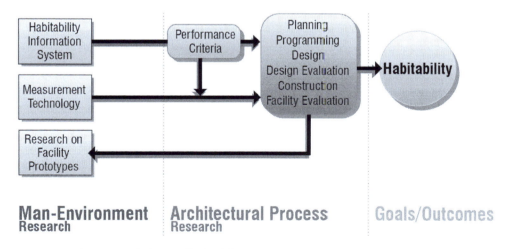

FIGURE A.3 Elements and phases of habitability research.
Source: Author, Jacob Wilhelm.

upcoming projects of a similar nature could also predict expected design problems. An effective design guideline database agglomerates decades of habitability research and prototype development to form parameters that constantly reference each other. They can also amass diverse analysis techniques for quantifiable and replicable standards to ensure a company's expenses and efforts.

The resulting data from these analyses is fed into a future, continuously updated habitability information system. Eventually, such a feedback loop, if instituted on a broad basis, will greatly contribute to raising the responsiveness of buildings to user needs.

A.4 Conclusion

The concept of 'habitability' is instrumental in a robust and viable paradigm for progressively programming, designing, constructing, occupying, and recycling high quality built environments. Beyond that, the BPE framework furthers conceptual integration by adding the 'glue' to tie the various building delivery and life cycle phases together in a temporal fashion.

A.5 Bibliography

Angier, N. (2015). Space, the Frontier Right in Front of Us. *The New York Times*. 24 Nov. 2015.

Barker, R. G. (1968). *Ecological Psychology: Concepts and Methods for Studying the Environment of Human Behavior*. Stanford, CA: Stanford University Press.

Bechtel, R. B., and Churchman, A. (eds.) (2002). *Handbook of Environmental Psychology*. New York: John Wiley & Sons.

Berlyne, D. E. (1960). *Conflict, Arousal and Curiosity*. New York: McGraw-Hill.

Cherry, E., and Petronis, J. (2009). Architectural Programming. *Whole Building Design Guide*. National Institute of Building Sciences, 9 Sept., https://www.wbdg.org/design-disciplines/architectural-programming. Accessed April 3, 2017.

Dewey, S., and Humber, J. (1966). *An Introduction to Social Psychology*. New York: Macmillan.

Emami, A., Gonbad, S. T. M., Barkhodar, F. and Milanizadeh, N. (2015). Historical Analysis of Environmental Psychology: A Review Article. *Trends in Life Sciences*. DAMA International. Vol. 4:2.

Fayn, K., and Silvia, P. J. (2015). States, People, and Contexts: Three Psychological Challenges for the Neuroscience of Aesthetics. *Art, Aesthetics, and the Brain*. Eds. J. P. Huston, M. Nadal, F. Mora, L. F. Agnati, and C. J. C. Conde. Oxford: Oxford University Press, www.oxfordscholarship.com/view/10.1093/acprof:oso/9780199670000.001.0001/acprof-9780199670000-chapter-3. Accessed April 3, 2017.

Federal Facilities Council (2002). *Learning from Our Buildings: A State-of-the Practice Summary of Post-Occupancy Evaluation*. Washington, DC: National Academy Press.

Gifford, R. (2002). *Environmental Psychology: Principles and Practice*. Colville, WA: Optimal Books.

Gifford, R. (2012). Applying Social Psychology to the Environment. *Applied Social Psychology: Understanding and Addressing Social and Practical Problems*. Eds. Frank W. Schneider, Jamie A. Gruman, and Larry M. Coutts. 2nd ed. Thousand Oaks: Sage, 311–318.

Green, H. (2010). *The Company Town: The Industrial Edens and Satanic Mills That Shaped the American Economy*. New York: Basic.

Hershberger, R. G. (1999). *Architectural Programming and Predesign Manager*. New York: McGraw-Hill. London: Routledge. (Reissued 2015.)

Mallory-Hill, S., Preiser, W. F. E., and Watson, C. (eds.) (2012). *Enhancing Building Performance*. New York: Wiley-Blackwell.

Maslow, H. (1948). A Theory of Motivation. *Psychological Review*, Vol. 50, pp. 370–398.

Pastalan, L. A. (1974). *Man Environment Reference Environmental Abstracts*. Ann Arbor, MI: University of Michigan.

Peña, W., and Parshall, S. (2012). *Problem Seeking: An Architectural Programming Primer*. 5th ed. New York: John Wiley & Sons.

Petersen, A. (2015). Secrets to Creating a Better Hotel Room. *The Wall Street Journal*. 30 Sept.

Petronis, J. P. (1993). Strategic Asset Management: An Expanded Role for Facility Programmers. In: Preiser, W. F. E. (ed.). *Professional Practice in Facility Programming*. London: Routledge. (Reissued 2015.)

Preiser, W. F. E. (1983). The Habitability Framework: A Conceptual Approach Towards Linking Human Behavior and Physical Environment. *Design Studies*, Vol. 4, No. 2, pp. 84-91.

Preiser, W. F. E. (ed.) (1993). *Professional Practice in Facility Programming*. New York: Van Nostrand Reinhold. (Reissued by London: Routledge 2015.)

Preiser, W. F. E. (2001). The Evolution of Post-Occupancy Evaluation: Toward Building Performance and Universal Design Evaluation. In: *Learning From Our Buildings – A State-of-the-Practice Summary of Post-Occupancy Evaluation*. Washington, DC: National Academy Press.

Preiser, W. F. E. (2003). *Improving Building Performance*. Washington, DC: National Council of Architectural Registration Boards (NCARB). (Republished in 2016: London: Routledge.)

Preiser, W. F. E. (ed.) (2016). *Facility Programming – Methods and Applications*. London: Routledge.

Preiser, W. F. E., and Vischer, J. C. (eds.) (2005). *Assessing Building Performance*. Oxford: Elsevier.

Preiser, W. F. E., Davis, A. T., Salama, A. M., and Hardy, A. (eds.) (2015). *Architecture Beyond Criticism: Expert Judgment and Performance Evaluation*. London: Routledge.

Preiser, W. F. E., Rabinowitz, H. Z., and White, E. T. (1988). *Post-Occupancy Evaluation*. London: Routledge.

Spivack, M. (1973). Archetypal Place. In: Preiser, W. F. E. (ed.). *Proceedings of the Fourth Annual Environmental Design Research Association Conference (EDRA 4)*. London: Routledge.

INDEX

Note: Page number in **bold** type refer to **figures**
Page numbers in *italic* type refer to *tables*

Aalto, A. 55
acoustic measurements 109, 111
activities 187
activity based workplace (ABW) 77; design
86–87, 89–93
activity simulation 65, 119
adaptability 30, 67–70, 72–75, 86, 93, 149,
153–154, 157, 176, 196, 198; cellular offices
89; formal 91–92; functional 91; open-space
offices 90–91
adaptive 77, 84, 114, 116–117
adaptive architecture 3; future trends 6–10;
historical development 4–6
adaptive environments 67–68
adaptive performance 65, 67, 72–75
adaptive reuse 125, 136, 144, 147, 183, 199
Adrian Smith + Gordon Gill Architecture
(AS+GG) 7
AEC industries (architecture, engineering, and
construction) 227
Affordable Care Act (ACA, 2010) 105
Aguilar, A., Petronis, J. and Whittemore, F. 125,
149–157
Aichi Children's Health and Medical Center
229–230
aid: bilateral 18, 22–24; humanitarian/
development 17–19; multilateral 18, 21–23
air rights 45
Airbnb 121
Albert, Prince 97
Alberti, L. B. 230
Alchemy Architects 9
alley culture 191–192

Amazon 255
American Institute of Architects (AIA) 228
Americans with Disabilities Act (ADA, 1990) 5,
54
Ames, W. J., *et al.* 116
Anfield, M. L. C. 126, 168–176, 178
antecedents 185–187
Apple 255
Application Programming Interface (API)
231
Arab Spring 57
Architectural Programming and Predesign Manager
(Hershberger) 201
Architectural Research Consultants (ARC)
149–150, 152, 154, 177
architecture 17–18, 24
Architecture Beyond Criticism (Preiser *et al.*) 254
art 191–192
artillery barracks 204–206, 210
arts, mechanical 10
Artspace 8
ASHRAE (American Society of Heating,
Refrigerating and Air-Conditioning
Engineers) 40–41
assembly-line education 10, 208–209
Assessing Building Performance (Preiser and
Vischer) 254
assessment grid 79, *80*, 82–83
AutoCAD 231
Autodesk Revit 230–231
autonomy 56–57
average distance to façade 78, *79*, 81–82, 120
average perimeter distance 81

Baker, B. 74
BBC/Pacific Quay 215
Beaver people 115
behavioral mapping 108, 110, *111*
Bell Committee 97
Bell, H. 97
Bell Report (1911) 97, 99
Belle Center of Chicago 55
benchmarking 78–79, 81, 83–84
Berlin: Brandenburg Airport (BER) 195; Senate
    Administration 195; TXL Airport, Terminal
    A 183, 195–196, 196–198, 202–203
Beuth University of Applied Sciences (Berlin)
    196–197, 202
Bielefeld University of Applied Sciences
    (Fachhochschule Bielefeld) 204, 206–207,
    209–211, 234
B.I.G. (Bjarke Ingels Group) 255
bilateral aid 18, 22–24
BIM Handbook (Eastman *et al.*) 228
BIMstorm 228
biosphere consciousness 9
BMJ (Boswell Mitchell and Johnson) Architects
    215
Bosch, S., and Nanda, U. 106
Boyarsky Murphy Architects 185, 192, *193*
Bringing Back Broadway 140
British Council for Offices (BCO) 81–82
Broadway Trade Building (May Company
    Department Store) 136–140, 144–147, 178
building: customizable 8, 35; energy
    performance 38–39; green 39, 42; intelligent
    209–211; life cycle 183, 195, 199, *200*;
    operation 154–157; performance 16, 34–37,
    44, 60, 199, *200*, 251, 253–254; reuse
    199; systems 152–154, 217–223; utilitarian
    204–206
Building Information Modeling (BIM) 160,
    183–184, 234–235; background 227–228;
    current literature 228; hospitals 229;
    important features 228; integrative 234; meta-
    227, 230–231
Building Information Modeling (Kensek and Noble)
    228
building performance evaluation (BPE) 4, 121,
    227, 230–231, 235, 249, 252–254, 256

Caesar, M. 223
campus architecture 204, 207–211
cellular offices 65, 83, 86, 91–93, 120, 211;
    adaptability 89; concept 88–89; German
    tradition 87
Central New Mexico Community College
    (CNM) 154, 157
Chandler Hospital 105
change 27–30, 54–55
Cherry, E., and Petronis, J. 254

Chicago: Belle Center 55; Center for Green
    Technology 190; Department of Environment
    190; Department of Transportation 190;
    Department of Water Management 190;
    Green Alley initiative 190
Chicago Children's Museum 54–55; Play for All
    54–55; *Therapy Play Guide* 55
Chicago Green Alley Handbook, The (2010) 190
chika 21
children's museums 52–57
Chubu International Airport 44
city landscape 44–45
climate responsive architecture 159–161
closed work environments *151*
Cold Climate Housing Research Center
    (CCHRC) 160
collection 95–97, 99, 103
Colquhoun, A., and Frampton, K. 222–223
communication 223–225; documentation 108,
    110, *111*; and knowledge 4
confinement 243, 246
Congrès International d'Architecture Moderne
    (CIAM) 48
construction technology 158, 160–161
consumption, democratized 7
Container House *170*
containers 126, 168–171, 173–176, 178–179
continuity 54–55
Cosimo I 90
Cosmonauts (2015) 99, *101*
Cota, L. *191*
cottage concept 135
Council for Tall Buildings and Urban Habitat
    (CTBUH) 81
Covenant Baptist Church 26, *27*
Craig Zeidler & Strong 68, *69*
Crosbie, M. J. 59–61, 119–121, 177–179, 233–235
cross-cultural context (accessibility) 20–22
Crystal Palace 97
cultural responsiveness 116–117
culturally adaptive architecture 17, 159–165
culture 191–192, 223–225; hubs 137, 145–147,
    178
customizable buildings 8, 35
customization, mass 7–9

Darvasi, A. 129
database development 249, 252–256
daylight: coverage 78, 82; penetration 79, 82,
    120
Decker, J. 158–159
deep floor plate 82
deep play 10
Déjà vu (Totty) 3
Della Pittura (Alberti) 230
democratized consumption 7
democratized production 7, 209

260 Index

design: ABW 86–87, 89–93; ego-less 137, 144–145, 178; evidence-based 105, 108, **132–134**; flexible 144; generic 136–137; healthcare 105, 108; inclusive 53, 57; interior 163–165; participatory 107–112; universal 4–5
design and behavior field 5–6
Design Like You Give a Damn (Architecture for Humanity) 55
design phase flexibility 152–154
design strategies 65, **74**, 125–126, 153, 178, 220; multi-performance spaces *36*, 39, 41; sustainable 35, 38, 42
Detmold School of Architecture and Interior Design 211
Dewey, S., and Humber, J. 252
diagnostic POE 107
digi-cities 8
digital revolution 3, 20–22, 67, 89–90, 93
digital technology 3–4, 15
Diné College (Navajo Community College) 116–117
disabilities, visual 127, 131
distance traveled 108, 110–111
Diyin Diné (Holy People) 115–116
Doctors Without Borders 24

East End Children's Museum 55
educational environments 34, 37–38
ego-less design 137, 144–145, 178
Einstein, A. 255
El Mac *191*
Ellin, N. 187–188, 191
Elzeyadi, I. M. K. 15–16, 34–43, 60
emergency department 105–106, 108–113
energy performance 38–39
energy utilization index (EUI) 38, *39*
Enhancing Building Performance (Mallory-Hill *et al.*) 254
entry-level learning 56–57
environment: adaptive 67–68; educational 34, 37–38; indoor quality (IEQ) 34–35, 38–39, 41–43; open work 149, 150, *151*, 152, 154; open/closed work 150, *151*
Environmental Design Research Association (EDRA) 230
ethics 52–53, 56
ethno-technologies 160, 163–164, 166
European Space Agency (ESA) 246
evaluation 67–68, *see also* post-occupancy evaluation (POE)
evidence-based design 105, 108; guidelines **132–134**
experimental office development 49–51
exterior skin 161–163

Facebook 255
Fachhochschule Bielefeld (Bielefeld University

of Applied Sciences) 204, 206–207, 209–211, 234
facility management 227–229, 231
Facility Programming (Preiser) 201
farm-to-table movement 57
Farnsworth House 32
Fawcett, W. 65–76, 119–120
Fay, L. L. 65, 105–113, 120
feasibility matrix 71, *72*
First Industrial Revolution 7, 10
Fisher, T., Hardy, A. and Preiser, W. 3–11, 35
Fitts, D. J., *et al.* 239–248
fixed-address system 51
FlatPak House 9
flexibility 25–26, 68, 72, 75, 149–154, 157; design phase 152–154
flexible design 144
flexible spaces 4–5, 218, 223
floor-plate 77–84; connectivity 78, *79*, 83, 120; visibility 78, *79*, 82–83, 120
FlowWorks (2014) 54–55
focus groups 109–110, 112
formal adaptability 91–92
Forrest, L., and Garfield, V. 159
Foster+partners 255
4d and a architects 168–170
Frampton, K., and Colquhoun, A. 222–223
Fraunhofer IAO (Institut für Arbeitswirtschaft und Organization) 87
free-address system 51
Frost, J. L. 60
functional adaptability 91
Functionalism 186
functionality 4–5
Funds for Humanity 19
funnel approach (gallery design) 56
future trends 6–10

Galaxy Soho 255
gallery 95, 97, 99, *101–102*, 103
Garfield, V., and Forrest, L. 159
GBBN Architects 106
GBQC Architects 27
Geddes, R. 27
Gehl, J. 187–188, 191
Gehry Partners 255
generic design 136–137
generosity 115–117
geometry driven models 84
Global Partnership Model 18
Global Village Project (HFHI, Ethiopia) 17–24, 59
Google 7, 54, 255
Grand Central Terminal 44–45
grasshopper parametric algorithm *84*
Great Exhibition (London, 1851) 97

Green Alley initiative (Chicago) 190
Green BIM (Krygiel and Nies) 228
green buildings 39, 42
green housing 168–169
green technology 176
grid of sustainability 190–191
gross floor area (GFA) 79, 81
growth 26–27

habitability 4–6, 239–247, 249–256; levels 251
habitability paradigm 5; and building
    performance evaluation (BPE) 254;
    and database development 254–256;
    definition 249–250; elements 250–252; and
    programming 253–254
Habitat for Humanity International Ethiopia
    (HFHE) 19–20, *21–23*
Habitat for Humanity International (HFHI) 15,
    17–24, 59
Haida people 159–160
hand-made heritage 164
Hara, H. 45
Hardy, A. 183–194, 233; Preiser, W. and Fisher,
    T. 3–11, 35; Wilhelm, J. and Preiser, W.
    249–257
Hartman + Majewski Design Group 153
healthcare design 105, 108
Heatherwick Studio 255
Hershberger, R. G. 253; and Smith, M. E. 15,
    25–33, 60
Hershberger-Kim Architects 26
Hibbs, K. E. 65, 95–104
historical development 4–6
Hodulak, M. 65, 86–94, 120; and Rath, U. 183,
    195–203, 234
holistic approach 183, 195–196, 199–200
Horton Plaza 30, *31*
hospitals 227, 229, 230–231
hoteling 151, 178
houses, not-so-big 121
housing: green 168–169; informal *169*
Houston Children's Museum 54–55
Hozhó 114–115
huddle rooms 150, *152*, 154
human space use 185–190
humanitarian/development aid 17–19
Humber, J., and Dewey, S. 252
Hume, I., and Miller, J. 68
HVAC (heating, ventilation and air
    conditioning) 35

Ideo.org 9
Ieiri, R. 228
Improving Building Performance (Preiser) 254
inclusive design 53, 57
Indianapolis Children's Museum 56
indicative POE 107

indoor environmental quality (IEQ) 34–35,
    38–39, 41–43
Industrial Era 17
Industrial Revolution 6, 186–187, 228; First 7,
    10; Second 7–10; Third 6–10, 57
informal housing *169*
Innovating the Industry (Yamanashi) 228
innovation centers 255
instructional space 154, 157
integral planning *202*
Integral Urbanism (Ellin) 188
integrative BIM 234
integrative planning 183, 195–196, 199–203, 234
intelligent building 209–211
Intelligent Building Technologies (InteG-F) 209
interdisciplinary networks 23
interdisciplinary planning 201, 203
interior design 163–165
internal volume configuration (IVC) 243
International Space Station (ISS) 243, 245;
    composition, modularity and adaptability
    239–242; habitability 242–244, 247; life
    aboard 242; net habitable volume (NHV)
    244–247; psychological factors and future
    roles 246–247
Internet 3, 24, 28, 231
interstitial space 28
interviews 110, 112
investigative POE 107
Isozaki, A. 44–45, 48

Japanese National Railways Company 45
Jerde, J. 30
JFMA BIM-FM Research Council 228
Jones, Z. M. 126, 158–167, 178

Kahn, L. I. 28
Kalkin, A. 169, *170*
Kato, A., Mori, S. and Taniguchi, G. 16, 44–51,
    60, 184, 227–232, 234
Kensek, K. M. 228; and Noble, D. E. 228
Keret House 233
Kirkbride, T. S. 55
Kish, K., and Liljegren, K. 125, 136–148, 178
Knappe Center 139
Kohn Pederson Fox Associates (KPF) 47
Kokuyo 49, *50*
Kyoto Station Building 16, 44–45

lateral learning 10
layers-of-light approach 40
Lazor Office 9
Le Corbusier 48, 186; versus Wright *186*
Leadership in Energy and Environmental Design
    (LEED) 16, 34, 38–39; post-occupancy
    evaluation of multi-performing building
    37–38

262 Index

learning: entry-level 56–57; lateral 10
Learning from Our Buildings (Federal Facilities Council) 254
Leed™ buildings 34–43
Lewis Integrative Science Building (LISB) 37, *38–39*, 40
Life Between Buildings (Gehl) 187
Liljegren, K., and Kish, K. 125, 136–148, 178
live science 97
"Live. Work. Play" paradigm 4, 240
Local First 191
long-term change 22–23
long-term developmental process 56
Los Angeles 136–137, 140, 147–148, 178
low-performance spaces 34, *36*, 41–42, 60

McDonough Braungart Design Chemistry (MBDC) 9
McMaster University Health Sciences Centre (MHSC) 68–70, 75, 119
Magley, A. L. 15–24, 59
Mail Order District (MOD) 146
maker spaces 26, 178
Malin, E. 162
Marriott International 254
Maruno-uchi Building 45
Maryland General Hospital (MGH, University of Maryland, Midtown Campus) 229–230
mass customization 7–9
Mass Design Group 9, 60
masterplan 95–97, 99–104
May Company Department Store *see* Broadway Trade Building
mechanical arts 10
Media Space 99
Medieval era 187
meta-BIM 227, 230–231
Metropolitan Life Insurance Company 45
Miami Children's Museum 55
Mies van der Rohe, L. 32, 48
Miles, D. *192*
Miller, J., and Hume, I. 68
MINT subjects (mathematics, information technology, natural sciences, and technical disciplines) 208–209
Mir space station 240
Modern Movement 223
Mojapelo, A. 175
monoculture 9–10, 208
Monte Carlo simulation 67, 70, 119
Montgomery Park Center 144
Montgomery Ward Center 144
Morgan, J. L. 65, 77–85, 120
Mori, S., Taniguchi, G. and Kato, A. 16, 44–51, 60, 184, 227–232, 234
MRV Architects 159, 161–162
Muf Architecture – Art 99

multi-performance spaces 35, *36*, *40*; post-occupancy evaluation of LEED building 37–38
multi-purpose spaces 217–223
multi-tasking spaces 126, 158, 165–166, 178
multilateral aid 18, 21–23
Murray, G. 183, 214–226, 234
museums 95–97, 99–100, 103–104; children's 52–57

Nanda, U., and Bosch, S. 106
National Aeronautics and Space Administration (NASA) 243–244, *245*, 249; Human Research Program (HRP) 246
National Institute of Flamenco (NIF) 157
National Museum Directors' Council (NMDC) 95
Navajo 66, 114–117, 121
Navajo Community College (Diné College) 116–117
Navajo Mission Academy 117
Navajo Nation 117
NBBJ 255
net habitable volume (NHV) 244–247
net leasable area (NLA) 79
net-to-gross area efficiencies 79–81
net-to-gross ratio 78, *79*, 81, 120
networks, interdisciplinary 23
New Mexico State Space Standards 150–152
New Urbanism 8
Noble, D. E., and Kensek, K. M. 228
non-invasive architecture 9
not-so-big houses 121
Nutzerorientierte Bedarfsplanung (Hodulak and Schramm) 201

occupancy counts 109, 111
off-limit zones 243
Office of Government Commerce (OGC) 214
offices 77–78, 82–84; experimental development 49–51; open-space 86–87, 89–93; planning 48–51, *see also* cellular offices
one size fits all approach 35, 42
Onuma, K. 228
open work environments 149, 150, *151*, 152, 154
open-space offices 86–87, 89–93; adaptability 90–91; concept 89–92
Operations Research 25

Paimio Sanatorium 55
Paint PHX 191
Pan Am (Met Life) Building 44–45
parametric 78–79, 81, 83–84
Parametricism 255
Parshall, S., and Peña, W. 254
participatory design 107–112

participatory planning 209
Partners in Health (PIH) 9
Parvin, A. 7–8
patterns 220, 222–223, 225
Paxton, J. 97
Peña, W., and Parshall, S. 254
performance: adaptive 65, 67, 72–75; BPE 4, 121, 227, 230–231, 235, 249, 252–254, 256; building 16, 34–37, 44, 60, 199, *200*, 251, 253–254; criteria 129–132; energy 38–39; space 35–37
Perkins School for the Blind 128
persons with visual disabilities 127, 131
Petronis, J. 253; and Cherry, E. 254; Whittemore, F. and Aguilar, A. 125, 149–157
Petzinger, T. 6
Phoenix Children's Museum 53–54
Pilosof, N. P. 69
planning 153–154, 157; integral *202*; integrative 183, 195–196, 199–203, 234; interdisciplinary 201, 203; participatory 209; standards 149–152
play 53–54
Play for All (Chicago Children's Museum) 54–55
Play Date (Children's Museum of Phoenix) 53–54
plug and play spaces 144
plug-in space 68
polyculture 9
Ponce City Market 144
pop up operators 144
post-occupancy evaluation (POE) 4, 34, 36, 65, 105–106, 112–113, 120–121, 125, 129, 132, 135, 177, 179, 210–211, 223, 230, 234–235, 242, 253–254; application 112; diagnostic 107; indicative 107; investigative 107; methodology 107–110; multi-performing LEED™ building 37–38; outcomes 110–112
Preiser, W. 107, 117, 129, 132, 249; *et al.* 132; Fisher, T. and Hardy, A. 3–11, 35; Hardy, A. and Wilhelm, J. 249–257; and Smith, K. 132; and Vischer, J. 132; and Wilhelm, J. 127–135, 177
Problem Seeking (Peña and Parshall) 201, 254
problem-seeking approach 25
Process Maps 215–216, 234
production, democratized 7, 209
Professional Practice in Facility Programming (Preiser) 253
programming 200–201, 249, 252–255
public interest, rise of 8–9

Queen, Her Majesty 99
questionnaires 109, 111–112
Quinn Evans Architects (QEA) 139

Rath, U., and Hodulak, M. 183, 195–203, 234
real options 67, 75
reciprocity 115, 117
recycling 168–170, 173–175, 177–178, 190, 199
redundancy 32
relativity theory (Einstein) 255
relocatable church concept *31*
Renaissance 230
repurposing 168, 173–174
research methodology 129–132
resilience 30–32
reuse, adaptive 125, 136, 144, 147, 183, 199
Rifkin, J. 6–10
Roessel, J. M. 66, 114–118, 121
Roessel, R. 114
Roosevelt Row 191
Roscosmos 240
Rudovsky, B. 114–115
runners 49
Ryder Architecture 183

Sakai, Y. 45, 47–48
Sakakura Associates 47
Salk Center 28
San Juan College 157
sand volume 244
scale/mobility 22–23
scheduling 157
Schramm, U. 183, 204–213, 233–234
Science Museum Group (SMG) 95
Scottish Government 214, 223; Review on Design-Led Construction Procurement 223
Scottish Public Finance Manual (SPFM) 214
scripting 30
Sears Roebuck Distribution Center (Sears Building) 136, 140–147, 178
Second Industrial Revolution 7–10
semiology 220, 225
sensory fusion 52
sharing economy 3, 24, 121
shell-and-core projects 77, 84, 137, 144
short-term change 22–23
Shpuza, E. 81–82
sick building syndrome (SBS) 39
silo effect 233
Silo Effect, The (Tett) 187, 190
silo-busting 190, 193
simulated demand profiles 70, *71*, 72–73
simulations 227–228, 231; activity 65, 119; Monte Carlo 67, 70, 119
single-performance spaces 34–36, 40–41, 60
sitters 51
Sliver House 185, 192, *193*
Smith, K.: and Preiser, W. 132; and Tauke, B. 16, 52–58, 60–61
Smith, M. E. and Hershberger, R. G. 15, 25–33, 60

264 Index

Sonnenkraft SA 174
spacecraft 243–247
spaces 241–243, 245–247; flexible 4–5, 218, 223; human use 185–190; instructional 154, 157; interstitial 28; low-performance 34, 36, 41–42, 60; multi-performance 35, *36*, 37–38, *40*; multi-purpose 217–223; multi-tasking 126, 158, 165–166, 178; performance 35–37; plug and play 144; request process (New Mexico) 150, *151*; single-performance 34–36, 40–41, 60; standards 149–153, 157
spatial utopian theories *186*
Spivack, M. 250–251
Springbok Barracks 206
standards, space 149–153, 157
starchitects 7, 255
State School for Construction and Engineering 206
Strong Museum 55
Susanka, S. 121
sustainability 35–38, 168–169, 171, 173–174, 178–179, 200, 223, 228, 235; grid of 190–191
swing rooms 106, 111
Symbolic and Literal Aspects of Technology (Colquhoun) 222–223
symbolism 223
systematic approach 75
Szczesny, J. 233
Szenasy, S. 166

tailored approach 28
Taisei Corporation Nagoya Branch Office 48, *49*
Tange, K. 44–45, 47
Taniguchi, G., Kato, A. and Mori, S. 16, 44–51, 60, 184, 227–232, 234
Tatsuno, K. 45
Tauke, B., and Smith, K. 16, 52–58, 60–61
Taylor, S. 175
technology: construction 158, 160–161; digital 3–4, 15; ethno- 160, 163–164, 166; green 176
Teicholz, P. 228
Terminal A (Berlin TXL Airport) 183, 195–196; conversion 202–203; program development 196–198
Tett, G. 187, 190
therapeutics 55–56
Therapy Play Guide (Chicago Children's Museum) 55
thermal boredom 40, 60
Third Industrial Revolution 6–10, 57
Thornton, T. 160–161
Tierra Adentro of New Mexico (TANM) 157
tiny house movement 121
Tlingit people 159–162
Tokyo Metropolitan Government Building 44–45, 47
Totty, M. 3

townships 168
train station complex 45
transfer of development rights (TDR) 45
Tsimshian people 159–160
TUNZA International Children's Conference on the Environment (Rio de Janeiro, 2012) 175
typological analysis 78–83

Uber 3, 121
Uffizi 88, 90
Umberto Eco (Caesar) 223
universal design 4–5
University of Maryland Medical System (UMMS) 229
University of Maryland, Midtown Campus (Maryland General Hospital, MGH) 229–230
Urban Heat Island effects (UHI) 185, 190
Urban Tech Republic (UTR) 196
US Army Corps of Engineers (USACE) 249
US Forest Service (USFS) 159
US Gemini program (1961–1966) 245
US Green Building Council (USGBC) 38
US Navy (USN) 249
US Space Shuttle 241, *248*
us versus them 211
utilitarian buildings 204–206
utilization 154, 157
Utopianism 186

Vischer, J., and Preiser, W. 132
visitor experience 95–96, 99, 103
visual disabilities 127, 131
Vitruvius 251

walk-through 129, 131–132
walkers 51
wall-to-floor ratio 78, *79*, 81–83, 120
Walters, H. 116
WASH (water, sanitation, and hygiene) 19
Wee House 9
Weeks, J. 68–69
Wehrmacht 204, 206
WeWork 3
Whitmire, A., *et al.* 246
Whittemore, F., Aguilar, A. and Petronis, J. 125, 149–157
Wiki architecture 7
WikiHouse 7
Wilhelm, J. 125–126; and Preiser, W. 127–135, 177; Preiser, W. and Hardy, A. 249–257
Wilkinson Eyre Architects 99
workplace change management 91
World Expo (Kazakhstan, 2017) 7
World Health Organization (WHO) 18
World Trade Center 45

World War II (1939–1945) 161, 206
Wright, F.L. 28, 186; versus Le Corbusier *186*

Yale Traffic Index 231
Yamazaki, N. *242*
Yanagisawa, M. 48

Yasui Architects & Engineers 229
yellow cedar 161, 178

Zaha Hadid Architects 99, *102*, 255
Zeidler, E. 68, *69*
zoning strategies 192